THE DEVIL AND BOBBY HULL

THE DEVIL AND BOBBY HULL

How Hockey's Million-Dollar Man Became the Game's Lost Legend

Gare Joyce

John Wiley & Sons Canada, Ltd.

Library and Archives Canada Cataloguing in Publication Data

Joyce, Gare, 1956-

The devil and Bobby Hull : how hockey's million-dollar man became the game's lost legend / Gare Joyce.

Includes index.

ISBN 978-1118065730

   1. Hull, Bobby, 1939-.   2. Hockey players—Biography. I. Title.

GV848.5.H8J69 2011   796.962092   C2011-902451-9

ISBN 978-1-118-06577-8 (ePDF); 978-1-118-06579-2 (eMobi); 978-1-118-06578-5 (ePUB)

Production Credits
Cover design: Mike Chan
Interior text design: Thomson Digital
Typesetter: Thomson Digital
Printer: Friesens

John Wiley & Sons Canada, Ltd.
6045 Freemont Blvd.
Mississauga, Ontario
L5R 4J3

Printed in Canada

1 2 3 4 5 FP 15 14 13 12 11

For the Giles family in memory of Mark,
the funniest, sunniest guy in the business.

Contents

Acknowledgments

I conducted 90 interviews in researching *The Devil and Bobby Hull*. To everyone quoted here directly or indirectly or those who supplied information on background I am deeply indebted. There were 90 more interview subjects that I couldn't chase down—at least, not in time for publication (some are only getting around to calling me when the book is in page proofs). I tracked down the former Joanne Hull, as well as Bobby Hull's first wife, but neither was inclined to talk to me.

I am sure to miss a name or two in trying to catalogue those who helped me in the research and writing of this book but I'll try.

There were dozens of folks down around Point Anne, Belleville, Picton and environs who offered me a wealth of anecdotes about Bobby Hull's youth and retirement. These include James Hurst, John McFarland, Clara Sheppard and Carrie Saunders.

Among those who volunteered their time to help me with this project I must thank Jamie Mercury and Mike Mercury, son and brother of Ben Hatskin's lawyer, Telly Mercury, who passed away at about the time I started to forage for facts about Ben Hatskin. They helped me apply the right color paint to the numbers in the portrait of the Winnipeg Jets founder.

Many friends helped steer me toward interview subjects and research materials and they include (but are not limited to) Tim Campbell of the *Winnipeg Free Press* and Tim Wharnsby of CBC.ca. Other professionals who volunteered their time include journalist David Roberts in Winnipeg, video archive expert Paul Patskou and Kevin Shea of the Hockey Hall of Fame.

Over my years in the business I've been lucky enough to befriend distinguished journalists who were lucky enough to work in NHL and WHA games during what I think was a better time. These gentlemen have been at once heroes and mentors to me and I appreciate them helping out. Red Fisher, Jim Kernaghan and Frank Orr didn't just help me with this book; over the years they taught me how to conduct my business. I was also a fan of Gerald Eskenazi when I was reading the *New York Times* back in school days and I was honored that he took the time to help me out. I didn't know Vic Grant in Winnipeg before working on this book, but after talking to him I wish I'd had the pleasure of meeting him a long time before.

Many thanks to those who read some or all of the manuscript at various stages of composition and de-composition, including Terry Koshan, Damien Cox, Craig Button and Mike Sands. Their advice was indispensible.

I'd like to thank my editor at Wiley, Karen Milner, my copy editor, Nicole Langlois, and other members of the staff, including Elizabeth McCurdy.

I'd like to thank my agent, Rick Broadhead, who again went to the wall for me on this project.

I'd like to thank my daughters, Ellen and Laura, who, again, understood that sometimes their father had to go into the Fortress of Solitude to work away on another book.

And, last but far from least, I'd like to thank Susan Bourette, who, again and again, suffered for my art.

Hell begins on the day when God grants us a clear vision of all that we might have achieved, of all the gifts which we have wasted, of all that we might have done which we did not do.

—Gian Carlo Menotti

1

Pitchfork

Bobby Hull is sitting in a booth at Wayne Gretzky's restaurant in Toronto. He doesn't notice that he's sitting beneath a Chicago Black Hawks sweater, No. 9.* Memorabilia collectors would designate it "game-used." It hangs from the ceiling and is preserved between

---

*Frederic McLaughlin, the founding owner of Chicago's NHL franchise, had been a commander in the Blackhawk Division in the 86th Infantry in World War I. The division took its name Chief Black Hawk, a ferocious leader in the Sauk tribe in the Midwest. In McLaughlin's original paperwork with the league filled out in the 1920s, the franchise was referred to as "the Blackhawks." Over ensuing decades, however, the team took the name "Black Hawks," the presumption being that the team was in fact named after the Chief. That was the case over the course of Bobby Hull's playing career in Chicago. In 1986, the original franchise documents surfaced and Bill Wirtz decided to change the team name to reflect McLaughlin's original intention. All uses of the team name in this book will reflect the accepted usage at the time of the reference. For example: Bobby Hull played for the *Black Hawks* in 1971; he had to wait 39 years to watch Jonathan Toews lead the *Blackhawks* to the 2010 Stanley Cup.

two sheets of hard plastic, like a prehistoric fly in amber. And even if you knew it was somewhere in the restaurant you'd have trouble finding it among all the sweaters and sticks and pucks and photos that hang on the walls or are displayed behind glass in showcases. Hull doesn't see the sweater. More troublesome to him, he doesn't see fans lining up to buy The Golden Jet, *an authorized coffee-table book that captures his playing days in Chicago. He has a Sharpie in hand but no purchases to sign. He's pissed off that the publicist assigned to promote this signing has somehow made it a well-kept secret, one known only to Hull, four guys familiar to him from signings at memorabilia shows and me, the guy sitting across the table from him. Between us are two glasses of draft, both his, a plateful of sliders, all his, and a data recorder, mine.*

Hull's 71 years old and, frankly, looks it. Aging isn't a crime but for Hull it's unimaginable. Those photos in the book show him in his 20s and early 30s, when he was a Canadian Adonis, something close to physical perfection. Yeah, his blond locks were thinning but his eyes were bluer than Paul Newman's. Broken nose, broken jaw, cuts: nothing marred his Hollywood-quality looks. The man sitting across from me is only somewhat recognizable from those images. Now he wears a rug that clashes with his temples. His face has thickened. He trembles. When he reaches across the table for a plate, his left hand steadies the right at the wrist. After a bout with pneumonia his heart went out of rhythm a couple of winters ago. Even before that, though, years in a hard game and a harder life than he could have imagined have caught up to him.

Hull is in Toronto for a limited book tour, nothing beyond driving distance of the city. He'll show up on a couple of television shows, go to studios for radio interviews and make appearances in book stores to sign copies of this glossy nostalgia tour in hardcover. It's the perfect Christmas gift for the fan of a certain generation, someone who either remembers his 71st birthday or is close enough to plan for it. And the book is well-timed, what with the Blackhawks still celebrating their Stanley Cup win the previous spring, their first championship since 1961. The 49-year drought came to an end two seasons after Hull and the Blackhawks set aside hockey's ugliest grudge. Hull was brought in as an "ambassador" for the team in December 2007, not as a hockey man charged with a role in management or the hockey side of the operation but no matter; events suggested that it could be viewed as the lifting of a curse.

To Hull's mind any curse has not lifted but just transferred to this book tour. The stop at Wayne Gretzky's is a disappointment. The midweek lunchtime crowd isn't enough to keep one waiter busy and the bartender is wiping down the taps. Hull ridicules the publicist "The posters for the signing weren't hung because they just said 'Gretzky's,' not 'Wayne Gretzky's,' which is what the owners want," Hull says. "I mean, what's the point of that? Does somebody honestly think it's Keith Gretzky's place?"

His voice is testosterone aged in oak kegs. It's growl and rasp. Even when he says "please" and "thank you" he sounds gruff. Maybe it's the by-product of 25 years of yelling for the puck, yelling to be heard above the cheers. Maybe it's hard living. No matter. When he wisecracks about Keith Gretzky, it's not clear whether he's making a joke of having to attach a given name to No. 99 or taking a shot at management burying the poster because of the publicist's oversight.

I try to get the conversation back on the rails. I tell Hull that the first thing I think about when I hear his name is a book I was given as an academic prize in fifth grade, back in Centennial year: Great Canadian Sports Stories. *"I remember that photo of you with a pitchfork and a bale of hay," I say.*

"I know the shot you're talking about," he says. "It's in the book."

He flips through the pages and arrives at a black-and-white shot from the '60s. He's shirtless and his chest and arms ripple as he heaves a bale. His face is tensed, just another muscle he's putting into his work.

"I'd sharpen the prongs of the pitchfork and then go out there all day in the summer," he says. "It was hard work. Each of those bales weighs 70 to 100 pounds, maybe more if they're wet. Other guys would get out of shape during the summer. Only later on did players figure out that you'd have to work out in the off-season. I just did farm work. Eight hours a day, in the hot sun or in the rain, it didn't matter."

The pitchfork, the hay bales and grueling physical chores made his game, he says. They gave him his gifts, incredible strength, grip strength, wrists, shoulders. "My father worked at the cement factory in Point Anne. I'd see kids in the countryside nearby, farmers out in the sun, and I said to myself, 'I'm going to get [a farm] someday.' I bought my first one with money I had left over from the season when I was twenty-one over on Big Island, just across the Bay of Quinte from Point Anne. I didn't hire anyone to work it or do something that I could do myself."

When Hull talks about the farm, he's animated, excited. For almost anyone, including many farmers, eight hours a day or more pitching bales of hay would be one of Dante's circles of hell. Not Hull. He had broken scores of hockey records, made millions and lived life to the absolute fullest but he gives the impression that working the farm made him happiest of all. There he had no bosses, no one trying to get something out of him, no onlookers, no complications. It might have been hot and dusty and dirty but it was honest and fair work that left him satisfied at the end of the day.

• • •

The photo that Hull showed me in his coffee-table book wasn't the one that had burned in my memory. In the shot

I remember, he happens to be pitching a bale of hay as well. It's quite possibly the same day and almost certainly the same farm, Hullvue Farm, a spread out on Big Island near Demorestville in Prince Edward County. Hull's face is out of view. Stripped down to the waist, he has his back to the camera. All that you can see are rippling lats, delts and traps, swelling triceps, and forearms on loan from Popeye. He's raising a pitchfork head high and hoisting a hay bale skyward. Even though you can only see the crown of his head, his blond hair thinning and sweaty, it could be no one else. It couldn't be Gordie Howe—even though Howe was also prodigiously strong he wasn't that thick from east to west. It couldn't be Tim Horton—he lifted weights, gym work not farm work. It had to be Bobby Hull, recognizable without a number, without a sweater, without his face being in view. When the National Archives of Canada staged its exhibition of defining portraits in 1993, culling four million paintings and photographs from over 400 years down to 145 items, those in the gallery saw Hull's back, not his front.

The shot of Hull from the back ran across a full page in *Great Canadian Sports Stories*, a book written by Peter Gzowski and Trent Frayne in advance of the nation's centennial year. Gzowski and Frayne made sure that no major athlete in any game, amateur or pro, could complain about being overlooked. Still, predictably, more pages were dedicated to hockey than to any other sport and almost all of those were given to the NHL. There were photos and stories in brief about legendary players: Howie Morenz, Rocket Richard and Howe. And then there was Hull. Richard had been the first player to score 50 goals in a season, but Hull was the first to beat that mark. Howe had broken Richard's career scoring record but Hull was on pace to pass them both. When the book was published in the spring of 1966, the NHL was not quite six decades old and still consisted of six teams that traveled by train from game to game. Changes were in the offing—the league would expand to 12 teams in the fall of '67. At that point, Hull wasn't just considered the NHL's defining player, but also the one all later stars would be measured against. Though Gzowski and Frayne stopped short of saying it explicitly, they suggested that Hull would lead the NHL and Canadian sports into the nation's second century.

Hull was the NHL's one crossover star. Back in 1956, Jean Beliveau had been the first NHL player to land on the cover of *Sports Illustrated*, a head shot that looked like it had been lifted from a hockey card. Jacques Plante made the cover a couple of years later, an action shot with the goaltender ducking below the crossbar and peering through traffic. By the late '60s, though, Hull had staked his claim to *SI*'s front. Over his career he would end up on the cover five times in a Black Hawks sweater. *SI* was the sports establishment's seal of approval. He was the face of the game. On the cover in February '64, with a headful of blond hair, he was glaring in a brawl with Red Wings defenseman John Miszuk. On the cover four years later he was standing at the Chicago bench, yelling at his teammates, with bare gums where his bicuspids used to be. He was the game's brightest star but even so not immune to or protected from the game's violence.

Those *Sports Illustrated* images didn't start to capture his influence. He changed the way the game was played.

Hull didn't invent the slapshot but he did more than any previous player to popularize it as an offensive weapon. At every neighborhood rink, kids spent hours imitating Hull's big windup and endangered others on the ice and bystanders. A big slapshot became a badge of masculinity, like a long drive in golf or high heat in baseball.

A by-product of his shot: Hull did more than any player to popularize facemasks for goalies, more even than Plante, who famously donned a mask back in 1959. Plante blazed the trail but Hull inspired fear. "When the Canadiens had a game with Chicago, Gump Worsley would always manage to pull a muscle in the warm-up, like a lot of guys," Montreal *Gazette* columnist Red Fisher said.

Hull was the one player in the era who dictated opponents' strategy. The Canadiens assigned Claude Provost, a smart, experienced winger and a strong skater, to follow him around all game. The Red Wings sent Bryan (Bugsy) Watson to jab and needle him. The shadows might have some success some nights but the scoring statistics suggest that he prevailed more often than not.

Prolific, iconic, influential, terrifying—and yet unfulfilled. The Black Hawks had won the Stanley Cup in 1961 when Hull was just 22. Though they had to like their chances a few times through the rest of the '60s, they fell short. In Hull's prime he developed the reputation of a talent but not a team player— someone who could get the fans out of their seats but at the end of the day leaving it to someone else to raise the Cup. Those inside the game knew that he often didn't have much of a supporting cast but still, the guy on the *SI* cover should be able to win it on his own. The guy with the pitchfork should be able to carry the team on his broad back.

Still, Hull was a certified star. The NHL was the second or third priority at best in New York, Boston and Detroit, but in Chicago Hull had the highest profile of all the stars of the city's hard-luck pro teams. The Cubs' Ernie Banks would make the Hall of Fame but, year in, year out, the team was either hapless or heartbreaking. The White Sox had no one to get excited about. The Bears' Gale Sayers was the most explosive running back of his era but injuries cut his career in half. His teammate Dick Butkus was the most intimidating linebacker in his day but his game should have carried a parental warning for violence. Even with both players, the Bears lost as many as they won in a good year. The Bulls weren't on the radar. Hull didn't own the city but of all the pro stars he owned the biggest piece of it. He made the Stadium Chicago's most exciting venue. Nelson Algren, the author who best captured life on the streets of Chicago, once said that loving the city was "like loving a woman with a broken nose." It fit that the city's sports fans embraced the athlete whose nose had been broken more often than their hearts.

Hull's hold on the Second City was noticed elsewhere. He stood as proof that the NHL could play in other major American markets. NHL bosses and entrepreneurial sorts believed that they could fill other arenas the way Hull filled Chicago Stadium. They believed that the league had to go beyond the Northeast and go west, as Major League Baseball had. It wasn't the Montreal Canadiens and their continued excellence that spurred expansion—if that would have been enough then the league might have expanded in the '50s. It wasn't Toronto—the city's staid culture seemed to have little to do with major American cities. It wasn't Detroit or the moribund teams in Boston and New York. It wasn't any team. It was Hull, the one with star quality, the one with genetic gifts you could see with his bare back to the lens. "There's no doubt that Bobby was the biggest factor that led to expansion," said Jim Pappin, his former Black Hawks teammate.

. . .

Full disclosure: I wasn't a Hull fan when I won *Great Canadian Sports Stories*. I was like a legion of kids in Toronto in my worship of the Maple Leafs. I was heartbroken when my parents sent me to bed during the third period of Game 3 of the 1967 Stanley Cup final—but I stood silently by a slightly open bedroom door and, in a feat of pre-adolescent endurance, stayed awake long enough to watch Bob Pulford, my favorite Maple Leaf, score the winning goal in the second overtime period.

Still, I was like every other Canadian kid of my generation. I knew enough about hockey to know that it was impossible to deny Bobby Hull his stature in the game. Street hockey games were like an occasionally car-interrupted tennis match, one slapshot east, one slapshot west, goaltenders grimacing, protecting their loins first and faces next. I knew that it was Hull and Stan Mikita who first experimented with curved sticks—within a couple of years every kid had to have one. Mine was a Victoriaville—Northlands like Hull's were rare and well beyond my price point. With hockey cards Hull's was the prestige item and I never managed to buy or win one—just an endless procession of Ab McDonald, Moose Vasko, Val Fonteyne and other journeymen pros.

I accepted Hull as portrayed in the sports sections, magazines and books. I thought he had less in common with other hockey stars than he did with comic-book heroes. Hull was Canadian Superman. Like Superman's, the outfit he wore to work concealed his physical gifts. His Black Hawks sweater was hockey's biggest cover-up. Gordie Howe summed it up best: "He gets bigger as he takes off his clothes." It went beyond musculature. The story of his origins read like Superman's too.

Robert Marvin Hull grew up in Point Anne, a town of 400 a couple of hours east of Toronto. If he was different than Superman in one particular area it was family. Clark Kent was an orphan. Robert Marvin Hull was the oldest son of Robert Edward Hull and his wife, Lena. He had four older sisters, three younger brothers and three younger sisters. His older sisters Maxine and Laura were supposedly the first to get him out onto the ice, the Bay of Quinte when it would freeze over, but his father took over his development as a player. Robert Edward was, by his son's estimation years later, "a fair country hockey player" and he knew enough about the game to recognize his oldest boy's potential. Father got on the ice with son, father coached son, father pushed son. Robert Edward was a caustic man. When a camera crew went out to Point Anne to do a profile of Bobby in the early '70s, Robert Edward criticized his son and not jokingly. "He should score two or three goals every game, but he stinks the place out every time a gang from Point Anne comes down to see him," he boomed. Bobby Hull seemed not to take the criticism to heart. "The best coach I ever had," he said at the end of his professional career.

Point Anne wasn't just similar to Superman's Smallville. Point Anne was a fit with the era in the game, so many of its stars coming from small towns. Morenz was born in Mitchell, Ontario, population 2,000. Howe grew up in Floral, Saskatchewan, where the one-room schoolhouse was in the shadow of the town's only landmark, a grain elevator. Point Anne was a fit with the nation at the time of Hull's birth. Back in '39, almost half of Canadians lived in rural communities like Mitchell, Floral and Point Anne. By the time Hull scored 58 goals in an NHL season, there were three Canadians in cities for every one off in the country.

As you'd expect he was a local hero in Point Anne and parts around. Not just a hockey hero but also a real-life hero. In August 1960, Hull, then 21, saved members of his family when a gasoline leak in his 22-foot boat exploded into flames. He pulled a cousin out of the boat and dragged his grandfather to shore. His mother was too severely injured to be pulled from the boat into the water, so Hull, swimming furiously, pushed the boat to shore and then rushed her to the hospital. "I don't know how we lived through the fire," his wife Joanne told the Belleville *Intelligencer*. "Bobby and his father reacted so quickly that they saved us all from getting killed."

He was the most famous man that Point Anne, Belleville and Hastings County had ever produced. He was still in his 20s when local political bosses talked to him about running for public office. They pointed out that Red Kelly managed to hold down a seat in the provincial legislature while he was playing for the Maple Leafs—he went from practice at Maple Leaf Gardens over a few blocks to Queen's Park. Hull respectfully declined—making his way from Chicago to emergency sessions in Ottawa or Toronto would be logistically impossible. Still, he left the door open for after his playing days, knowing the most powerful men in his home riding would back him.

Hull couldn't yet turn his talent, character and fame into votes but he didn't have to wait to turn them into a commercial windfall with an array of endorsements. Fantasy: his name was on Munro table hockey games. Function: his name was on Bauer skates. Child-friendly: he and his sons took the ice in a Milk Duds commercial. For adults only: he vouched for

Algonquin beer. If Hull was plugging a product, it didn't even have to make sense. The second most ludicrous: in an ad for Jantzen Actionwear, the muscular Hull, with chest hair like Sean Connery's, stood on a Hawaiian beach in a swimsuit beside basketball star Jerry West and retired NFL star Frank Gifford, who looked scrawny, boyish and uncomfortable by comparison; the phallic imagery was hardly subtle with Hull standing a surfboard upright and West holding a skateboard. Most ludicrous: the balding Hull was the celebrity pitchman for a dandruff shampoo. (Later, and far more credibly, he was a spokesman for the House of Masters, retailers of pate recoverings.)

Other sports stars of his era compared as unfavorably as West and Gifford. Even a follicle-challenged Hull was cooler than Johnny Unitas with his high-tops and his brush-cut. Hull was more accessible than Bill Russell and Wilt Chamberlain— simply a matter of altitude, with Hull an everyman's 5-foot-10 and the basketball stars at 6-foot-9 and 7-foot-1. Hull resembled one star from the other games: the Yankees' Mickey Mantle. They shared rural backgrounds and prodigious physical gifts. They were photogenic, aspirational figures. American kids wanted to grow up to be The Mick, while Canadian kids imagined they'd be Bobby Hull someday.

At the start of the '70s, it was unthinkable that Bobby Hull was going to end up being the player no one wanted to be. That he'd go from having it all to having nothing at all. From pride to shame.

That's exactly what happened.

• • •

When Wayne Gretzky and Mario Lemieux and other great players emerged after Hull's fall from grace, they knew his story.

They knew that fans perceived him, fairly or not, as a talent but not a winner. They knew he was punished for his hubris, never forgiven for taking on the Black Hawks' owners and the National Hockey League. They knew his private life became public scandal. They knew the commercial image he had cultivated was exposed as a fraud.

Gretzky, Lemieux and the rest had very different talents and very different games on the ice but a common approach to the management of their careers and the protection of their images. They were as cautious as Hull was bold. They kept their private lives as private as possible. They sought and won the approval of management and, in return for this and their other virtues, they became management or took other places of prominence in the game.

Bobby Hull could have or should have been like Jean Beliveau in Montreal, like Steve Yzerman in Detroit. In Hull's prime, it was hard to imagine that he would ever play anywhere but Chicago. If he were going to play elsewhere, the door should have been open to him and he should have been able to go out on his own terms, like Wayne Gretzky did. He should have been able to find work in the game, like Lemieux as an owner, Yzerman as a general manager, Gretzky as a coach and Orr as a powerful agent. Instead, Hull walked away from the team that he led and years later was denied a chance to return. His career ended not with glory and tribute but rather a humbling, his release listed in agate type in the transactions column and accompanied by recriminations. And he was outside the game, a famous name who, for almost three decades, never made another dollar from the league except for an NHL pension that paid him not even a grand a month. Some great players walk away from the game and don't look back, but the Hawks and the NHL couldn't walk away from Hull fast enough for their liking.

It was Hull's bad luck to come at a time of sweeping change in the game off the ice. The rules of the business. The public spotlight. And he made decisions that burned powerful people with long memories. Maybe it could have been forgiven but no one could muster sympathy when he violated taboo. When he brought disgrace on himself, they believed he brought disgrace on the game. Others who came after him went to school on Hull's experiences. No giving in to inner demons. No giving in to temptation. No deals with the Devil. No one wanted to fall like he did, from fairy tale to cautionary tale.

● ● ●

Will Gretzky or Lemieux one day be sitting across from someone like me, flogging a book with Sharpie at the ready and not a customer in sight? Will Sidney Crosby or Alexander Ovechkin? Never say never. Everything they've done so far in their hockey lives seems like a big production, nothing so small-scale and haphazard, but then again that's how it once seemed for Bobby Hull. They shouldn't have financial need to do something like this, but then again that's how it seemed for Bobby Hull. Maybe at age 71 they'll be more like Hull than they'd ever suspect. Middle age is sometimes unkind to the game's stars, old age even more cruel.

I tell Hull that I once sat at the same table as Rocket Richard and he smiles. "A great player," he says. "There was no one like him. For a young player back when I was growing up, no one was more exciting."

I don't go into detail about the occasion, because it's painful. Back in the mid-80s I attended another publishing event: a small imprint was flogging another Canadian sports-history book. The publisher wanted to get a dollop of publicity and miscalculated, believing that it needed to do more than offer sportswriters a free lunch and beer tickets. They brought in sports celebrities, the most famous being Richard. I took a seat at the table opposite Richard and the former *Globe and Mail* sports columnist Dick Beddoes embedded himself at the Rocket's left shoulder and, when not waxing nostalgic, asked him a couple of questions. Richard had no answers. He looked blankly ahead. He had too much to drink that day and, by appearances, it was a recurring theme in his life. Not bombed so much as embalmed. He seemed unwell—might have been a touch of the flu though it looked like it could have been something chronic. He was fine for photo ops—cameras could focus on him even if he couldn't on them. Just no stories.

It's noon. Hull is fatigued by the flight from Chicago the night before and a Bloody Mary or two en route. He's in far better shape than Rocket Richard was. He's having a couple of small draft beers and he'll be switching over to red wine and more. I don't imagine that a few drinks will loosen his lips. There are stories that he'll tell and there always have been. There are stories that he'll avoid and always has. That's why he has authorized a book collecting old photos. The narrative would be far more troublesome. Images are kinder than the facts.

2

Crawling Through
a Knot-Hole

After talking to Bobby Hull for a while, trying to put his NHL career in perspective, it's clear that he divides it evenly between individual accomplishments and shoulda-beens in the collective. No surprise. He has one Stanley Cup ring but his CV catalogs an impressive list of NHL honors and trophies: 10 First Team All-Star selections from 1960 to '72, three Art Ross trophies as the league's leading scorer, two Hart trophies as its most valuable player, a Lady Byng Trophy for gentlemanly play and a Lester Patrick Trophy for service to hockey in the United States.

It seems like his memory of the near-misses eclipse that single Cup victory, back in '61 when he was just 22. "Back then I thought I'd have a bunch of these," Hull says, making a tight fist and raising it to show a ring big enough that it would fit through the nose of one of his prize bulls. "I knew it was hard to win a Stanley

Cup but I really felt like we were going to win a few of them. I was confident in that."

He seems to remember less about '61 than his next trip to the Cup final, when Chicago made it all the way to Game 7 against the Canadiens at the Forum. "Was it '64 or '65?" he says. I tell him it was the latter. "I was still playing beside Phil Esposito at that point," Hull says. "A lot might have been different if Chicago had held on to Phil."

The day before meeting Hull at Wayne Gretzky's, I watched film from Game 7 in '65. It was a decisive 4–0 win for the home team. Even with the game out of reach in the third period, the Black Hawks played with the desperation of a team down a single goal. Coach Billy Reay double-shifted Hull beside Stan Mikita, even though they had rarely played together at even strength. The Hawks generated chances but nothing close to a game-changer.

What struck me about the film was Hull in the post-game. Hull was the first player that Hockey Night in Canada *chased down for an interview. Frank Selke Jr. flagged him while the rest of the Black Hawks skated off the ice and headed to the dressing room. We've grown accustomed to athletes down-hearted in defeat: head bowed, damp eyes, a struggle for words. This was precisely what Hull wasn't. He stood up straight, looked straight ahead and spoke the simple truth. "We were beaten by a better club," he said. "That first period they out-played us and that told the story. Tommy Ivan came in and told us—and Billy Reay both—if we can hold them in the first period maybe we have a chance. As it happened they stormed out and had one in the net fifteen seconds in and it was history after that."*

The broadcast made it seem like the story of the game was defeat for Hull and the Hawks as much as Montreal's triumph. You might presume that Selke and the Hockey Night in Canada *crew went to Hull first because the Canadiens were too busy celebrating, but that wasn't the case—in fact, Jean Beliveau could be seen standing to Hull's side, waiting in line to be interviewed. Hull was a constant theme when the microphone was thrust in front of other Canadiens. Selke asked Claude Provost about his assignment, shadowing Hull around the rink. "Very tough job and I'm very proud he didn't score any goals against me," said Provost, a former Second-Team All-Star.*

Hull was all rectitude and sportsmanship after the loss. After talking to Selke Jr., he skated over to shake hands with Montreal coach Toe Blake and he made a point of personally congratulating Canadiens players even though he had already passed through the handshake line. He was the last Black Hawk on the ice.

"That one didn't hurt as bad as '71," Hull says. He winces.

He doesn't need to fill in the details. I remember watching the '71 final. Chicago vs. Montreal. The Montrealers were the hockey equivalent of The Over-the-Hill Gang. They had missed the playoffs for the first time in a generation the previous spring, and general manager Sam Pollock had to coax Jean Beliveau to put off retirement to lead the team through what management had presumed to be a rebuilding year. When Montreal staggered though October and November of 1970, Pollock fired coach Claude Ruel and replaced him with his assistant, Al MacNeil, who had one full year's experience in the organization, having worked as a playing-coach with the Canadiens' American Hockey League affiliate. It looked like management was throwing in the towel, but under MacNeil's direction the club went 31–15–9 down the stretch and finished third in the Eastern Conference with a respectable 97 points. The face-saving looked like it would quickly come to an end in the first round of the playoffs when Montreal faced the Boston Bruins, who had placed four players on the NHL's First All-Star team. That season Boston's Phil Esposito set an NHL scoring record with 76 goals in 78 games and Bobby Orr set another with 102 assists. In an improbable upset, the Canadiens knocked off the Bruins, famously coming back from a 5–1 deficit to win Game 2. The Canadiens advanced past the Bruins and then Minnesota to the final against Chicago largely on the goaltending of Ken Dryden, who made his NHL regular-season debut, a brief one, in the late spring of '71. In the final, Chicago and Montreal traded wins on home ice through the first five games. After Game 5 Henri Richard, frustrated by sparse ice time and line juggling (including 14 combinations of forwards in one period), told reporters that MacNeil was "incompetent." MacNeil received death threats and lived under guard of 30 Montreal plainclothesmen leading up to Game 6. Champagne was chilling in the Black Hawks' dressing room when they took a two-goal lead into the third period that night at the Forum. The Canadiens seemed to be fresh out of miracles, but again rallied for three goals in regulation to send the final back to Chicago for Game 7.

The capsule version does the series no justice, really.

I tell Hull there's no video of that famous Game 7 in its entirety. It's not to be found at the Hockey Hall of Fame. When I asked officials there about it, they told me that many famous games have gone missing over the years, game films chopped up for highlight packages, videotape recycled. It turns out that Game 7 in '71 is one of the most requested videos, but somewhere along the line tapes of Jean Beliveau's last game and Ken Dryden's emergence on the scene went missing. I had hoped that the Paley Center in New York, the former Museum of Broadcasting, would have it on file, since the Paley Center has kept on file virtually every broadcast aired by the major U.S. networks going back to the '40s and CBS had decided to pre-empt regularly scheduled programming, including the top-ranked show that season, All in the Family, *to air Game 7 in prime time on a Tuesday night. I drew a blank with the Paley Center as well. I had hopes that there might be a copy on the black-market of hockey videos. No luck there either—all kinds of famous contests, hundreds of obscure contests, thousands of fights, but not Game 7.*

"I've seen highlights of that game but I've never thought about watching the whole thing," Hull says. "If I just had a ring from that year, with '61, that would have been enough. That would have been enough for me."

I ask Hull if he'd look back on his career in a different way if his team had won Game 7 at Chicago Stadium.

"I would," he says. "I tell people that I don't second-guess . . . that I'd do it all again. That one got away. Things would have looked different. Maybe things would have turned out different."

• • •

Go to youtube.com and you can find a couple of minutes of highlights from Game 7 of the '71 final, a newsreel narrated by Dan Kelly, then the voice of NHL broadcasts on CBS. The highlights include four of the five goals, a few near-misses and the final seconds of the contest. Some plays are shown in slow-mo. Others are at real speed with the camera jiggling enough to induce motion sickness.

Beyond those clips, there are only words left from that Game 7 in '71. The words tell the story.

The eyewitness accounts in newspaper and magazine stories: these were incomplete, most often jumping right past what had happened and how it happened and focusing on why it mattered. Square miles of copy were as tired as the players were at the end of what had been the longest season in professional sports, 222 days in all. The outcome of the game would remain in doubt right up to the final horn and at the end of the night the scribes in the press box tapped out profundities about destiny and dynasty, about the moral order of all things that were bound to come to pass on the ice, about the Stanley Cup somehow belonging in Montreal. Not about how it came to pass.

The testimony of the principals: every narrator has grown more unreliable with every passing year and so, four decades after the fact, plumbing the truth about 60 minutes one night in May '71 is like trying to breathe life into the coldest cold case. One would overstate a minor role in the proceedings and another in the white-hot center of action would remember only a blur.

The best surviving account of Game 7 was never committed to paper or broadcast on television: the play-by-play and color commentary on WMAQ, the Chicago radio station that carried Black Hawks games. Lloyd Pettit provided the play-by-play and sidekick Harvey Wittenberg offered the color commentary. Theirs isn't an entirely reliable narration—Pettit and Wittenberg were homers. They went from the third person to the first when talking about the team—the Hawks became "us." Still, this was history in real time, exactly what was happening, how it was happening. The lines, the match-ups, the sequences of events, they're all there. Occasionally Wittenberg had to break away from the game during stoppages to read a spot for STP ("Power to Clean with Power to Burn"), Skil Power Tools ("See Why No One Was Sorry He Bought the Best There Is"), Su Casa ("For Exciting Mexican Food, Drinks and Entertainment") or Leon's Polish Sausages ("When Your Goal is Pleasing Everyone"), but even this seemed to serve as a needed reminder that the NHL in general and the Black Hawks in particular stood at the intersection of sport and commerce.

• • •

It's no surprise that the highlight reel looks dated. The film looks like it has been put in a hot-water wash. What's surprising is that the game sounds dated. With nothing more than the recording of the radio broadcast, a hockey fan in the new century will quickly realize that this was another era. Not because of the names, including 14 members of the Hockey Hall of Fame on the ice. Not because of the broadcast's brassy theme music, which sounds like it had been lifted from a '60s action series canceled after one season. No, it's the game's rhythms that give away its vintage.

The game in the modern era is played at a dead sprint, in 40-second shifts. A forward who logs 25 minutes of ice time in a regulation game is almost unheard of. Yet in Game 7 of '71, Bobby Hull was on the ice for seven of the first 10 minutes of the first period, more than four minutes in one stretch.

When Al MacNeil elected to send out his top line, Frank Mahovlich, Yvan Cournoyer and Jean Beliveau, for the opening face-off, Billy Reay, with last change, tapped Stan Mikita, Dennis Hull and Eric Nesterenko. For Chicago, that was the desired match-up: Mikita using his game and guile to make Beliveau play both ends of the rink and Nesterenko fully occupied with nullifying the Big M.

After 45 seconds of uneventful play, Hull came on with his linemates, center Chico Maki and Cliff Koroll. He stayed on the ice until the six-minute mark. By today's measure that would be the equivalent of eight consecutive shifts. A minute after stepping on the ice, and with the Canadiens clustered around him, Hull fired a pass to put Maki into open ice, which led to Canadiens defenseman Terry Harper taking a holding penalty. Harvey Wittenberg suggested that the call raised hopes that referee John Ashley was going to call a fair game.

Maki and Koroll came off but Hull moved back to the right point—a better angle for his slapshot from the blueline— and stayed on through the entire power-play, a cautious and uneventful one. When Harper stepped back on the ice, Hull kept right on going, not waiting for a stoppage to move back up to left wing, anticipating Maki and Koroll coming back on. With just the recording of the radio broadcast, a little imagination is required to visualize what is happening, but just when you'd imagine that Hull was finally heading to the bench, Pettit describes a pass from Hull to Mikita, who had just come on again.

Hull's game and energy didn't drop off. At the end of the extended shift he decked Henri Richard with a clean check in the Chicago end. When Richard got back onto his skates, Black Hawk defenseman Doug Jarrett slammed him again. "A clean and legal check in the opinion of referee John Ashley," Pettit noted. When Jarrett scored the second knockdown, Hull broke for open ice down the left wing and generated the game's first scoring chance, blowing by J.C. Tremblay and bearing down on Dryden. Hull had scored on dozens, even hundreds, of lesser scoring chances but this time it came undone. The puck caught a rut or two in the soft Chicago Stadium ice, never the league's best and worse than normal because of the heat and months of wear and tear. Hull tried to get the puck on his forehand but he couldn't get it to sit down. Dryden recognized this and charged far out of his net. A backhand shot, almost an afterthought, rolled into Dryden's torso.

The game was scoreless but it was a promising start for Hull and the Black Hawks. He seemed to be on his game, his teammates were carrying the play and the Canadiens were reeling.

Hull was "a machine," Cliff Koroll said. "In a situation like that Bobby would come off not because he had to catch his breath but just so everybody could get into the game. He went at it harder than anyone else could and he didn't get tired. What made Bobby so hard to shadow was the fact that a guy might be able to stay with him a minute, but another minute or another minute on top of that? No way."

• • •

Bobby Hull didn't know the kid who rolled over the boards when the Hawks first took the ice against the Canadiens in the final, though he might have thought No. 14 looked familiar. Then again, Hull would have looked into the faces of thousands or tens of thousands or maybe hundreds of thousands over the decade of his stardom.

Back in early winter of '66 a 17-year-old kid, unimposing at 150 pounds, stood deep in the throng outside the side door of the Forum where the Black Hawks bus was idling. Dozens of men, women and children were between him and the open bus door, where Bobby Hull stood and signed autographs. The teenager didn't have a pen or a program or any desire to get an autograph. He just wanted to meet Hull, just wanted to shake his hand. Eventually the police waved the crowd away and Hull stepped up onto the bus. At that point the teenager burst through the crowd, dodged the security detail and jumped up on the bus just as the door was closing and the driver was putting the bus in gear.

Hull was already in his seat, talking to a teammate, when the intruder said in thickly accented English: "Mr. Hull, one day I'll play against you."

Hull took it in his usual good humor. The words are lost in Hull's memory and the young man's then only emerging English. Hull shook his hand and offered something like, "You hang in there, pal" to the star-struck kid.

In the '71 final, Rejean Houle kept his promised appointment. From the first shifts of the series right up to the start of Game 7, Houle reprised the role previously filled by Claude Provost but went about it in an entirely different manner. Provost, like Bugsy Watson, like others drawing the assignment, had tried to push and shove Hull, a thankless task. "Hull was so much stronger than everybody else that usually he'd hurt you more than you'd hurt him," Peter Mahovlich said. "Reggie had to skate with him, stride for stride, denying him the puck, beating him to spots."

In the first six games of the final, photographers, as always, tracked Hull around the ice and Houle was in the frame every time, spoiling most of their shots and Hull's. He was effective. Hull had 10 goals through 11 games in the first two playoff rounds but just one at even strength against the Canadiens.

When Rejean Houle made his appointment with Hull it wasn't as laughable as it sounded. In '66, his first year of junior hockey, he was a first-line forward with the Thetford Mines Canadiens and played in the Memorial Cup that spring. A season later he joined the Montreal Junior Canadiens, scoring more than 50 goals that season and leading the team to victory in the 1969 Memorial Cup. By that time he was touted as the next great Canadiens star—he and his Junior Canadiens teammate Marc Tardif ended up as the last players that Montreal general manager Sam Pollock could lay claim to through a territorial exemption from the NHL draft.

Yet 12 months before the Montreal–Chicago Cup final, Houle didn't look like an NHLer at all, toiling with little distinction for the Montreal Voyageurs, the Canadiens' AHL affiliate. "When we went to training camp [in '69] it was still the Original Six approach, with a team adding one rookie—maybe—and the veterans owning the room and setting the culture of the team," said Peter Mahovlich, who had been acquired in a trade from Detroit a few years previously, and had played with Houle with the Voyageurs. "For Reggie, for all of us, it was institutional resistance. It was trying to break into a family, not a lineup."

When the Canadiens canned Ruel and gave MacNeil the reins it was the best possible news for those who had played for him with the Voyageurs: defenseman Guy LaPointe and Dryden, both future Hall of Famers, along with Peter Mahovlich and Houle, among others. "It was a tough situation for us until Al came in but once he did we played with confidence because he had confidence in us," LaPointe said.

Despite MacNeil's confidence, Houle didn't seem equipped to reprise the role that Provost had played in the Canadiens' tense seven-game win over Chicago in the '65 final. Houle's linemates, center Peter Mahovlich and tough-guy winger John Ferguson, seemed up to the task. At 6-foot-5 and with a gait encumbered by heavy metal knee braces, Mahovlich sometimes looked like Dr. Frankenstein's monster. On the left side, Ferguson was a horror show of another sort, a feral, long-time nemesis of Hull. Inevitably, when the Black Hawks faced the Canadiens the crowd waited for Hull and Ferguson to cross paths and then for the fireworks. When Hull arrived at a regular-season game in Montreal with a helmet and facemask to protect a broken jaw, Ferguson tried to rip it off in an angry scrum and the Forum turned on their tough guy. For Ferguson, the dislike of Hull was part of his old-school code. He would cross the street in the summer to avoid an opponent who happened to be walking his way. The ice wasn't big enough for the two of them to peacefully co-exist.

Imagine a Stanley Cup contender of the '50s sending out a 20-year-old rookie to face Maurice Richard. Or a team in the early '60s taking the same strategy with Gordie Howe. It would have been sending a lamb to slaughter. The defining stars of the game who came along before Hull were capable of Gothic violence. They played with a fire that burned darkly. Any coach who sent a rookie in to chase them would leave the arena in defeat and with the kid's blood on his hands.

Al MacNeil's conscience wasn't troubled by assigning Rejean Houle to shadow Hull. As Houle and Pete Mahovlich acknowledge, Hull was a comparable talent to Richard and Howe but he went about his game differently.

"With the Rocket or Gordie Howe, other players feared them," Houle said. "Bobby was fair, not dirty. He would try to beat you but he wouldn't do anything to beat you. He was going to beat you clean—within the rules."

"Gordie would slash and elbow and spear you to get room on the ice," Peter Mahovlich said. "You couldn't send one guy out against him every shift. You had to rotate guys so he didn't know who'd be checking him and couldn't get that mad at any one guy."

As Houle, Mahovlich and all the principals from the '71 Cup final say, referees called a different game in that era. Lloyd Pettit noted in the warm-up that the fans booed the introduction of the officials. "John Ashley, as usual, did not receive a warm welcome," Pettit said. Harvey Wittenberg added: "The fans are chanting 'Ashley's a bum' . . . referring to that Game 3 when we had a 2–0 lead and the Canadiens defeated us 4–2." The radio team hinted at Ashley never seeing things the Hawks' way and in particular Hull's way, something just short of a league-wide conspiracy. Reay had aired his frustration with reporters after Game 4, saying he saw "a lot of holding and grabbing" by Houle and his shutdown linemates. The coach spared himself a fine but not the message with his withering parting spot: "The refereeing was terrific."

"That was always the story with Bobby," Cliff Koroll said. "Today the best players get fair treatment—they might even get protected by the referees. [But in those days] the refs would let [opponents] get away with all kinds of things. The refs knew it was the only way that anyone could stop Bobby."

The referees didn't protect Hull and neither did his equipment. Hull had worn the same shoulder pads since he broke into the league—they were relics by '71 and they lasted him to the final shifts of his career. A photo of them can be found on the Internet: sweat-stained, paper-thin, frayed and scuffed with tape marks from high sticks, slashes and hooks. When Hull was knocked into the boards, cleanly or not, his shoulder pads would have afforded him no more protection than a down-filled jacket.

"[With] the amount of ice time, the style of game he played, the equipment, everything, I have no doubt that Bobby Hull took more physical punishment on the ice than anyone who ever played the game," Jim Pappin said. "He didn't start things and he didn't retaliate, so a lot of the toughest guys in the league took liberties with him. He figured if he stayed in the game, rather than end up in the penalty box, he gave his team its best chance of winning."

• • •

In histories of the NHL, Hull is usually cast—typecast, really—as a one-dimensional scorer whose game consisted of a booming slapshot and a blinkered focus on the opponent's goal. That reputation was deserved early in his career, but not in 1971. There was no Selke Trophy for the league's best defensive forward in that era—it didn't come along until 1978. If there had been, Hull wouldn't have won it—it was then and is now far easier for a 20-goal scorer to be noted for his two-way play than a 50-goal player. Yet Hull would have deserved votes in any election of the game's most defensively responsible forwards. In fact, when the Montreal *Gazette* offered a list of Conn Smythe Trophy candidates before Game 7, Hull's name was at the top and his contributions at both ends of the ice were cited: "The Super Hawk [is] winding up his best all-around season. [He] not only has emerged as Chicago's leading scorer [but also] has been the whole spark of the team in each series. He ran wild in the Hawks' four-game sweep against Philadelphia, bagged two winners in the drag-em-out round with New York and has come up with four big goals in the final . . . Besides his regular shifts and power-play efforts, Bobby has worked as a penalty killer and defensive performer when necessary. Thursday [in Game 5] his best play of the game was an extra skating effort to catch Frank Mahovlich on a breakaway."

Reay tapped Hull to kill a tripping penalty to his brother Dennis midway through the first period. At first Hull was paired with his usual center, Chico Maki. After a whistle 40 seconds into the penalty, Maki came off and Hull stayed on, working beside Stan Mikita. Just a few seconds before Dennis came back on the ice, Hull carried the puck up the ice and led a shorthanded three-on-two break, sending Mikita in alone on Dryden. Bad ice, a rolling puck and a hard-charging Dryden kept the game scoreless, but it was a measure of Hull's game that not only did he stay on through the full two minutes and effectively kill the penalty, he also generated the best scoring chance in that stretch.

A quote has drifted down over the years since the early '70s. The Soviet coach Anatoli Tarasov said that Canada's two best players were Bobby Orr and Bobby Hull. Not Canada's two greatest scoring threats but the two best players. Orr's status was beyond dispute, but Hull, who was bumped off the NHL's First All-Star team by Johnny Bucyk that season? Tarasov wouldn't have bestowed high praise on Hull if he had been a one-dimensional player who brought a shot and not a lot else to the game. He wouldn't have mentioned him in the same breath as Orr if that had been the case. Tarasov, though, studied the whole game and wasn't subject to popular opinions in the media and the public. He saw Hull the player, not the image. Four decades later commentators compare Alexander Ovechkin to Hull as an indictment, the notion that both are great with the puck but possess no interest in the drudgery of the defensive game. What might be true of Ovechkin was not true in any way of Hull in '71.

• • •

The Black Hawks scored the game's first goal a little over a minute before the end of the first period. Again, Hull was putting his stamp on the game. It began at even strength when Houle struggled to keep up to Hull and John Ashley whistled him for a holding penalty. On the power-play, Hull again was back at the right point and when the puck came over to him all four Montreal penalty killers overcommitted to his side of the ice, trying to put themselves in his shot's and harm's way. Dryden also was well over to his glove side of the crease to cut down the angle. Hull's shot drifted wide but caromed off the back boards to Dennis Hull who was wide open at the hash mark on the left wing. The younger Hull brother had a yawning cage and plenty of time to fire the puck before Dryden could recover. Chicago: 1, Montreal: 0. It was the 12th shot on Dryden, twice as many as Tony Esposito would face in the first period.

Fourteen men on the ice that night would go on to election into the Hockey Hall of Fame. Eight of them were in Canadiens sweaters. (Montreal would have had a ninth, but defenseman Serge Savard missed the playoffs that spring with injury.) The Black Hawks had three: Tony Esposito, Stan Mikita and Bobby Hull. The other three? Trick question: referee John Ashley, and linesmen John D'Amico and Matt Pavelich. Teams win Stanley Cups with and because of Hockey Hall of Fame players. The Canadiens of the '60s and early '70s had an unusually large cluster of them. But a lot of teams that have but three Hockey Hall of Famers get only so close to a championship.

Unlike most star players, Hull rarely played with All-Star talent in support. He was the ultimate big fish in a very shallow pool of talent with the Black Hawks. The '71 final was a glowing example: Frank Mahovlich, the Canadiens' left winger and the skater who most closely matched Hull in gifts for the game, lined up beside two other Hall-worthy players: center Jean Beliveau and Yvan Cournoyer. No offense intended but they were a significant step up from Hull's linemates, Chico Maki and Cliff Koroll. "Bobby never had a center who could really help him be the player he was capable of being," Jim Pappin said. "He had Espo [Phil Esposito] for a while but [the Black Hawks' management] didn't give him the time to develop and traded him to Boston."

Pappin and others suggest that the best center that Hull played beside was Bill (Red) Hay, his linemate on the '61 team and through the early half of the decade. Hay had only 11 goals but still led that championship team in point-scoring with 48 assists. He was a nice fit as a set-up man for the most prolific scorer in the game. Yet in 1967 an oil company, one that Hay had worked for in the off-seasons, made him a job offer that he couldn't walk away from, not for the money that Chicago management was putting on the table.

That Dennis Hull had opened scoring in the game to decide the '71 Stanley Cup championship was no surprise. The younger Hull played beside Mikita that season and racked up 40 goals, good for fifth in the league and only four behind his brother. Dennis Hull was like several players in Chicago's lineup: not quite Hall-worthy, but useful. Bill White and Pat Stapleton were the most effective blueline pairing in the league that spring. Their ice time might have been the equal of Bobby Hull's. Like Dennis Hull, White and Stapleton would have been charter members of that next level below Hockey Hall of Famers, sometimes called the Hall of Very Good. Fact was, Chicago's was a top-heavy roster and the Black Hawks had to ride their best as long as they could stand it.

• • •

Danny O'Shea wasn't up to the standards of the Hockey Hall of Fame or even the Hall of Very Good. O'Shea had been a junior star with the Oshawa Generals, and a key player on Canadian national teams that competed in world championships in the mid-60s. He was still a lot closer to sea level than the summit occupied by Bobby Hull and Mikita and a long line of names on the Canadiens' roster. Going into Game 7 against the Canadiens he had only one goal in the playoffs and that was all the way back in the opening round against Philadelphia.

Hubert (Pit) Martin would have been a candidate for the Hall of Very Good. Martin scored as many as 32 goals in a season and played 1,101 NHL games with four teams, yet his career would always be defined by something beyond his control: he was the consolation prize in arguably the most lopsided trade in league history. In May 1967 Chicago sent Phil Esposito, Ken Hodge and Fred Stanfield to Boston where they emerged as three cornerstones of the highest-scoring team in league history en route to two Stanley Cups, and Esposito shattered Hull's single-season goal-scoring record. In return the Black Hawks received Martin, journeyman defenseman Gilles Marotte and goaltender Jack Norris. Marotte lasted less than three seasons in Chicago and Norris played all of 10 games for the club, leaving Martin as the only lasting reminder to fans of general manager Tommy Ivan's folly.

Seven minutes into the second period, O'Shea and Martin combined for a goal that seemed like it would clinch the Cup for the Black Hawks. A near-miss came first: Jim Pappin got the puck from the left wing to the slot, where O'Shea fired a shot that beat Dryden but hit the post. The Canadiens cleared the puck in a panic and were called for icing. It was a brief reprieve. Off the ensuing face-off Martin's forechecking behind the Montreal net forced a turnover by Jacques Lemaire. Martin found O'Shea in front of the net. O'Shea's one-timer was saved by Dryden but it bounced right back to him, between his skates. In one motion he kicked the puck up to his stick and fired the puck past the Montreal goaltender. It was what they like to call a goal-scorer's goal but it was scored by a guy who'd never be accused of being one.

The fans littered the ice with popcorn boxes and plastic cups. "Happy debris," Lloyd Pettit called it.

"I remember looking over to the Canadiens' bench after that goal and their heads were hanging down," Cliff Koroll said. "I thought right there that we had them."

Peter Mahovlich said that might have been a sign of fatigue but nothing like resignation. "We came back from five-to-one down to beat the Bruins in the opening round and from two goals down twice already in the series against the Hawks. We knew it wasn't going to be easy but we knew it was still possible. We just couldn't let them get another."

• • •

Despite Mahovlich's professed resolve, the Black Hawks looked poised to run the Canadiens out of the rink. Every Canadien but one: Rejean Houle. Houle had been celebrated for his work against Hull. Before Game 6, the Montreal *Gazette* had run a large sketch of Houle in pursuit of Hull, the rookie's eyes transfixed on his quarry. The title: "Me and My Shadow." The caption: "Rejean (The Peanut) Houle figures to be a key man at the Forum Sunday as he again checks Bobby Hull. The Chicago ace was held to three shots and no goals Thursday night [in Game 5] and that effort will have to be repeated . . ."

Houle's job wasn't complicated. It was simply a matter of maintaining constant awareness of Hull's whereabouts from the time he stepped on the ice until the point when the gate closed behind him. "It was a hard thing to do but that's all that was really expected of me and I did it . . . except for that one time," he said.

"That one time" came on the shift after O'Shea's goal. "That one time" is the image that has lingered with the principals and Black Hawks fans for years. "That one time" could have or should have won the Cup. "That one time" would have been a crowning achievement for Hull.

Billy Reay sent Hull back on the ice with linemates Maki and Koroll on the shift immediately after O'Shea's. Al MacNeil sent out Houle to give chase. The Canadiens looked fragile and Koroll wasn't the only Black Hawk to sense it. Hull and his linemates controlled the puck in the Montreal end for a long stretch. It was white-knuckle stuff for Houle. Like a cornerback on a dangerous wide-out, his job was to stay with Hull for as long as possible, but there was no staying with him forever, not with Hull weaving through traffic without the puck. By the time Hull skated into the slot, he had shaken his tail. "I only lost him for one second the whole game," Houle said. "When I looked for him, there he was in the slot and I'm thinking, 'I just lost the Stanley Cup. It's my fault.'"

Hull unleashed his shot: a wicked wrist shot, one that would have been harder than 99 percent of the slapshots around the league. And at the moment when Houle thought he'd lost the Cup, Hull had empirical reason to presume that he had just won it. Dryden waved his right arm at the puck but, holding with his blocker and stick, he couldn't raise it fast enough. It was cleanly past the Montreal goaltender. He went down as if struck by a blast from a musket. For Chicago fans it was a moment that the French like to call *la petite mort*, the moment just before ecstasy. For Houle, it was just death. If he could have, he would have asked for a blindfold.

Even blindfolded, though, Houle would have heard enough to hold out hope: the sound of a shot finding metal. And if he had peeked, Houle would have seen that the puck had hit the crossbar so squarely that it ricocheted right back into the slot, almost waist-high on Hull. A 100-m.p.h. rebound. "I believe it hit the crossbar and came right out," a hyperventilating Lloyd Pettit said. "There will be people who say that puck was in." Harvey Wittenberg restored order during the next stoppage when the broadcast team had a chance to watch the replay. "Another half-inch and that puck is in," he said.

It wasn't a bullet dodged, just a bullet errant by a minute margin.

Houle had lost Hull for that single moment but his job was going to get easier. He would get relief in his shadow's role from an unexpected source: Chicago coach Billy Reay. In a CBC documentary in 1964 Hull described Reay as "a perfect coach [who's] three moves ahead of them all. He instills confidence in his players." This night in Chicago Reay ended up too many moves ahead of himself and tried to instill confidence in players not up to the task rather than relying on his best.

• • •

There were 11 minutes left in the second period when Hull dented the crossbar. Over the first 11 minutes of the game, Hull had played close to eight minutes. But around the half-way mark of the second period, with the Canadiens reeling, with Chicago outshooting Montreal by a two-to-one margin and leading 2–0, Billy Reay must have believed that his team had all the goals they'd need to win the Stanley Cup. Over the last 11 minutes of the second period, Reay played Hull for less than three minutes on three shifts, including a stretch on the Black Hawks' power-play. The most prolific goal scorer in the NHL's history and the favorite to win the Conn Smythe Trophy, Hull was cut back to a third- or fourth-liner's ice time for no apparent reason.

Making it all the more curious was the fact that Reay was presented with situations that seemed to favor Hull's game, the teams playing four-on-four. Instead of sending out Hull or even Stan Mikita, Reay chose to go with Lou Angotti and Eric Nesterenko, nine- and eight-goal scorers respectively during the season, as the first option when both teams were playing a man short. Angotti's place in the lineup was only opened up by an injury to another center, Bryan Campbell, in the Black Hawks' opening-round victory over Philadelphia. Reay's thinking was that, however mediocre Angotti and Nesterenko might be in generating offense, they'd be defensively responsible enough to shut down the Canadiens.

It turned out to be too cute on a couple of counts.

First, the last line of defense was compromised. Tony Esposito was gassed. Reay should have known that. When Gerry Desjardins was hurt in midseason, Esposito had no relief. His backup, Ken Brown, had played part of one period that season. (In fact, those 18 minutes would constitute Brown's entire NHL career.) If Reay hadn't guessed it, he should have seen it. Lloyd Pettit and Harvey Wittenberg noticed. Three times during the broadcast they had mentioned the flagging goaltender's body language. Once, Wittenberg said: "Tony is looking really tired. He's got that arm resting on the crossbar.

It's really hot down there." Pettit later noted Esposito draped over the crossbar during a stoppage and said that he "looks pretty well beat."

Second, the second-last line of defence had a hole too. Bill White and Pat Stapleton ate up 30 minutes of ice time each night through the playoffs and kept the Chicago end of the rink neat and tidy. White would lead all players in the playoffs in plus-minus and Stapleton was right behind him. They were going to play major roles for Team Canada against the Soviets in the Summit Series a year later. But the other defensemen had issues. Doug Jarrett was no better than a journeyman and struggled to cope with the Canadiens' speedy forwards. Keith Magnuson was hobbling on one leg, trying to play through injury.

Over a very short stretch toward the end of the second period, the Black Hawks gave the Canadiens a breath of life, then a fighting chance and ultimately the Stanley Cup.

• • •

With less than six minutes to go in the period, with Magnuson and J.C. Tremblay off with minor penalties, Angotti carried the puck out of the Chicago end and up to Montreal's blueline. Nesterenko was behind the play and across the ice, indecisive on a line change. Angotti opted for a dump and chase— which might have worked if he had gone ahead and chased the puck. Instead, he just folded back into the neutral zone. Jacques Lemaire had an unmolested run down the left wing, no Black Hawk forward in the frame with him on the replay, none in Lloyd Pettit's radio call. "Lemaire carries it out, down the near side of the rink, he skates to the blueline . . . the center line . . . winds up . . . and a goal," Pettit said, to the bass accompaniment of 18,000 groans. "Jacques Lemaire, from about ten feet outside the blueline, wound up and took a blistering slapshot."

It didn't win the Cup but Lemaire's goal would become the enduring image from Game 7 '71. The radio team struggled to describe what happened. Wittenberg said: "It handcuffed him. He might have been partially screened 'cause a Black Hawk defenseman [Bill White] was backing up on the play." Pettit and Wittenberg also suggested that a haze that hung over the ice had something to do with Esposito's difficulty picking up the long shot.

It's hard to fault the broadcasters for their uncertainty. Tony Esposito has offered conflicting accounts of what happened on the play. "I didn't lose the puck in the haze," Esposito told reporters after the game. "I just missed it. I saw it all the way. The problem was that I went down and the puck went over my shoulder." Years later he gave a different version: "I just don't know if I saw it," he said. "I can't tell what happened. I know I got my arm on it and I thought I had it."

Lemaire's recollection of the play is clear and vivid. "All I wanted to do was get to the red line and shoot the puck and get off," he said. "I was dead tired. I was about twenty feet from the boards near the bench. When I got near the red line, I took a shot and went toward the bench. I didn't even watch the shot. All of a sudden, it went really quiet in the building. And the guys started to yell. I turned around, and I could see the puck in the net. It was the strangest goal I ever scored that was so important. We started to skate better and play better. They dropped. It was a matter of time after that. It turned the game."

The goal did precisely that, though it was helped along by Billy Reay, who continued to neutralize Hull better than Houle and the Canadiens ever could.

• • •

Even though the Canadiens were carrying play to the Black Hawks, Reay kept Hull off the ice until the 17:30 mark of the period. Hull might have been able to jump-start Chicago's offense with a couple of good shifts, but 26 seconds after he stepped on the ice defenseman Doug Jarrett went off with a minor penalty for hauling down Rejean Houle. The boys from WMAQ once again saw it the Black Hawks' way. "It looked like a good check but in the opinion of John Ashley Jarrett grabbed hold of him after the check," Pettit said.

Hull stayed out for the penalty kill but those listening to the game were left in the dark after the subsequent face-off and likely took refuge in their basements. Nine seconds into the penalty, just as Lloyd Pettit told listeners that Bill White had retrieved the puck and seemed well-positioned to clear it, WMAQ's feed from Chicago Stadium cut out and after a brief pause the station's airwaves gave way to a deep voice, uninflected by accent, in the slow rhythm of dire news that must be understood on its first reading. "This station interrupts its regular programming to bring you emergency information from the National Weather Service. The National Weather Service has issued a tornado watch for central and most of northern Illinois, portions of southern Wisconsin, a portion of northwest Indiana, south and central Lake Michigan, southeast Iowa and a portion of northeast Missouri. This includes the Chicago area. The threat of tornadoes will extend from now until 4 a.m. A few severe thunderstorms, large hail and damaging winds are also forecast."

Again, WMAQ went silent. When the station returned to the game, Lou Angotti and Eric Nesterenko were on the ice again, matched against Henri Richard and Lemaire. During the weather warning, John Ferguson had taken a penalty on Montreal's power-play, so the teams were again playing four-on-four. Reay was still reluctant to use Hull in a situation that seemed to play into his strengths—if Hull was hard to shadow five-on-five, he'd be significantly harder to mark with open ice in a four-on-four. Disaster ensued. Off the face-off, Nesterenko fired the puck around the boards behind Esposito, intending to get the puck up to Angotti on the left wing. Instead, the puck took a strange bounce off the boards, caromed off the net and landed on the stick of Lemaire who found a wide-open Richard in front of the Chicago net. A one-timer gave the punchy-looking Esposito no chance to recover. The game was tied.

• • •

Insanity is supposedly the repetition of the same thing with the hope of a different outcome. So it was that Reay's mis-begotten strategy reached another level of madness after the intermission. He had barely used Bobby Hull for half a period, believing it was the best way to protect a lead. In the third period the coach seemed afraid of overworking Hull in the event of the game going to overtime. Thus Hull and his linemates had only one shift through the first five minutes.

That shift, however, suggested that putting all their chips on Hull might have limited effect for the Hawks. The reason: John Ashley seemed to be working in concert with Reay in taking Hull out of the game. If you were a Black Hawks fan you might have presumed that John Ashley was, like a wrestling referee, always looking the other way when the villains in a piece were doing their dirty business on the babyface as a way of heightening the drama. "It always seemed like there was one set of rules for the guys who were checking Bobby and another for everyone else," Cliff Koroll said.

At even strength two minutes into the third period, Montreal's checking line of Ferguson, Houle and Pete Mahovlich was back out against Koroll, Maki and Bobby Hull. Houle had the puck behind Chicago's net and centered it to Ferguson whose one-timer from the right side hit Esposito's pad shin-high. The puck rebounded into the slot where Hull gathered it and sped up the middle with open ice ahead of him. A long three-on-two break looked imminent. Pete Mahovlich, who had just sent Keith Magnuson into the net behind Esposito, was a step and a half behind Hull and leaning in the wrong direction. As skaters, there should have been no contest between them— Hull was one of the league's most fluid and explosive skaters while the younger Mahovlich was awkward, even ungainly— but Mahovlich reached out and hooked Hull high, under his right armpit, and hard, hard enough to spin him halfway around. Hull struggled to break free and he pushed off on each stride with a physical violence but barely advanced. Mahovlich smothered him and then, just before the Canadiens' defense took possession of the loose puck, Hull raised his arms as if to say, "I surrender; don't shoot." Ashley made no call.

A few shifts into the third period, Hull was back out with his usual linemates and again matched against the Canadiens' designated checking line. A good minute had passed without a stoppage, some adventurous play that went from Dryden's doorstep to the Hawks' defensive zone and back. Peter Mahovlich was the first Montreal forward to reach the bench and Henri Richard came on—barely avoiding a too-many-men call. Houle found Richard on the left wing a stride outside Chicago's blueline—the far side of the ice from Hull. It must have looked like a harmless position, a one-on-one match-up that would lead to a routine lock-up. But it was the fleet Richard against a wounded Black Hawk defenseman, Keith Magnuson. Richard wheeled down from the left wing and blew by the hobbling Magnuson to break in alone on Esposito. Magnuson dove and reached for the puck. He swung his stick at Richard's skates and made him wobble, taking his right hand off his stick to try to keep his balance. Barely under control, Richard skated over a bad patch of ice—a few minutes earlier, the officials had held up play to try to repair deep ruts in the spot, the ice being almost unplayable at the end of a long season and in the early summer heat. It looked like Richard was going to lose an edge, but he recovered in time to grab hold of his stick again and put the puck past the sprawling Esposito. Montreal: 3, Chicago: 2.

A couple of years after this game, Keith Magnuson wrote *None Against!*, an autobiography with the help of magazine writer Robert Bradford. Magnuson's first reference to that awful moment in 1971 did not appear in the text until page 177, the fourth-last page of the book. *None Against!* is not a straight chronology. Magnuson talked freely about the Black Hawks' run to the Stanley Cup final in the spring of '73. Obviously, however, '71 was the cause of a deep and enduring wound.

"Later people made excuses for me. My knee problems for one. The stiffness and the pain. Richard had picked up the pass coming straight off his bench. Never mind that either. As I've said I don't buy alibis. All that counted was that I was too slow trying to cut him off. He passed me and scored. At least I should have tripped him which in the third period of a tied-up Stanley Cup final would have been a good penalty."

• • •

Peter Mahovlich maintains today that he and his teammates were confident that they were going to win after Richard's second goal. "I don't think that Chicago had any great chances after that," Mahovlich said.

The video and audio record of that game suggests otherwise. So too would the recollection of the Chicago players. True, during what must have seemed like great, awful stretches for the Black Hawks and their fans, J.C. Tremblay managed to rag the puck or control it in his corner of the Montreal end, moving it along the boards about six inches at a time, letting the seconds waste away. Tremblay and the Canadiens iced the puck with an instant and default desperation whenever there was a remotely threatening situation. Bobby Hull managed to draw a hooking penalty on Terry Harper, and another on Peter Mahovlich five seconds after Harper stepped out of the box, and yet the Black Hawks failed to generate a meaningful scoring chance over that four-minute stretch. Hull, out on the ice for a full six minutes, was pushed out to the boards when he poured down the wing and couldn't find an open shooting lane when the puck came back to the point. The other forwards on the home team skated into five rush-nullifying offsides— in fairness, they had to have been discombobulated by yet another line shuffling by Reay in the waning minutes. (Reay had Hull move onto Pit Martin's wing and Koroll onto Mikita's. The coach put Hull out with Gerry Pinder, heretofore unused, and benched Angotti and Nesterenko, the first option on the four-on-four in the previous period.) Nonetheless, in those last 14 minutes, with the Cup hanging in the balance, Ken Dryden eliminated any doubt about the Conn Smythe Trophy.

Jim Pappin had Chicago's two best chances to tie the game and send it into overtime. First, he crashed the net, literally, bowling over Terry Harper and Dryden, but couldn't control a pass from Pit Martin that rolled between his skates. A better chance came seven minutes from the end, when Jacques Laperriere, usually as reliable as a metronome, turned the puck over in the Canadiens' end, much like Nesterenko had in the previous period, firing a routine pass off the side of Dryden's net. Pit Martin gathered the puck on Dryden's glove side and slid it across the crease to Pappin, wide open on the far side of the net, five feet from the goal-line. Pappin one timed the puck cleanly and without pause and started to raise his stick over his head in celebration. Pappin's stick only came high enough to cover his eyes as Dryden kicked out his right leg across the open crease, his skate all the way to the post and the puck deflecting away off the blade.

"One play and a lot of sleepless nights," Pappin said of the thwarted chance.

Thereafter, however, the game moved along with grim inevitability, as if the save on Pappin left the Black Hawks resigned to the inevitability of the outcome—that there was going to be no beating Dryden.

• • •

Hockey Night in Canada's Howie Meeker took the unusual step of naming Al MacNeil the game's first star. MacNeil had pushed all the right buttons, especially compared to Billy Reay's strange management of his personnel. MacNeil hugged

Richard at center ice and the coach was carried around the ice on the shoulders of Pierre Bouchard and Marc Tardif, a clear message of solidarity to put an end to the death threats. After the game, hints were dropped to suggest that the Canadiens intended to bring back MacNeil. The hints were apocryphal. St. Louis Blues coach Scotty Bowman already had a deal done with the Molsons in Montreal.

In the Chicago dressing room, Nesterenko wept. He blamed himself for Richard's goal late in the second period. "I blew it and it cost us the Stanley Cup," he said.

In his book, Magnuson tried to describe the awful guilt he felt in the Black Hawks' dressing room after that loss, "the most terrible and isolated moment" of his life. Magnuson wrote that the entire team was in tears and that he wanted to quit the game on the spot, considering himself "washed up" and disgraced. Even if he never played the game again, he thought he'd have to move away from Chicago and never return.

Hull was wistful. He put the loss in a perspective that only a veteran could have. "I'm getting along in years for this game," he said. "I don't know how many more chances I'll have to be on another Cup winner."

This was unintentionally prophetic. It would turn out to be his last best chance. The Black Hawks were going to make the playoffs again in the spring of '72, but they folded their cards quickly, going out in four straight to the Rangers. By that time Hull suspected and even hoped that he wouldn't play for a Stanley Cup.

● ● ●

"It will take a while to forget this one," Hull said overly optimistically in the Black Hawks' room after the game. "We can only blame ourselves. Because of a few mistakes I have to have a soft drink instead of champagne."

In the wake of a soul-crushing loss like that, even a troop of Boy Scouts would be tempted to knock back something stiffer than a soft drink. And the Black Hawks did. "We always went out after games and we'd have been out that night," Pappin said. Hull and his wife Joanne attended almost every post-game session and after a few drinks, they would be embroiled in an argument—"mostly fun," Pappin said. Hull's teammates got a good laugh out of it, Joanne saying things to her husband that his teammates would never dare say. And it wouldn't have been one drink that night before farewells. "The Hawks went at it hard," Hockey Hall of Fame sportswriter Frank Orr said. Others might have gone harder than Hull but it hit none of them harder than Hull. "Bobby was a nice enough guy until he got a drink into him and then it could turn pretty dark," the Montreal *Gazette*'s legendary Red Fisher said.

The nanny who gave up working for the Hulls after eight years, just two months before the '71 playoffs, saw that darkness long after last call. "He was always worse at home after a game," the nanny said. "It didn't matter if it was a win or loss, he was always worse after drinking. He didn't really keep [alcohol] in the house. He just drank when he was out. It just seemed to affect him that way, turning aggressive and violent, arguing, getting out of control. It had gotten worse over the years. I wouldn't have wanted to be around when he got back that night."

Even Hull realized that those hours after a game ate him up. "If I play a bad game, I feel like crawling through a knot-hole somewhere," he told Scott Young in a CBC documentary in 1964. "I feel terrible. It goes on not only an hour afterwards but through the night. Usually I don't sleep a great deal . . . until I play the next game and possibly play a little bit better."

After Game 7 in '71, with no next games to wake up to, with a growing sense of his athletic mortality, with tornadoes touching down not so very far away, that night in May would have been among the most terrible nights of Hull's career.

• • •

"The problem was we had the wrong people out on the ice. The guys who got us there were Mikita's line and Chico Maki and I. At the crucial time, with the Stanley Cup on the line, Bobby Hull and Chico Maki are sitting on their asses on the bench and Stan Mikita. They had a couple of guys out there who hadn't played one shift in the three series we played to get there. They were out there not just once but twice to get scored on and then a guy with a bad leg by the name of Magnuson was out there with the game tied and the Pocket Rocket went by him like shit through a tin horn. The wrong people cost us the Stanley Cup. I would have been satisfied with this . . ."

Hull raises his hand and shows a ring with '61 engraved on the side.

". . . and '71. We got out-coached in '71."

When Hull works his way through his seasons in Chicago he figures at the very least he should have played for three Cup winners. And that doesn't include the '67 season when the Black Hawks ran away with the regular-season title, leading the six-team league in goals for and goals against before being upset by the Toronto Maple Leafs in the first round.

"We got out-coached when we lost to Montreal in seven games back in '64 or '65," he says. "Instead of starting our line so that Montreal had to put their checking line out against us, they put

some 165-pound center out there and the Canadiens put out a 6-foot-4, 212-pound center named Jean Beliveau. That's poor coaching.

"I never had a good coach in my career. You know what a good coach is? A traveling secretary. They have your room keys. They have your airplane tickets. They run a quick short practice and get the fuck out of there. That's it."

Hull readily throws Lou Angotti under the bus, blaming him for the first two Montreal goals in Game 7. Hull doesn't note that it was Angotti who set him up for the winning goal in Game 7 of the semi-final against the Rangers. Hull readily throws Nesterenko under the bus even though he had been Hull's linemate for years. And he throws Magnuson under the bus even though he was gutting out a torn-up knee. Hull sounds through it all like he's the only party aggrieved.

After surgery to repair his knee, Magnuson spent months in a cast that ran from his ankle to his hip. It turned out that his leg would heal before his psyche. One night in the summer of '71, hobbling on crutches, Magnuson went out for drinks with Cliff Koroll, his roommate. Magnuson and Koroll were seated at a table when another patron, "a loud-talking clown" as described by Magnuson, approached their table and started to bait them about the loss in Game 7. Magnuson couldn't even walk away and had to sit and suffer through the drunk's abuse. Later that night, while Koroll was away from the table, Magnuson wandered out of the bar and into the street and stood in the rain, crying inconsolably. Koroll feared the worst when he came back to their table to find Magnuson gone. He hunted Magnuson down, flagged a taxi and got them home. Koroll ended up carrying Magnuson, cast and all, up the stairs to his bedroom. It was at that point, Magnuson wrote, that the real healing started. Only at the very bottom did Magnuson see the loss *in the best perspective. In* None Against! *he wrote: "I suddenly realized that part of being a true professional is learning to leave all your karma and guilt behind and not to carry your losses around like an enormous bag of yesterdays: the one thing Bobby Hull never did."*

Maybe that was true at the time, but 40 years later Hull is only too ready to reach into his bag of yesterdays.

3

All That Money
Can Buy

"The Black Hawks never offered me a contract," Hull says. His expression is a helpless shrug. His delivery is strictly what's-a-guy-to-do.

That's always been Hull's line: The Hawks didn't offer me a contract. He has always characterized it that way so that the fault could not lie with him but rather with the team that he had led to the Stanley Cup final three times. He has always characterized it that way so that he didn't choose the World Hockey Association over the NHL, or the Winnipeg Jets over the Chicago Black Hawks. He has always characterized it that way so that he was somehow backed into a corner and that his only choice was to play for Winnipeg or not at all. His version: if you were an NHL fan or Chicago fan and thinking of looking for fault, it lies with Arthur and Bill Wirtz, not with the Golden Jet. His version: if you were a WHA fan or Winnipeg fan, the Wirtzes gift-wrapped the most dynamic forward of his generation.

Hull is sitting in a bar owned by and named after the guy who couldn't wait until age 18 to turn pro in the NHL and so signed up with the WHA and went to Indianapolis at an age when most kids are taking their first driving lessons. Hull is sitting in the place owned by the guy who later cried crocodile tears at a press conference announcing his trade from a four-time Stanley Cup winner with a Canadian city in its thrall to Los Angeles, a franchise bereft of history and cachet. In the performance of his life (at least, off the ice), Wayne Gretzky wept in front of the cameras about a trade he could have blocked and didn't and then scapegoated the handiest unsympathetic figure, Peter Pocklington, then owner of the Edmonton Oilers. When in doubt, blame the guy who signs the checks, the one who never played the game. Gretzky's game was never like Bobby Hull's. Hull's wrists were thicker than Gretzky's biceps. But Gretzky went to school on Bobby Hull. What Hull makes the Wirtzes, Gretzky made Pocklington: the villain in the piece.

The truth trickled out about the Gretzky trade. He was a willing and involved participant in the deal. In the years after, the picture became even clearer. His image as the unfailingly modest prodigy evaporated. He couldn't conceal his self-importance and lapsed into the third-person when describing what he cast as his plight: "There was a calling for me . . . that the game was bigger than Wayne Gretzky," he told filmmaker Peter Berg in King's Ransom, *an episode in the 2010 ESPN documentary series* 30 for 30.

Hull has always stuck to his single line: "The Black Hawks never offered me a contract." He has always portrayed himself as the object

of the Wirtzes' neglect. Hull's story had to be like Gretzky's: more
complicated than first reported, than first portrayed.

• • •

Joanne Hull, age 32 though she preferred that it not be mentioned, stood in front of the television camera with a reporter
from CBS holding a microphone in front of her. Her thick, light
brown hair fell to her shoulders before curling up. Her mod dress
looked like it was fresh off Carnaby Street. Black and white and
checkered, it had to leave viewers rubbing their eyes. It was 1968,
the first season after the NHL expanded from six to 12 teams,
and this was an intermission bit on a broadcast going out across
the United States over the network on a Sunday afternoon. CBS
was looking for games featuring strong teams in the biggest
media markets. The game booked by CBS Sports' programmers
looked good back before the season started: Chicago, the team
that led the league in goals for and against in its last Original Six
campaign, was hosting the Toronto Maple Leafs, the defending
Stanley Cup champions. Unfortunately for CBS, that Cup run
had been an old Maple Leafs team's last gasp and so the Black
Hawks were hosting an also-ran. No matter, the broadcasters
focused on Bobby Hull. They wanted to get up close and personal with the game's biggest star. Hull was the owner of many
trophies and Joanne was one of them.

The reporter made small talk with Joanne about the life of
a hockey wife.

"Is there a bit of worry about him?" he asked. It was an
allusion to the physical risks attached to the game. She admitted she did worry. "Bob has had some very bad injuries,"
she said. "I'm upset about his treatment [by opponents on

the ice]. It's unfair to the game and it's unfair to Bob." She also suggested that she was worried about hockey's violence, though she said that the Hull boys had only seen their father in one fight on the ice.

The reporter asked Joanne about the game's grind on a player's family. When he asked her about the time her husband was away on road trips, she broke into a pained expression on reflex. He asked her about the possibility of her husband's retirement in the not-far-off future and his love of farming; she described country life as "marvelous" and said she thought spending time on the farm year-round was "going to be wonderful for my boys." She kept a straight face when she said she and her husband were "looking forward to being full-time farmers."

When the camera pulled back, Joanne was standing in front of an oil painting of her husband, a portrait of Bobby Hull in action. On the canvas Bobby Hull was in a red Black Hawks sweater, making a sharp turn a step from the boards, leaning almost at 45 degrees, holding his stick in his right hand and keeping his left out to keep his balance against the centrifugal force.

The reporter noted that Joanne's hobby was painting and asked her about this portrait of her husband, one she had done during one of those road trips. "This started out as a gift for Mr. Wirtz, our boss," she said. "Every time I take the youngsters in to see Mrs. Knowles [Arthur Wirtz's secretary], she has a bag of peanuts for them. We were talking and she suggested that Mr. Wirtz might like something like that."

Joanne said the painting ended up not being a gift to the Black Hawks owner after all. She said that Bobby had come home from a road trip at 3 a.m. when he saw the portrait for the first time and immediately decided that they were going to hold on to it. "I'm afraid Mr. Wirtz will have to wait until I paint the next one," she said.

Joanne went on to say that her style was usually "more in the impressionist school" and that her husband's time on the road gave her time to paint. She showed another portrait, this time of a young, melancholy boy who in exhaustion has laid his head on a dining table. She said that she had started sketching one of her sons—"tow-heads, I like to call them," she footnoted—but then she decided just to make the portrait "a boy."

The reporter wrapped up the interview quickly. "Pretty well-adjusted boys, pretty well-adjusted parents."

Of course, as would become common knowledge years later, even the most impressionistic of Joanne's canvasses bore a greater likeness to reality than the picture she painted for the television viewers. The farm: born in Los Angeles and raised in Chicago, Joanne didn't like the farm and the idea of retirement there appalled her. The tow-heads: Joanne dyed Blake's dark hair blond so that he was a neater fit at public appearances and in commercials. The violence: the young Hull boys might have seen their father in only one fight on the ice but they didn't have to leave the family home to get more than a heavy dose of real-life violence.

Nothing was farther from the truth, though, than her calling Arthur Wirtz "our boss." It suggested a level of respect that the Hulls never had for Wirtz and his family. "Hate" is not too strong a word—in fact, it keeps popping up in the coverage.

• • •

The Black Hawks were at many levels like the other organizations in the league. They enjoyed all the benefits that went with a monopoly position. Players lacked organization and leverage.

General managers could tell them to like the offer in front of them or to lump it. Well into Hull's career many veterans had to hold down summer jobs and real-life concerns.

"When we sat down to talk with [general manager] Tommy Ivan he'd tell us that the team lost two million dollars last season," Jim Pappin said. "It wasn't a lie exactly. Fact was, the team made a twelve-million dollar profit two years before and then only ten million. Of course we didn't find that out until we all retired."

Chicago was and remains a city of family dynasties. There was "The Family," Al Capone's Mob network that owned and ran the town in the Dirty '30s. Richard Daley served as the almost feudal mayor for a couple of generations and by the time his son Richard Jr. was voted into the same office, the Daley name was all over Chicago, attached to all manner of buildings and programs. The sons and grandsons of William Wrigley Jr. ran the family's chewing-gum business for more than a century before letting an outsider into the executive fold. In Chicago, nobody blinked when the NFL franchise's founder, George Halas, handed off the Bears to George Halas Jr. That was just the way things were done.

The Wirtzes fit right in. The patriarch was Arthur Wirtz, son of a Chicago cop. He had the goods to follow his father onto the force—he was 6-foot-5 and meaner than George Halas. Arthur Wirtz, though, didn't envision himself walking the beat. In his early 20s, fresh out of college, he founded the Wirtz Corporation and made a small fortune in real estate in short order. The Depression was a catastrophe for almost everybody but an opportunity for Wirtz, who snapped up everything from small office buildings to lakeshore high rises from distressed sellers for nickels on the dollar. He formed a partnership with James Norris, a Canadian who moved to Chicago and founded the Norris Grain Co. Norris bankrolled and Wirtz looked for opportunities. The Olympia in Detroit went into receivership and Wirtz and Norris took it over for $2.5 million, and landed the Red Wings franchise in the bargain for another $100,000 in 1933. Two years later they bought Chicago Stadium for $300,000, indisputably their biggest score given that it was built at a cost of $7 million just before Wall Street crashed. They added the St. Louis Arena and, by the end of the Second World War, took over Madison Square Garden.

Wirtz diversified as aggressively as he accumulated properties. If you bought a 40-ouncer in Illinois it was likely that the liquor distribution arm of Wirtz Corp. had a piece of it. If you were depositing a check in the state, there was a good shot that Wirtz Corp. controlled the bank. Still, Wirtz and Norris determined that their arenas' profitability rode on having the lights on for as many nights as possible. They produced Sonja Henie's figure-skating shows. They put hardwood down on the arena floors for hoops, college and pro. Their boxing subsidiary, International Boxing Club, ran the sport in the United States in the '50s under the cloud of fight-fixing and tainted by links to the Mob. Though the Feds' investigation into boxing eventually resulted in jail time for IBC associates Frank Carbo and Blinky Palermo, Wirtz and Norris were slapped down only on anti-trust violations. The courts ruled that IBC constituted a monopoly and, though the partners appealed it all the way to the U.S. Supreme Court, they were ordered to divest themselves of IBC. Thus boxing was the only business that the Wirtzes had to get out of rather than take over. "In those days there was always a 'Mob' feel to the Wirtz business empire, like you'd find around an old boxing gym or in the Bada Bing

Club in *The Sopranos*," said Gerald Eskenazi, who covered the
NHL for the *New York Times* in the '60s and '70s. Eskenazi
suggested that the Wirtzes didn't run from the appearance of
ties with a "rougher" element. "They had a guy named Murphy
on their payroll as the Hawks' PR man, the worst in the league,
a 'dese-dem-and-dose' ex-boxer who had been owed a favor,"
Eskenazi said. "He was typical of those you'd find working in the organization or at Chicago Stadium, nothing like
you'd find around the Canadiens or the Maple Leafs, the real
image-conscious franchises at the time."

Wirtz was already a big hitter in the NHL when he and
Norris took over the Black Hawks in the early '50s. (Norris
positioned himself as a minor partner to those who ran the
estate of franchise founder Frederic McLaughlin. Soon after,
Norris died and Wirtz wrested control of the franchise.) The
Black Hawks had been perennial also-rans and they were drawing crowds of 3,000. Their failures on the ice and at the turn-
stiles were the inevitable product of the organization run on a
shoestring under the previous ownership. In 1955 they hired
Tommy Ivan, who had coached the Red Wings to three Stanley
Cups. Ivan poured money into scouting and coaching with
the team's junior affiliates and made the big club competitive
and profitable in the '60s. Because of this investment in scouting, the Black Hawks found and developed the likes of Hull
and Mikita.

During the Black Hawks' good run in the '60s, Arthur Wirtz
handed over more responsibility in the franchise's day-to-day
operations to his son William Wadsworth Wirtz, who ascended
to the team presidency in 1966. "Dollar Bill" Wirtz was a character in his father's mold. A self-styled tough guy, the younger
Wirtz bragged about an almost certainly apocryphal barroom
brawl with former heavyweight champion Rocky Marciano.

It probably said more about the Brown grad's self-image than his fighting ability and though he never squared off with any of the Black Hawks, contract negotiations got his testosterone flowing.

• • •

When Hull was setting scoring records and featured on the covers of *Sports Illustrated* in his mid-20s, he wanted to be the highest-paid player in the league. Arthur Wirtz and general manager Tommy Ivan assured him that he was, though they offered no proof of the fact. Hull thought he was getting played and he had good reason. The Hawks' bosses made up the rules as they went along.

In the mid-1960s Hull retained Lyman MacInnis, a Toronto accountant, to serve as a financial advisor and to represent him in negotiations with the Black Hawks. Even before MacInnis sat down with Arthur Wirtz, his son Bill and the Hawks brass, he realized that they played by their own rules. "I'm flying into Chicago for the first contract that I did for Bob and I booked into the Bismarck Hotel," MacInnis said. "Bobby and I were in my room at the hotel and going over some details and numbers. I could tell that Bobby was bothered by something but I didn't know exactly what it was. Then, at one point, he raised his finger to his lips and quietly said, 'Shush.' And then he said in a loud voice, 'I could really use a drink but there aren't any glasses in here.' Ten minutes later there's a knock at the door and a bellman had a tray of glasses for us. I didn't know that the Wirtzes owned the Bismarck."

This was business as usual with the imperious Wirtzes— they would stop at nothing. On one occasion Hull believed he had an agreement with Bill Wirtz and signed two documents, one a standard player's contract, the other a separate benefit agreement between the two parties. When he later made an inquiry about the agreement, Wirtz said he knew nothing about it, denying its existence. When Hull went to look for his copy of the agreement, it was gone. Hull might have lost it, but he suspected that it had been lifted by a second-story man on the Wirtz payroll.

According to MacInnis, Bill and Arthur Wirtz went far beyond eavesdropping and pilfering paperwork in their negotiations with Hull. "I had heard stories about the criminal element and the Wirtzes but I didn't put a lot of stock in it at first," MacInnis said. "But that changed as soon as we sat down with them. The Wirtzes scared the hell out of me. They were used to getting their way and they could hurt you in a lot of different ways. The Wirtzes said they could get companies to drop Bob from endorsements. They made veiled threats that had us looking around and thinking that they could be unveiled pretty quickly. They didn't say it directly to Bob but their people said to him that he 'should watch your kids,' basically threatening them. Bobby always thought people were ripping him off and many times they tried. To his mind nobody was worse than the Wirtzes. 'Hatred' would not be a strong enough word."

The relationship between Hull and the Wirtzes worsened with every round of contract talks. A few months after Joanne told CBS viewers about her painting for the Wirtzes, her husband and MacInnis went to the Hawks' owners determined to come away with a contract that would pay him $100,000 for the 1968–69 season. He wanted to be the first NHL player to earn six figures.

The Wirtzes played hardball. They told Hull that he was already the highest-paid player in the game. They bumped up his salary to just over $60,000. Hull and MacInnis suggested the contract could contain performance bonuses based on goals scored. Arthur Wirtz shot down that idea. He told Hull those bonuses would be pointless because he could get dropped down to the third line and see his ice time slashed when he closed in on the targeted numbers.

Back in that era, player salaries weren't disclosed but Hull's was well over twice the league average. According to MacInnis, Hull doubled his salary with money he earned in endorsements. His pursuit of the top dollar wasn't a case of hardship, just a point of pride, and he was never going to get over the sting of being shorted. The hard feelings didn't affect his play—for that $60,000 Hull went out and scored 58 goals, a league record. He could set aside resentment for 60 minutes at a time.

With negotiations at an impasse in the summer of '69, Hull went to reporters and aired his grievances. He accused the Wirtzes of reneging on promises they'd made. He called general manager Tommy Ivan and coach Billy Reay "puppets" of the owners. He said he was going to retire "with regret and much sadness." He said he was going to become a full-time farmer, looking after 300 head of Hereford cattle on his farm in Demorestville. Everyone thought it was an empty threat and Joanne prayed that it was. Hull missed games at the start of the season but never made it to the farm.

Hull went back to the Black Hawks and told the Wirtzes he wanted to play again. His act of defiance ended up costing him: a fine of $17,000. The Wirtzes made him get on the carpet. He had to publicly apologize to the owners, general manager and the coach in front of reporters and cameras in the executive suite of the Bismarck.

"After careful consideration, I have abandoned my desire to retire from organized hockey and I wish to rejoin the Chicago Black Hawks as a player in good standing. My request to return to play has been granted, subject to my playing condition being approved by the club's general manager and coach . . . Differences arose between my advisors and the club on matters which I now realize are entirely unrelated to my functions as a hockey player and I have now abandoned my position I have taken in the past. I regret having made certain statements which were printed out of context and offer my apologies to William W. Wirtz, Tommy Ivan and Billy Reay."

The scripted groveling wasn't enough for the Wirtzes. The Black Hawks put out an announcement that Hull would no longer serve as a "team spokesman." He had liked to bring his sons to practices and let them hang around the dressing room but the team put the kibosh on that going forward. Hull hung on to a shred of his dignity when he refused a conditioning assignment to the Black Hawks' Central League affiliate in Dallas, but management didn't let up when he was returned to the lineup. Billy Reay cut Hull's ice time and made him focus on defensive play—the league's greatest scorer was being recast as a checker. Hull's production plunged—either disenchantment or a crisis of confidence. Eventually Hull's scoring rebounded but the hatred never abated.

• • •

Sport Magazine assigned a freelancer, John Devaney, an author of children's books, to follow Hull on a road trip in the spring of '72. The resulting story, "The 15 Years of Bobby Hull," appeared in the May issue. Teams often suffer a season-long hangover after a run to the Stanley Cup final but the Black Hawks racked up 107 points and finished in first place in the Western Conference in 1972. Tony Esposito showed no after-effects of Jacques Lemaire's Game 7 goal and ran away with the Vezina Trophy—the Black Hawks gave up only 166 goals across the 78-game schedule, a margin of 25 goals better than any other club. Hull was a year older and still the target of shadows but his play didn't fall off either—he would end up with 50 goals for the fourth time in his career. When the *Sport* editors assigned Devaney to the Hull profile they did so fully expecting the team to make another run in the playoffs and maybe land on prime time on CBS again.

The portrait of Hull that emerges in Devaney's article is that of a world-weary superstar. He had always talked about his love of the game but none of that shines through the story. Devaney's wasn't a cynical take—in fact, he sympathized with Hull in his strained dealings with the Hawks management. Hull may have endured physical punishment on the ice but his words in Devaney's article showed that the years of fighting with the Wirtzes had taken a crushing emotional toll.

"Ten or fifteen years ago I just wanted to play hockey," Hull told Devaney. "I loved hockey. Just give me that old biscuit and let me shoot it. Let me go. I just want to chase after the puck and race all over the ice. Now it's less racing around. Maybe there is less enthusiasm. It's more of a business now, scoring goals to win games. Instead of my legs I use more of [what's] upstairs."

"I still like hockey. You get all this money for what? One or two hours of work a night for doing what I love. It's all the other bullshit that I hate. It's all the time you waste. Like we had a meeting at 11 this morning. Now it's 12 o'clock and I have nothing to do until 7:30. At home we practice in the morning and the rest of the day is shot. Maybe it's my own fault. Maybe I should have some other things to do. But when you have business interests, it can take your mind off what you're paid to do—play hockey."

Hull went on to say that he hated the months living out of a suitcase and all the time he spent away from his family. But he admitted a "hate-on" for management that dated to the dealings leading to his retirement and "un-retirement." If you had looked at the standings you might have liked Chicago's chances of winning a Stanley Cup. If you had read between the lines of the *Sport* profile, you didn't, not if they were planning on riding Hull once more.

• • •

Most NHLers accepted their lot in their professional lives. They accepted that management had all the leverage and used it to full and brutal effect. They didn't bother to look up into the stands and figure out the nightly take for the owners. Hull did. He sensed that he gave more value than he received. He didn't just want to be the game's best-paid player. More than that, he expected to be treated well by the owners. His ideas of how a worker should be treated by his bosses dated back to his youth.

Hull grew up in what might seem like a dreary place: Point Anne, Ontario, an isolated village on the north shore of the Bay of Quinte, seven miles east of Belleville, Ontario. There's just one road into Point Anne—it comes to an abrupt end at the grounds of Canada Cement, the company that founded the village back in 1905. Robert Hull, Bobby's father, arrived in Point Anne with his new bride in the 1930s and took a job on a kiln in the plant, a job that he'd hold down for 40 years. It wasn't that he was just a loyal employee but that the loyalty went both ways. The Hulls' home was, like the others there, built by the company and provided for them. So were the grade school, the community hall and four churches. So were the first hockey rink Bobby ever played on and the baseball diamond. To Bobby Hull's mind, these weren't just perks. They were what made Point Anne special to him. When a film crew came in at the height of his fame, he talked about the town like a Chamber of Commerce spokesman. Point Anne was, he said, "where everyone in town went to the same school [and] where kids grow up to play hockey."

Point Anne was less defined by the school and hockey than it was by Canada Cement. Robert Hull and his co-workers in Point Anne were sheltered from the Great Depression, earning good wages and having job security. There had only ever been a single labor stoppage in the history of the company in Point Anne. "Everyone had a positive feeling about Canada Cement," said Clara Sheppard, who grew up in Point Anne and went to school with the Hulls, a few years ahead of Bobby. "The union and the company worked quite well together. I never remember it being disagreeable."

Point Anne was just one of hundreds of company towns that were founded in North America in the late 1800s and early 1900s. "Companies had to go to the frontiers to get the resources for production," said Neil White, a historian who has studied and written extensively about the company towns. "Wages tended to be higher than average and the cost of living low. Elsewhere in the world you might have found labor unrest in company towns—management and the workers equally obstinate, neither giving an inch. You were much more likely to find an acquiescent, collaborative relationship between labor and management in Canadian and American company towns and companies would have looked after those who had specialized skills. The company and the townspeople recognized that, with smaller communities, everybody knew everybody else and it was more important that everybody got along. Living in close confines and living next door to your co-workers provided a greater impetus for social cohesion."

Sports were central to Point Anne's social fabric. Robert Hull was a star of the company's hockey team and one of the mainstays of the Point Anne Cement Men, a team that won a provincial baseball championship over all-star squads from the big cities. Teams in other company towns were national powers in hockey—the Trail Smokeaters and the Cornerbrook Royals won the Allan Cup, the Canadian senior hockey championship.

"Those who played [for the company teams] helped organize the boys' games at the rink and on the diamond," said Clara Sheppard. "All winter long, kids would skate on the bay when it froze over and play in the park all summer long until sunset. Lots of the boys followed their fathers to work for Canada Cement and to play for the company team."

"People who leave company towns almost inevitably say that it was great to grow up there," Neil White said. "Values they learn there they take with them wherever they go."

Hull never had a good word to say about the Wirtzes and never a bad one about Point Anne. He might have not followed his father into the factory—none of his brothers did—but he only wanted from the Black Hawks what Canada Cement gave his father and others in Point Anne: fair value, security and respect.

• • •

Hull was expansive when *Sport*'s John Devaney raised the subject of the World Hockey Association, a league that was ramping up to take on the NHL in the fall of '72. Devaney even noted that he "felt like a pipeline to NHL owners" though Hull's statements were entirely intended for the Wirtzes' ears. "The WHA will happen. A lot of guys making $15,000 a year will be offered $30,000 and they won't think twice about leaping . . . you have to be a mercenary."

Hull told Devaney that he didn't intend to jump leagues. "When I sign with the Hawks next time, they will look after my wants," he said. He went on to rework the scripted apology from his un-retirement speech. "I was wrong when I was at odds with management the other times. I let other people talk for me. This time I will sit down with them and my accountant. My accountant knows exactly the boundaries of what can be realistically acquired. He's no pusher."

It's hard to imagine the Wirtzes took Hull's words at face value. They knew that he had never changed his mind about them and believed that they had taken advantage of him. If they didn't smell a rat when he admitted that he was wrong they should have. When he said that the new league "will happen," he was operating on inside information. It was more like he was going to make it happen. "The 15 Years of Bobby Hull" was his kiss-off to the Wirtzes. In his own mind he already had a new boss.

● ● ●

If Ben Hatskin had been born in Montreal he'd have been the real-life model for a roguish character in a Mordecai Richler novel, comically drifting between high and low society. If Hatskin had been born in Chicago, he would have served well as a picaresque protagonist in the mold of Saul Bellow's

Augie March. To literature's loss, Hatskin's parents left Russia
and settled in Winnipeg's hard-scrabble North End, a neighborhood made up of ethnic blue-collar workers and a Jewish
community shut out of better parts of the city. The Hatskins'
two sons took up the family business, something so dreary and
utilitarian that Richler and Bellow might well have scripted it:
the Hatskins made boxes. Crates, corrugated cardboard. When
something of value was delivered, the Hatskins' contribution
was the part you threw away.

The family business never manufactured a box that would
have easily fit Ben Hatskin. Physically and socially he could not
be contained. He was a massive man. He went to Oklahoma to
play football, likely the only way that he would have set foot
on a college campus. He came back to spend a stretch on the
Blue Bombers' line, though with less distinction than he'd later
claim. He remained involved in sport, owning and running the
Winnipeg Junior Jets hockey team in the '60s. He bought race-
horses and hung around with the railbirds at the Assiniboine
racetrack.

Hatskin did take over the family business—his only sibling,
Ruben, wasn't quite up to that and walked in his older brother's shadow. But Ben Hatskin wasn't content to be the King of
Cardboard. He diversified, going from boxes to jukeboxes. If
you dropped a dime in the slot to hear a song anywhere on the
prairies, it landed in Hatskin's pocket.

Credulous folks might have thought he was just an enter-
prising businessman. Reality was more complicated than that,
however. Jukeboxes were as much a racket as a business and
not simply because it was an all-cash enterprise. Hatskin didn't
pay owners of establishments where his jukeboxes could be
profitably placed and they didn't share in his take. They had

to see things his way, not because he was garrulous and good-natured. They had to because it was common knowledge that he was connected.

Boxes and jukeboxes were his businesses in plain sight but Hatskin was involved in other matters. He liked to think of himself as a financier. Others outside of polite company would label him a loan shark. Both labels fit. That he provided a needed service lent a little dignity to this line of work. Many of his people—North Enders, Jews and others outside the Winnipeg establishment—were leery about going to banks to take out loans. Many who went to Hatskin couldn't get money any other way. For Hatskin it was serendipitous synergy: many who needed to get floated happened to own businesses where he could set up jukeboxes.

Hatskin might have given more bear hugs and back slaps than anyone in town but he could afford to keep a friendly face in his line because it was believed that he was a phone call away from gentlemen who packed heat. His long-time mistress "worked" as his secretary and had been the moll of several men who did time. One guy who was unaware of her history took her on a date, only to be ambushed by a pistol-wielding ex-boyfriend and told to beat it. But none of her former suitors seemed to resent her employment and enjoyment with Hatskin. Their understanding might have been a matter of self-preservation.

A Winnipeg lawyer provides an instructive anecdote about the company Hatskin kept in the '60s. "A lawyer friend and I went to Florida on an impulse not long after we were out of law school," the lawyer said. "We booked into a hotel in Miami and after a time we realized that there were no women around. Gay? No, not that. Guys in very expensive suits with a very rough way of talking. Then we realized that we'd stumbled into something like the Mob summit in *The Godfather*. Now we're wondering what kind of jackpot we've got ourselves into. We realize that we're pretty clean-cut professional guys and that they're making us for G-men. We could be in all kinds of trouble. All of a sudden, in the lobby, we see Ben Hatskin. We're saying, 'Ben, what the hell are you doing here?' Ben tells us that he has come down because he did some sort of deal with a guy here. He didn't get very specific at all—he made a point of that and we didn't ask because we didn't want to know. He says that he'll let them know that we're okay."

Two months after this chance meeting in Florida, the lawyer picked up a copy of the Winnipeg *Free Press* and in the social notes found an item about Hatskin and a partner acquiring an Arizona mansion formerly owned by Dutch English, a Chicago mobster. Those who had taken out loans with Hatskin could read between the lines.

This reputation was useful when it came to collecting accounts outstanding but the city establishment frowned on it. But even if Hatskin had been a Boy Scout he still wouldn't have had any hope of getting into the Manitoba Club—into the early '70s it was still all-Gentile. Even reputable Jewish businessmen looked down on him, regarding him as a stain on the B-list at best.

Hatskin never set down roots in Dutch English's former home. His business was portable but he knew his act played best in Winnipeg. He had his network of contacts in the city. He had powerful friends, most notably the Simkin family. Friends from his youth in the North End and owners of a large construction company, the Simkin brothers backed Hatskin on larger ventures that required major capital.

Hatskin was both a loyal friend and loyal Winnipegger—
he fiercely defended the city to those who would knock it.
Predictably, he was bent out of shape that the NHL awarded
an expansion franchise to Vancouver in 1970. He thought
Winnipeg was a better hockey town. He told Clarence Campbell
as much when he bumped into him in the lobby of the Chateau
Lacombe in Edmonton. He asked the league president what it
would cost to put an NHL team in Winnipeg and was told that
$7 million would be a starting point. Campbell spun on his
heel and walked away, considering the matter dead.

Wild Bill Hunter, owner of the junior team in Edmonton,
also thought his town was a better fit for the NHL than
Vancouver. He had also approached Campbell and been sum-
marily dismissed. Rather than grouse about the slight, Hunter
phoned Hatskin and they concluded that there had to be a way
to get in the game without laying out $7 million.

Hatskin was 55 years old, an obese two-pack-a-day chain-
smoker, not a candidate for longevity. He was beginning to
think about leaving a legacy. He and his long-suffering wife,
Cecilia, had no children and he had no blessed accidents
with his mistresses. A hockey team would resonate with
Winnipeggers more than a shopping plaza bearing his name.
He was also thinking about crashing Old Money Winnipeg's
party, striking a blow for the North Enders. He claimed to be
worth $3 million and might have been worth a good part of
that, but even at his most generous self-valuation he was at
best a welterweight in the establishment. He thought that a big
splash with pro hockey would win him the high-society acceptance he craved. A variation on Richler's Duddy Kravitz: a man
with a team is somebody. Others would have been daunted and
denied because they'd have tried to play by the NHL's rules.

Hatskin sought out the help of those who had rewritten the rules once already.

• • •

Dennis Murphy, Gary Davidson and Don Regan, three young lawyers from southern California, had gained some measure of fame in sport in the late '60s. They had founded the American Basketball Association, a maverick rival league to the well-established National Basketball Association. By the fall of 1970, however, they were squeezed out of the ABA and happened to be looking for new horizons when Hatskin and Hunter came knocking with an idea: a rival pro league to compete with the NHL. When Hatskin and Hunter arrived for a meeting with Murphy, Davidson and Regan in Newport Beach, the three lawyers wondered who these Canadians were and if they were on the square. They were somewhat surprised that Hatskin and Hunter didn't blink when they were asked for $25,000 each up front before they opened a file, and cut a check for $5,000 on the spot. A little due diligence confirmed, to their surprise, that Hatskin's and Hunter's money was real. Either they didn't know or were willing to overlook questions about some of Hatskin's sources of financing and associates. They were even more impressed that Dave Simkin would be taking a 50 percent interest in a franchise in Winnipeg and putting the family's war chest behind the venture.

The three lawyers had never seen a hockey game. They couldn't have told you the difference between offside and icing but they needed no lessons about the business fundamentals of professional sport. The ranks of sports franchises and owners had exploded. The AFL had launched in 1960 and won a merger with the NFL before the decade was out. Hatskin and Hunter had sought out Murphy, Davidson and Regan because they had founded the American Basketball Association and by '71 the league was in full flight—not up there with the NBA in terms of media exposure and revenue but decent quality entertainment, attracting talent, competitively catching up to the NBA. By the early '70s a merger between the two hoops leagues seemed inevitable (though it was still several seasons off).

Hatskin and Hunter wanted to go that same route—starting a new league wasn't the goal but the means to an end, a way to force a merger and bring NHL teams to Winnipeg and Edmonton.

Hatskin and Hunter had sought out the California lawyers but they weren't blindly determined to go ahead with their scheme. They needed to be convinced about its viability. "We gave them the greatest pitch job of our lives but our business plan was a pretty good business plan," Don Regan said. "[Hatskin and Hunter] wanted to get into professional hockey. If they got an NHL expansion team, they'd spend five million or so. They'd get to draft, who? Mother Teresa and you and me and they'd finish last forever. They'd probably be ten or fifteen million upside down before they'd be competitive and making any money. Starting up a rival league they'll lose a million or two but be able to go after good players like the AFL did and like we did in the ABA. At the end of three or four years they'll have a good team and they'll have lost four or five million dollars and be able to force a merger with the NHL. That looked good to [Hunter and Hatskin]."

Murphy, Davidson and Regan came up with a plan that drew on their experience from the ABA, something that would enhance the league's credibility and put a merger on the fast track. "Early on we determined that for the league to succeed at the gate and to get a television contract we needed to get a superstar," Regan said.

They had tried the same approach when starting out the ABA but with disastrous results. They had it only half right: they believed a famous name from the NBA would win them needed publicity. Though the ABA founders successfully landed a Hall of Famer, they miscalculated. They recruited George Mikan, long retired, to be the league's commissioner. "George was a neat guy but he was seven feet tall, had thick glasses and was awkward, physically and socially," Regan said. "And I don't think George was captain of his GE College Bowl team either. He wasn't on the court. He wasn't an icon to kids. And in the end, because George ran the show, our influence diminished."

The object lesson: land an action hero, not a figurehead. The hockey neophytes trusted the task of strategizing to Max Muhleman, a sports marketer who could dine out for life on the fact that he convinced Goodyear to be the first company to position its corporate logo on the side of a stock car. "After a year of research we determined that the guy who was most likely to sign on with us was Bobby Hull," Regan said. Hatskin went through back channels with contacts he had made in junior hockey to make sure that Hull's contract was up at the end of the season and that he was fully disenchanted with the Wirtzes. Affirmative on both counts.

"We started to negotiate with him and Stan Mikita," Regan said. "We only pursued Stan because we thought we might need to get him to sign on to get Bobby. But Bobby was the key player. We concluded that a million dollar check would do the job."

They would hit their target. Down to the dollar. That it would be just one slice of the biggest player contract in sports history didn't make any of them hesitant—any of them, including Hull.

• • •

In the film *The Devil and Daniel Webster*, a stranger mysteriously appears on the scene and offers a down-on-his-luck farmer the promise of great prosperity for seven years in return for his soul at the end of the term. The stranger, Mr. Scratch, lives up to his end of the Faustian bargain but the farmer has second thoughts and enlists the great lawyer Daniel Webster to argue his case against the Devil. An adaptation of Stephen Vincent Benet's short story of the same name, *The Devil and Daniel Webster* provided an allegorical lesson on greed as seduction against better judgment.

No less than Mr. Scratch, Ben Hatskin understood the magnetic pull of a dollar and he knew that it might be the single enticement that he could offer Bobby Hull. And like Mr. Scratch, Hatskin arrived on the scene unannounced. He first made contact with Hull when the Black Hawks were in Vancouver in November '71. Hatskin was in town, ostensibly for the Grey Cup, but he had a stealth mission. The Black Hawks were staying at the Hotel Vancouver, so Hatskin set up shop across the street at the Georgia. He had a well-placed intermediary to deliver a message to Hull: Bob Turner, a former NHLer who had had a stint with the Black Hawks. A Winnipegger, Turner was willing to do Hatskin a favor and he convinced Hull to give Hatskin a call without specific details. When Hull did call, Hatskin simply told him that he had a business proposition and if he wanted to talk about it, away from rubbernecking fans and teammates, to walk over to the Georgia.

There had been rumbles about the rival league's launch but few in the NHL, from the front office to the dressing room, gave it much of a chance of ever getting off the ground. Hatskin had a good feeling about Hull from the handshake on. He had reason to. Hull's motivations went beyond the simple vice of greed. He wanted revenge for the Wirtzes' betrayal. If it was any sort of shot he could fire over the bow of the Wirtzes' yacht, Hull was all ears. In *Paradise Lost*, John Milton's Satan said it was "better to reign in Hell than serve in Heaven" and for Hull, reigning in a hockey netherworld had it over submitting as the Wirtzes' serf, no matter what the spotlight glories were.

In that first meeting Hatskin dropped a couple of bombs. First he mentioned one million dollars. Hatskin would later tell people that he picked the number out of the air, a tall tale. Hull would later tell people that, asked to name a price, he decided to ask for something outrageous just to scare off a nuisance, another tall tale. It was in fact a price point that the founding team determined after months of research. Hatskin also spelled out to Hull a vision: that Hull would have significant influence, if not quite control, on the team and even the league. He would be the playing coach—he'd always thought he could do a better job than anyone else and this presented a chance to prove it. He would be out in front of the league. His wouldn't be a standard playing contract but rather a personal-services contract. The million bucks appealed to Hull's greed and the position of star and boss went straight to his ego.

Regan called Hull "a quick study" for a small-town boy who didn't finish high school and had never been out of the province of Ontario until the Black Hawks called him up from St. Catharines. He wasn't shy either. He set down conditions in that first meeting—that the WHA founders would pay him the million up front, that there'd be money on the back end and that they would pick up any costs if the matter went to court. And Hull told them that he was going to take it back to his advisor on financial and contract matters. Mike Royko, the famed Chicago newspaper columnist of that era, once proposed that the city's seal should have been a hand, palm extended, and its motto *Ubi Est Mea* ("Where Is Mine?" in translation from the Latin). Hull had long asked the question. He didn't find it. It found him. He knew where it was going to come from. Only the brokering remained but he already had his hand out.

• • •

In the early '70s, Hull had cut back on the use of Lyman MacInnis's services, using him only for tax preparation and advice, and had retained a Chicago accountant named Harvey Wineberg to handle contract negotiations with the Black Hawks. Wineberg had made an end-run around the International Management Group, the powerful sports agency, to handle Hull's business affairs.

IMG wasn't representing any NHL players at the time. Most of its clients were PGA golfers and pros from the tennis circuit. The agency's executives, however, believed Hull had the potential to cross over from a niche sport into the commercial mainstream. IMG could offer Hull the full benefit of its network of industry contacts for endorsements—the agency was essentially one-stop shopping on Madison Avenue for celebrity athletes to serve as commercial pitchmen. Hull was already making more off the ice in endorsements than any other player in the NHL but IMG believed he was only just starting to tap his earning potential. The agency contacted Wineberg to set up a meeting with Hull and the accountant set a date. The agency also sent along a proposal with a marketing strategy, along with some preliminary paperwork about the terms of a business relationship.

Wineberg ambushed IMG. When the boys from the agency showed up in Chicago, Hull wasn't on hand, only Wineberg, and there were words but no discussion. Wineberg advised them that Hull had just signed an agreement to have him look after both his client's hockey and off-ice deals. And the accountant then expressed his regret that they had come all the way to Chicago for nothing. What had happened was that Hull had taken one look at the paperwork and didn't trust IMG because of what he thought was an unfair commission— Wineberg would remember it as 15 percent on salary and 20 percent on endorsements. In the meeting with IMG, this point led to an angry exchange. "I suggested they go represent someone who was not so important, someone who could really be helped with all of that expertise they were implying they possessed and I lacked," Wineberg wrote in his memoir, *Thanks for Your Trust: Memories of an Untamed Accountant.*

That was Wineberg's style. Where MacInnis had been coolly dignified, even ironic, in handling personal affairs, Wineberg was aggressive. MacInnis was tai chi; Wineberg, full-contact karate. Wineberg's first sports client had been Chicago Cubs manager Leo Durocher (a.k.a. "the Lip") and they were abrasive soulmates. When the Wirtzes told Wineberg they intended to negotiate only with Hull and with Wineberg out of the room, the accountant turned it around on the owners and said they didn't need to deal with his client but to go to him directly. Wineberg dismissed Alan Eagleson even more bluntly than IMG when the head of the NHLPA tried to elbow his way into representing Hull.

Eagleson was representing Bobby Orr when he made overtures to Hull. Hull made no secret of his hatred for Eagleson and low regard for lawyers in general. Eagleson, however, thought he could get past Hull's antipathy with money on the line. "Bobby just wanted nothing to do with him," said Lyman MacInnis. "He didn't trust him at a gut level, which was probably a good reading of [Eagleson] as it turned out."

By the early '70s, Bobby Orr was fully eclipsing Hull. The arcs of their careers were a sharp contrast. In Hull's second season he was still learning the game—he called a post-season tour of Europe with the New York Rangers "when I really learned to play the game." By Orr's second season, he was redefining the game—winning the first Norris Trophy as the league's best defenseman. By 1972, it was written in stone that Orr was the greatest defenseman in the history of the game and arguably the greatest player ever.

Hull wanted to win a Stanley Cup but, above all else, he wanted to be the highest-paid player in the game—which would mean making more than Bobby Orr. It might have seemed like overreaching but, then again, Hull looked at it as a matter of career achievement. He had been the face of his team for more than a decade and his career was winding down. With Hull's ambition in mind, Wineberg met with Arthur Morse, the Wirtzes' lawyer, in the fall of '71. Morse wanted Hull at the meetings, presumably because Hull would get tempted by the first number that was thrown out in talks. Wineberg responded that he was to serve in his capacity alone on Hull's behalf. Today it's commonplace for athletes to play the contract game in the media, to negotiate in print and over the airwaves.

With the Wirtzes and Morse, it worked the other way around. What was said by Wineberg in confidence in the meetings with ownership landed in the sports section the next day, always leaving the impression that the agent and player were greedy and unreasonable.

Morse told Wineberg that the reports were that Orr made $150,000 a year and that the Hawks might be reluctantly willing to step up that high. Wineberg, echoing Hull, said the offer was never fully in place. It didn't get far because the accountant had only the Black Hawks' word on Orr's salary. "I didn't know what it was and they did," Wineberg said.

The talks hit an impasse.

The Wirtzes knew that a rival league was in the planning stage. They were confident that no one could take on the NHL. They were confident that as valuable as Hull was to the Hawks, so was the team to its marquee player. And they were confident that time would wear down Wineberg and Hull. The owners' hubris would come back to haunt them.

When Hull was back in Chicago after his first meeting with Hatskin, he filled in the accountant about the details of his conversation with Hatskin. "Bobby told me, 'They're talking in millions,'" Wineberg said. "I told him there might be risks attached but Bobby was a risk taker. I don't think that he wanted to take this risk at the start. He wasn't looking to leave Chicago. He didn't want to leave Chicago in the worst way. He understood the risks. A lot of people wouldn't have done what he did [in the same situation] because they aren't risk takers like he was. He felt he had no choice in the end. This wasn't a risk he was anticipating or even happy about."

The next stage brought Regan and Wineberg together. Regan did a double take when he looked at the copy of Hull's contract with the Black Hawks. But for Bobby Hull's name and the dollar amount, it was a standard player contract used by all NHL teams. "My first reaction was, 'This isn't a contract,'" Regan said. "I showed it to friends, experts in contract law, and they also said it wasn't a contract. You didn't have to be an expert to reach that conclusion."

Simply put, the line in the contract binding a player to his team "at a salary to be determined" was void. In any contract, the terms have to be specifically stated to be legally binding, and in this case, the salary was left unstated. It was insufficient to leave any significant condition as "to be determined." What was known as the reserve clause, the single line that bound a player to a team in perpetuity, What was known as the reserve clause, the single line that bound a player to a team in perpetuity, effectively and artificially limited salaries—it denied players access to a free market to get fair value for their services. The reserve clause had gone almost unquestioned and unchallenged by professional athletes in North America to that point in the 20th century. Major league baseball players had tested the reserve clause twice, by George Toolson in the early '50s and by Curt Flood in 1969, taking the matter to the Supreme Court where they struck out with the nine justices. The media, pro-management at the time, demonized Toolson and Flood, labeling them everything up to and including Trotskyites for challenging the system. Nonetheless Regan believed that hockey's reserve clause wouldn't stand up to a legal test and he believed that Hull's character and history with management would embolden him for an ugly court fight. It was little wonder the Wirtzes and other owners didn't want lawyers in on contract negotiations. The reserve clause would have tripped the alarm for any lawyer who had ever drawn up a contract in some other field. The door was open, Regan believed, and he convinced Hull and Wineberg of the same. At the end of the season Hull was free to walk through it. And others would follow.

• • •

Regan, Hull and Wineberg met in Denver and hammered out the numbers. At the end of the day, they had an agreement in principle: $1 million up front, $1.75 million on the back end across the life of a 10-year contract. The task of drawing up the contract was passed on to Telly Mercury, Hatskin's lawyer, who spent weeks sweating out a 37-page document.

As fast as Regan danced, Hatskin had to be even lighter on his feet when he presented his fellow franchise owners with the proposition that each kick in $100,000 to cover Hull's million-dollar signing bonus—up front, before the league had played a single game. The other franchise owners were, in Regan's words, "not overly capitalized" and a couple bowed out of the project as soon as Hatskin floated the proposal. Mercury's billable hours on the contract might have been for naught but over the course of weeks Regan used his powers of persuasion to squeeze as much as he could out of as many as he could. Hatskin, with the backing of Dave Simkin, made up the shortfall.

If Hull and Wineberg had been privy to what was going on behind the scenes, they might have been scared off. Regan, Murphy and Davidson had made their bones with the ABA but otherwise it was amateur hour.

The original pitch to franchisees, a painfully plain-language document, was sent out to interested parties. It promised candy. It noted (in abridged form):

Hockey is a lucrative sport, especially for the original teams . . . The professional sport of hockey has enjoyed a steady growth in attendance in the United States during the last six years . . . The franchise price rose to $6-million each for the most recent franchise purchases by Vancouver and Buffalo . . . The franchises operating in warmer climate areas have had a problem with a lack of familiarity on the part of the fans . . . The hockey superstar, like his counterpart in other sports, is the one who creates the excitement to cause fans to come to the arena . . . Television, closed circuit and cable TV, will become an increasingly important factor . . . The bottom [sic] for all sports franchises, in addition to the all-important financial wherewithal, is to have experienced competent management . . . History shows us that once a professional sports franchise in any of the four major sports is established, a very few [sic] have ever gone out of business.

In ways they couldn't have imagined based on this pitch, the WHA was going to make a lot of history.

The would-be owners were also provided examples of team budgets, including:

- Arena rentals: $58,500 ($1,500 for 39 games)
- Training camp: $10,000
- Team insurance: $5,000
- Equipment and uniforms: $12,000

These, of course, were simpler times but not as simple as the founders presumed—the Toronto Toros ended up paying $50,000 (Canadian) a night to rent Maple Leaf Gardens. In the end, Regan, Murphy and Davidson proposed $1 million as a budget for teams, with the largest expense being player salaries, which they pegged at $340,000 (17 players at an average of $20,000). To say they were going to overshoot the mark on that would vastly understate it.

If Harvey Wineberg had seen the fundamentals on paper, he might have advised Bobby Hull not to pick up the phone at the Georgia.

• • •

The WHA was at this point something more than an idea. Hull was the biggest piece of business but there were hundreds of lesser pieces of business that the franchise owners had to move on. Hull's signing was going to be the defining moment but dozens of journeymen had already decided to make the leap of faith. In February 1972 Norm Beaudin was a 30-year-old forward who had played a grand total of 25 career NHL games with St. Louis and Minnesota. He had one career goal. Even with two rounds of NHL expansion, he remained a career minor-leaguer. He was the prototype of the player targeted by WHA franchises and the first signed by the Winnipeg Jets. "I got scouted in Cleveland in February and I liked Ben," Beaudin said. "At that stage of my career I wasn't worried about uncertainty. I signed pretty quickly. There was still more than two months left in the [AHL] season but I committed to them. They told me that Bobby Hull was going to Winnipeg. They were pretty definite about it. They said that he had agreed to go. I wasn't going to give up a chance to play with Bobby Hull."

Beaudin was clear about the timeline: he committed to the Jets with weeks left in the AHL regular season. Well before Hull was telling *Sport*'s John Devaney that he expected to finish his career with the Black Hawks, that he was sure the Wirtz family was going to look after him, Bobby Hull was expecting to be playing in Winnipeg the next season, which would look after the Wirtzes in a totally different way. He was keeping up appearances in case the WHA and, more specifically, the million dollars, fell through.

• • •

A couple of months after Beaudin signed with the Jets on the basis of Hull playing in Winnipeg, Hull led the Black Hawks into the playoffs. The Black Hawks rolled over the out-matched Pittsburgh Penguins in four straight games to set up a second-round series against the New York Rangers for the second consecutive spring. Chicago had beaten New York in a tense seven-game semi-final the year before and Hull had been the defining player in the series in '71. Now Hull was coming off a 50-goal, First All-Star season. By virtue of a first-place finish in the Western Conference in the regular season, the Black Hawks owned home-ice advantage in what promised to be a memorable match-up. The Rangers, however, obliterated that home-ice advantage, winning the first two games in Chicago with the Black Hawks looking surprisingly flat. After a hard-fought loss in Game 3 in New York, Hull's team laid down and were routed in the clinching game 6–2.

In the Monday-morning quarterbacking that ensued, many believed that the team ran out of gas after the long run to Game 7 of the final a year before. It was an under-achievement, to be sure, but fans and management presumed that Hull and the Hawks would be in a position to make another run to the Stanley Cup final the next spring. They had it half right: the Hawks were going to get that close again in 1973, losing again to the Canadiens. But in the aftermath of the second-round loss to the Rangers in 1972, the only people in Chicago who suspected that Hull had played his last game for the Black Hawks that night were Hull and Wineberg.

• • •

It was hard to get a hockey player on the cover of *Sports Illustrated* during the hockey season. Harder when his season was over. Two weeks after the Rangers knocked Chicago out of the playoffs Hull pulled on his Black Hawks sweater for a cover shoot with *Sports Illustrated*. His picture appeared below the line "The Man They Want to Steal." He was, in fact, The Man Who Had Already Accepted a Pre-emptive Offer. Hull told *Sports Illustrated* that he had an agreement in principle with the WHA, the Winnipeg Jets and owner Ben Hatskin. "If they make good they've got themselves a hockey player," he said. They were making good, getting the money in place, and the WHA and the Jets were getting themselves a hockey player. The NHL was going to be coming down with a multi-million dollar headache. Hull didn't say anything about having a higher cause—nothing about blazing a trail for other players to land a fair deal. He was pretty plain about his intentions. He was interested in what he thought was a fair deal for him and him alone.

• • •

The espionage element kicked in during the wee hours on the morning of June 27, 1972. At 4 a.m. Bobby Hull met Ben Hatskin and a small entourage who had chartered a plane to fly to St. Paul, Minnesota. For tax advantages, it was key to Hull that his contract be signed in the United States. Under normal circumstances there'd have been no need for the stealth. The Wirtzes, however, were making a desperate stab, not their last one, to hold on to Hull and had won an injunction to prevent Hull from signing on with the WHA until the matter was put before the court. The issuing of the injunction, however, wasn't by itself enough to block Hull's signing: it had to be served on one of the parties, either Hull or the WHA principals. If the contract was already signed, however, the injunction wasn't worth the paper clip holding it together.

Leaving nothing to chance, Hatskin might have directed the pilot to fly under the radar. However, once they landed, once the contract was signed and witnessed, they were going to announce the deal in befitting style. Unbeknownst to the WHA brass, Hatskin and Hull and the rest, the Minnesota Fighting Saints, another of the WHA charter franchises, had hired a 1934 Phaeton Rolls Royce and an armed escort for a procession to the exclusive Minnesota Club where they staged a press conference. Then it was back to the airport and back on the plane for the return trip to Winnipeg.

A few hours later Hull and Hatskin stood in the middle of 5,000 fans clogging the sun-bathed intersection of Portage and Main. The two shook hands and held the mock check aloft. At about that time Don Regan stepped off the plane in Chicago and was served with the injunction. Regan just flashed the freshly signed pact. The Wirtzes were a day late and $2.75 million short.

• • •

"The Hawks never offered me a contract," Hull says, omitting the fact that he was already promised to another.

At Wayne Gretzky's Hull is, as ever, rewriting history. When the facts are laid out, when the gaps in his story are filled in, the optics are bad. He knows how bad he looks if it's known that he was donning the sweater of the team that made him the game's greatest star and yet had already packed his bags and emotionally checked out. He knows how bad he looks if it's revealed that he was carrying the Black Hawks into the playoffs in '72, expected to give another transcendent effort and yet committed, at least verbally and seemingly emotionally, to the WHA. It was the sports version of going on a blind date when you're engaged and the wedding is on the weekend.

And, in fact, the notion that the Black Hawks didn't offer Hull a contract, that they didn't put anything on the table, is a bit of a fudge. Milt Dunnell of the Toronto Star *had a long-standing relationship with Hull, one going back to his very first NHL regular-season game, a 1–0 win over the Maple Leafs in Chicago. Dunnell was on the plane with Hull and company when it touched down for the signing of his contract with the WHA. Dunnell wrote the next day: "There is no doubt that Hull would have signed, a year ago, for what the Hawks had finally offered him—a million for five years. They didn't do it then because they didn't have to do it. By the time they realized that the discussions with Ben Hatskin were not about the price of wheat, Hull had the smell of fresh money in his nostrils." Hull had confided in Dunnell and later others that the Wirtzes, once convinced that the WHA threat was real, recognized the urgency and upped the ante, offering him $200,000 a year over a long term. All they really ended up offering him was a chance to gloat.*

On its face, Hull playing out the season with the Black Hawks while intending to jump to the WHA would violate our sensibilities about the game and sport in general. In fact it's commonplace, just in the case of Hull a little more obvious. Every day, every game, in any sport, you'll find an athlete who knows he's already gone. He vows to give it 100 percent but knows he's playing out the string.

Before he became the first million-dollar pro athlete, Hull was one of the first to feel the tugs of compromised loyalties. What Hull has tried to avoid or deny or rationalize, NBA star LeBron James turned into a reality show almost four decades later: James announced his leaving behind the Cleveland Cavaliers and signed with Miami during The Decision, *which aired on ESPN in the summer of 2010. Where he would land might have been in some doubt but there was none about James's departure from Cleveland. Against Boston in the playoffs, James put in a perfectly somnambulant performance, one that would have boxing fans crying, "Fix."*

By the spring of '72, Black Hawks fans were beginning to boo Hull, Devaney noted in Sport Magazine. *It would have been unthinkable in years past but never question the wisdom of crowds: at some level those at Chicago Stadium knew that Hull had checked out, the same way Clevelanders would know that James was going through the motions in his last games with the Cavaliers. Hull has consistently claimed that Hatskin came to him after the end of the Black Hawks' season and that he, Hull, picked a figure of $1 million for an upfront signing bonus out of thin air to scare off Hatskin. With that version of the story Hull escapes any appearance of cynicism like James's. That's not how it played out, however. He had entered into a Faustian bargain with the WHA and played an active and even aggressive role in setting the terms while still drawing checks from the Wirtzes. He suggested that NHL journeymen were going to "have to be mercenary." He claimed otherwise at the time and he'd always try to dance around it, but he was the ultimate soldier of fortune. He went to war for money and money alone.*

4

Invitation Rescinded

Gretzky's décor is like a walk through the Hockey Hall of Fame. It documents the modern history of the game, focusing on the span of No. 99's career but extending back to those he would just remember from Hockey Night in Canada *broadcasts and hockey cards. Thus does the Black Hawks' No. 9 sweater hang above the booth where I'm sitting across from the man who used to wear it.*

Most of the memorabilia has been drawn from the NHL: photos of NHL stars, sweaters and sticks used in NHL games, pucks with the NHL logo on them mounted above plaques that detail an NHL scoring landmark. You might be able to find something left over from Gretzky's time in the WHA. More substantial space has been given over to international play, appropriately given that Gretzky first skated into the public consciousness at the 1978 world junior tournament in Montreal. And though he raised the Stanley Cup five times, many of the best and worst memories of Gretzky's career were those when he played for Canada.

You need to be of a certain age and firm memory to remember a time before the best Canadian pros from the NHL played against foreign national teams. Bobby Hull came into the NHL when it was essentially an all-Canadian league and when the best NHL players never had a chance to play for their country. In Hull's prime, the best Canadians were pros and the teams that played in the worlds and the Olympics were amateurs assembled by Father David Bauer seemingly to gain Canada marks for attendance. That's a bit harsh, but the underlying truth: the era when Canadian amateur teams could win against other nations' best passed in the late '50s. Had Hull come along at a slightly different time, he might have played for the Belleville McFarlands team that won the worlds in 1959, the last time a Canadian club team came away with international gold. Eventually, Canada stopped sending teams altogether.

Generations of NHL greats never knew what it was to wear the Maple Leaf unless they played for Toronto, and no one really gave much thought to what they might have done in international competition. There was the NHL and there was amateur hockey and never was the twain going to meet. That was the conventional wisdom.

Back in '72, just days after Hull made history by signing the last line of a 37-page contract with the WHA, another piece of history was announced: the roster of the Canadian team that was going to compete against the Soviet Union that fall. Hull's name wasn't on that roster. Paul Henderson's was and three months later he became the center of the most famous photo in hockey history when he leapt off the ice after scoring the last-second, series-winning goal in Game 8 in Moscow.

A few days before Hull came to Toronto to sell his coffee-table book in the late fall of 2010, Paul Henderson was making the media rounds to publicize a cross-country tour that would give hockey fans a chance to come out and look at the sacred garment: his game-worn Team Canada No. 19.

Hull isn't much for being wistful. He has a full range of emotions. He can do angry. Hard-done-by. Phlegmatic. Amused. Indifferent. Only one aspect of his life story makes him wistful. "Not getting a chance to play in the Summit Series is still my greatest regret in hockey," he says.

• • •

The story of Team Canada at the Summit Series has been told and retold so many times that it seems impossible, nearly four decades later, to say anything new about it. Yet there is a persistent error in the writing and rewriting of the story and it goes directly to Bobby Hull's non-involvement. But before detailing that error, it's important to define the national mood circa the summer of '72, because that mood is the backdrop to the unsatisfying subplot with Hull at its center.

Everything purchased in memory comes at the cost of another memory and for something taking up as much space as the Summit Series, the cost is considerable: Team Canada's victory emptied the memory banks of the entire year that preceded it. In many ways, the year had been a downer. On July 1, 1972, on the occasion of the 105th anniversary of Confederation, the *Globe and Mail* issued a lead editorial on the state of the Dominion that captured a national ennui. The headline, "Canada '72—dull and grey, but still very real," was in fact less gloomy than the opinion piece beneath it.

The editorial began with a look back five years to Centennial Day and evoked the "colour and spectacle, music and laughter, when we dazzled the world with Expo." Canadians had "dazzled [themselves] with dreaming of dreams become real." In 1967 Canadians had embraced an attitude of relentless optimism and pride of country, almost un-Canadian, more American than anything else. For want of other words, it was a sun-bathed time of Canadian exceptionalism. Over the course of five years, however, clouds had blown in over the country and Canadians were "awakening to dull, grey reality" when the *Globe and Mail* hit their doorsteps that morning. "The old doubts and problems crowded back. The Centennial magic had not changed them much and [Pierre Elliott] Trudeau in the trappings of a prime minister looked more and more like just another Liberal (though brighter than most) trying somewhat waspishly to survive . . . The times seem very ordinary. Inflation is coming back and unemployment is still with us. There are strikes and lockouts. Everything is taxed to distraction . . . There is one visionary political movement left in Canada—the Quebec separatists and their Parti Quebecois."

Instead of celebrating, the *Globe* offered a damning. Canadians were "disillusioned," needed a "release from self-deception, exaggerated expectations and the word of false prophets." A few lines in the editorial could have been printed in purple ink but still it captured the mood of the nation. Or at least most of the nation.

Just days before, Bobby Hull had stood at the intersection of Portage and Main, holding up a million-dollar check. Hull's signing had given rise to an outpouring that was Centennial-like. Winnipeggers were elevated in a way that Canadians elsewhere longed for. The nation needed a defining moment, a cause, a hero. The nation needed a hero like Hull was to Winnipeg. The most likely candidate was Hull. If he could inspire the people to crowd the streets of downtown Winnipeg in midsummer, he could do it everywhere else. And a moment to make it all possible loomed.

• • •

For months Hockey Canada officials and Canadian diplomats had negotiated with their counterparts in the U.S.S.R. and the International Ice Hockey Federation to clear the way for a series with no precedent: a team of top Canadian pros against the world-champion Soviets. Those on the Canadian side of the table had already convinced the NHL's top executives on the merits of sending their best to represent their country. It had long been presumed impossible to stage such an event because an amateur would lose his eligibility if he competed against professionals, but in fact that had read into the words of the statutes an inflexibility that wasn't there— professionalism wasn't viral or contagious, contracted upon physical contact on the ice. That distinction made the Summit Series possible. The deal was sealed at a meeting in Prague with only a few scheduling details to hammer out. For two months ahead of the tournament conversation in the media and among hockey fans inevitably wound back to the roster for the Canadian team that would take on the Soviets that fall.

Uncertainty attached to the two names atop the list. One was Bobby Orr. After leading the Boston Bruins to the Stanley Cup and winning his second Conn Smythe Trophy and his third consecutive Hart Trophy, Orr had undergone knee surgery and all summer long Canadians awaited updates on his condition. In June, Orr expressed his hope that he would be fit to play for Canada. He had dispensed with his crutches and said he was aiming at a return for the four games in Moscow in late September. Too optimistic as it turned out. The other was Bobby Hull. Hull was physically able but his signing with the Winnipeg Jets and the WHA was the X factor. On July 1, 1972, the same day the *Globe and Mail* ran its gloomy editorial, the paper's sports columnist, Dick Beddoes, offered up a missive dedicated to assembling the Canadian roster. He expressed concern about Hull's availability to Team Canada. Beddoes: "Robert M. Hull could be another exception, if his promotional chores as playing coach of [the Winnipeg Jets] prevent him from full-time attendance at the camp. The directors of Hockey Canada, nominal sponsors of the Canadian team, do not plan any special dispensation for any player." Otherwise, Beddoes wrote, Hull had "a lock on left wing if he wants it." On the left side the fall-off after Hull and Frank Mahovlich was precipitous, in Beddoes's estimation. Paul Henderson was the last name on the columnist's list.

Reasons for concern about Hull's availability had nothing to do with the Jets' or the WHA's proprietary interest in its marquee name. Hull taking a star role against the Soviets would have been great exposure for the new league and Ben Hatskin's fondest dream, payback for Clarence Campbell's snubbing him. Hatskin had reason to believe that Hull was going to be on the ice with Team Canada.

In June, Harry Sinden, Boston coach and now the coach appointed to head up Team Canada, contacted Hull. Hockey Canada and the NHL had sent out forms to players under consideration for the team. Not that there'd have to be much consideration of Hull on merits—those forms landed on the doorsteps of players far less accomplished, many who weren't going to be selected. Hull suspected that his jumping leagues might have repercussions or, at least, complicate his situation and he sought out Sinden for clarification. Sinden offered him nothing but reassurances. As Hull remembered it after the team was announced: "Harry Sinden and I talked about it before and I asked him about this. He said, 'I'm picking the team and I'll have the players that I want on my team.'" Sinden told Hull that he could consider himself invited. Hull's apprehensions were well-founded.

On July 12, 1972, Sinden announced the roster of the team. Hull's name wasn't on it. It wasn't that he was not invited—which has become accepted fact over the years. That actually understates the case. Fact is, Hull had had his invitation withdrawn. Hull was in Winnipeg on the day of the announcement and had planned to do the rounds to publicize and celebrate his chance to play for his country. There would be no reprise of the euphoric scene that greeted his signing. *The Canadian Press* account described Hull's voice as "strained with emotion" when he spoke about being left out. "So I guess they've changed his mind too," Hull said when he was reached that day. "But I think Harry Sinden has got more guts than that."

Sinden might have had the guts to fight the league on the point, but having lost the fight, he didn't have the guts or decency to phone Hull with the news so that he wouldn't be ambushed by the announcement of the roster.

The dull and gray reality: the league and the owners had the leverage to dictate who was going to play and who was not. And though the contest for hockey supremacy was going to be waged between Canada and the Soviets, a critical issue had been left to the whim of a born-and-bred Chicagoan with an agenda, Bill Wirtz. Wirtz had represented the NHL in negotiations with Hockey Canada that previous winter. He had a clause inserted into a signed agreement that he must have thought was a stroke of genius, one that failed to register with Hockey Canada officials. Then again, they had never done business with Bill Wirtz, so they wouldn't have seen it coming.

With Hull's contract expiring at the end of the 1971–72 playoffs, the Wirtzes had reason to expect another protracted negotiation with Hull and maybe a threat to jump to the WHA or another threat to retire to the farm, both empty but time-wasting. Wirtz saw Team Canada not as a patriot would but as a businessman—he understood the players' motivations and saw their eagerness to represent their country as something he and other owners could exploit. More to the point, he could exploit it with Hull. So Wirtz inserted a condition into the league's agreement with Hockey Canada: all participating players had to have signed an NHL contract in advance of the tournament to participate in it. When Hockey Canada asked him about it, Wirtz dissembled, saying that it was a matter of taking out insurance on the players. In fact, it offered him an opportunity to squeeze Hull in contract talks—the Hawks could run the clock, knowing that they had no particular rush to offer him the best deal and that Hull would desperately want to play for Canada and thus take something less than full value to be eligible for the series.

When Hull announced, on June 27, 1972, that he had signed with the Jets and the WHA, Doug Fisher had a sinking feeling about the clause that Wirtz had inserted into the agreement. Fisher, chairman of Hockey Canada's executive committee, felt Hockey Canada had been played. He contacted Sinden. "We had to check with Harry when Hull signed to see if he had been invited," Fisher said. "Harry told us the invitation had already gone out and, of course, the number one point on the information sheet each player received explained that no one would be on Team Canada until he signed with the NHL."

Sinden had given Hockey Canada hope that Hull would still be invited but that hope was gone later that day when he received a phone call from NHL president Clarence Campbell. "[Campbell] wanted to know if we intended to stick by our agreement," Fisher said. "And of course we did."

Of course Hockey Canada did. The NHL had the hammer and Hockey Canada was a nail.

Fisher tried to defend Hockey Canada's shortsighted agreement with the NHL. During negotiations in April 1972, the WHA's status was "extremely mixed up," Fisher said. Fisher admitted that it was the government-supported organization's mis-step that had left Hull excluded. "Harry Sinden shouldn't be blamed if Bobby Hull doesn't play," Fisher said. "Hockey Canada, the organization formed by the federal government, business and hockey interests, is merely returning a favor to the NHL for its initial cooperation. If there's any blame it falls on us."

Hull was outraged. The decision to cut him out of the momentous series, he said, "sounds like the NHL . . . typical pettiness on their part. That's like slapping a child's hand. It's about time everyone realized what type of organization they are." Even though many in the media were, like Hockey Canada, nails to the NHL's hammer, they were strident in their protests. "If Team Canada is to have any meaning at all and this country is to be represented by the best hockey players we have, Bobby Hull must play," Jim Vipond wrote in the *Globe and Mail*.

Hull had the media's support but none from the other key principal in the negotiations that would deliver NHL players to Hockey Canada: NHL Players' Association executive director Alan Eagleson. Eagleson was no friend of Hull and (witness his later dealings that delivered Bobby Orr to Chicago) a very good friend of Bill Wirtz. He wasn't going to go to bat for the star player who had snubbed him when he was bidding to become his agent. Years later, Eagleson said that Hull killed his chance for selection to the squad by telling reporters about it in advance. Disingenuous as best: it's impossible to find the logic in that version. Eagleson, more than anybody, understood the implications of the condition attached to the NHL's agreement and, further, he was in a position to advise Hockey Canada officials, given that he sat on the organization's board. To what degree Eagleson advised Wirtz or worked an inside game behind the scenes will never be known—no denial would be believable and any admission would never be taken as the whole truth.

At the grassroots, the furor over Hull's "dis-invitation" was palpable. On Parliament Hill, however, the nation's power-brokers didn't pounce on the issue. On the day of the announcement of the roster, Prime Minister Trudeau and Health Minister John Munro told reporters that they weren't going to intervene in what they believed was a Hockey Canada matter. When the outrage escalated, they put their fingers in the wind and reversed directions—given that the federal government was underwriting Hockey Canada, they risked being lumped in with the NHL as the villains in the piece. Declassified minutes, from closed-door sessions where Trudeau met with his cabinet in the days after the announcement of the Team Canada training-camp roster, noted: "The suggestion was put forward that the government might make known, to Hockey Canada, its view that Hull should be permitted to play on the Canadian team . . . While the NHL was in a position to create difficulties for Hockey Canada by refusing permission to NHL players to play on the Canadian team, the NHL had been prepared to withdraw some of its earlier demands." Trudeau wanted to hear more from Hockey Canada officials but nothing they told him showed up in any transcripts made public, so it's not clear which demands the NHL "had been prepared to withdraw," if any at all.

Mail flooded in to Hockey Canada's office. From Allan Johnston of Powell River, B.C.: "I am a hockey fan, eight years old, and I very much would like to see Bobby Hull playing on the Canadian team playing against Russia." Mail flooded in to the Prime Minister's Office. From Toronto mayor William Dennison: "The failure to include Bobby Hull, a Canadian who next year will play for a Canadian team, is a serious omission and will do great harm to not only this upcoming series but possibly the future of professional hockey in Canada, due to the suggestion that Canadians are not responsible for the destiny of their National Game."

Trudeau recognized that it was a sensitive position, one that the Tories, in particular former prime minister John Diefenbaker, made a political football. Hockey Canada's brass were called into Trudeau's offices. "Trudeau gestured to stacks of messages. Most demanded he insist Hull play. If Hull could not, some people wanted him to block the Soviets from coming. The prime minister thought we should go ahead and play Hull," Douglas Fisher later wrote.

In the end, the federal government was as toothless as Hull without his bridge. A tersely worded telegram was all it could muster. "You are aware of the intense concern which I share with millions of Canadians in all parts of our country, that Canada should be represented by its best hockey players, including Bobby Hull and all those named by Team Canada, in the forthcoming series with the Soviet Union. On behalf of these Canadians, I urge Hockey Canada, the NHL and the NHL Players' Association to take whatever steps may be necessary to make this possible . . . I would ask you to keep the best interests of Canada in mind and to make sure that they are fully respected and served."

No amount of symbolic pressure was going to change the minds of Wirtz and Campbell. "It's just typical of the NHL and maybe typical of Canadian politics that they let the NHL run things," Dennis Hull told the *National Post* in 2002. The younger brother who was selected to Team Canada had threatened to quit the team if Bobby wasn't aboard. Bobby talked him into sticking with the team, but Dennis still fumed 30 years after the fact, his triumph coming with a significant asterisk attached. "You'd think Trudeau had a little more clout than [Campbell] did," he said.

Not even voices from within league ranks were going to budge Wirtz and Campbell. Harold Ballard, the Toronto Maple Leafs owner, took Hull's side against the NHL's. "I don't care if he signed with a team in China," Ballard said. "He's a Canadian and he should be on the Canadian team." Again, how sincere Ballard was is an open question. If he had supported the league's position, the position denying Hull a chance to play

against the Soviets, he would have opened himself to popular blowback in Toronto, a public-relations nightmare for
his franchise. He wanted at least to appear patriotic, though
he might have been just joining the chorus, standing in the
back row and mouthing the words. His support of Hull's position was seemingly a matter of convenience not conviction.
His objections to Campbell's and Wirtz's end-run weren't so
deeply felt that he was going to decline having his arena as
Team Canada's training-camp home and site of Game 2 of the
Summit Series.

Bobby Hull was out. It wouldn't be the last time the NHL
left him twisting in the wind.

• • •

Canada and the Soviets played to a dull and gray 4–4 tie at the
Winnipeg Arena on September 6, 1972. During stoppages in
play television cameras zoomed in on Bobby Hull sitting in
Section 2. Joanne sat beside him and he signed autographs.
Before the series Hull had told people that he considered the
Soviets a real threat to win the series, an opinion that put
him in a small minority, though one that numbered, among
others, Harry Sinden. After the game he hustled out of the arena
but was stopped beside Ben Hatskin's black Imperial before he
could get away. He later told reporters that a tie was a fair result
for both teams though Canada needed the victory more than
the Soviets. He said that he liked the Clarke–Henderson–Ellis
line. Said he liked the Soviets' skill and skating. Rated the series
a toss-up and said that he couldn't be in game shape if Hockey
Canada called him before the series headed back to Russia.

Any hard feelings Hull kept to himself. If it wasn't a tragedy, it was an irony. He was a Canadian who was excluded from the most momentous series in the history of the sport because he had left an American team for one in the country of his birth, where his roots were. It was, as he had said immediately after hearing that he had been "dis-invited," Team NHL, not Team Canada. But there was no re-opening wounds. His signing and the prospect of his playing for the Jets was the biggest hockey news in the history of Winnipeg sports—for two months, until Winnipeg hosted Game 3 of the Summit Series. Thus did the NHL try again to throw Bobby Hull into eclipse. He didn't owe the NHL any respect for its shabby treatment of him and he didn't gloat about it—he had too much respect for those who were on the ice and in straits.

And then he and Joanne rode away in Hatskin's Imperial.

● ● ●

At Gretzky's, Hull keeps the retrospection and introspection to a minimum about the Summit Series.

"How would things have been different if you had played?" I ask him.

"Impossible to say," he says. He won't take the bait. Again, respect for those who played.

A few years back Hull was asked where he watched Henderson score the winning goal in Game 8.

"I have no idea where I was," said Hull. He said he had only ever seen it on video. "No, I was likely busy," Hull said. "I guess I had more important things on my plate at that particular time. I was probably trying to join my new teammates in Winnipeg."

Sitting across from him I'm thinking that he might be the only person in the hockey world who won't put forward an opinion about the impact he would have had on the series. Then again, if he really doesn't recall where he was when Game 8 was played and wasn't watching the live broadcast, he might be the only Canadian of a certain age who can say that. It has to be hard to talk about when he has heard about Henderson's goal all these years, when Henderson's sweater is going out on a countrywide tour. Henderson's, not his.

5

Prior Total Dominance

The majority of wall space at Wayne Gretzky's is dedicated to photographs of players who'd be the most familiar to hockey fans in their 30s and early 40s. Those who are likeliest to spend their money in the bar that bears Gretzky's name can look around the room and see the players they grew up with in the '80s and '90s. The patrons see Hull's Black Hawks sweater but most aren't old enough to have ever seen him play in Chicago colors in anything but video transfers of grainy film. Most of the photos feature Gretzky and those he played with and against. Most of the sweaters were worn and sticks held by players who made hundreds of thousands of dollars early in their careers and millions later. Never during their NHL careers, not even as the lowliest rookie, did any live like Hull did as a teenager with the Black Hawks. None ever lived in a basement apartment. Those who came along after Hull prospered because he took on the establishment and was on the winning side.

At one level he was an unlikely rebel. He wasn't a long-haired radical who searched for causes to protest. He wasn't the type to rally others to a cause. He wouldn't form or join a picket line.

"It was wrong," Hull says. "The system was wrong. I took it on because it was wrong. I wouldn't have and couldn't have if the system was right and fair. And we got [a fair shake] because of that black judge in Philadelphia, a real good guy."

Hull sounds satisfied. They got theirs because he got his. To his credit, he doesn't claim that he took on the establishment so that others after him could get rich. It wasn't about a higher cause. He seems content foremost with what he got out of it, that million-dollar check and more. That his fight immediately and vastly improved the lots of all those players on the wall remains a happy by-product.

• • •

Clarence Campbell, Bill Wirtz and the NHL had shut Hull out of the Summit Series but they weren't going to stop there. "The NHL isn't going down without a fight," Campbell said. "As far as I'm concerned Hull is still under contract to the Chicago hockey club and if [the Jets and the WHA] want to gamble this kind of money to take him on, then all I can say is good luck to them. But if I were in Chicago's position, I would fight it to the end."

Campbell told reporters that the league had no policy in place that would blackball defecting players if they gave up the WHA and wanted to return to the NHL clubs owning their rights. "If this was a mass exodus I'd be concerned. But it isn't and I don't think [Hull's] move will create such an exodus," he said.

Campbell vowed to legally challenge every player who jumped to the WHA and he expressed confidence in the NHL's chances before the courts. He had a compelling reason to and it had little to do with right or wrong. The NHL had been a cash machine for decades and the league could count on its greater wherewithal to take on the nascent WHA, which was, as Don Regan tactfully described it, "not overly capitalized."

The day of Hull's signing, Campbell was in Washington. Three days later, when he made his vows to get nasty, Campbell had been stopped by reporters as he emerged from a committee room in the U.S. Senate. He and other high executives of the major sports leagues had been cordially invited there to testify before senators who were proposing new regulations for the business of sport. Campbell had gone to Washington to advance what he considered the highest cause of all: the status quo.

Today, sports fans expect the chief executives of leagues to be forward-thinking and visionary. Clarence Campbell was of another and simpler time. He had both black Oxfords squarely in the past. This shouldn't be taken as a measure of limited intelligence. Back in the 1920s he had attended Oxford University on a Rhodes Scholarship. He wasn't just a drudge who held down the job of league president and did not know the game. Before he moved into an office job with the league he had spent several seasons working on the ice as a referee. And he knew something about higher causes, having left the league to join the Canadian Forces when the Second World War broke out. Then, after the Allies' victory, he served as a prosecutor of Nazis on trial for war crimes. He had an informed, values-rooted sense of what was right and wrong.

The case that Campbell had taken to the U.S. Senate was a losing one. It was of another time. If he knew this was the case, no one can know but, given his significant accomplishments as a lawyer, he had to at least have suspected it. Don Regan said Campbell had to know. "A first-year contract law student would know just looking at it," Regan said.

The essential emptiness of the NHL's position requires little explanation beyond Campbell's testimony that day. The league's chief executive wasn't treated as a hostile witness—the senator who took the lead in questioning, Marlow Cook, a Republican from Kentucky, at one point referred to "the WHA pirates." Campbell wasn't being pushed for reform by Cook. It was kid gloves.

At first Campbell invoked the good-of-the-game principle—that he did not oversee the league as a business but rather as an organization that had the interests of hockey at heart. He suggested that the NHL was generously underwriting the development of coming generations of players, giving a junior team $3,000 for a player selected in the first two rounds of the draft and $7,000 more when that player signed with his NHL.

Senator Cook: That is a substantial sum of money, isn't it?

Clarence Campbell: This is the lifeblood of our business.

Senator Cook did seem to have trouble processing the idea that a team could sell a player to another club for $40,000, yet that same player would make only half that sum as a yearly salary. Campbell laid it on thick about teams sinking thousands of dollars into player development.

The transcripts record a few thousand words dedicated to the good work the NHL was performing, the value that it provided the paying customer. Campbell was running the clock until Senator Cook asked him about the challenge the new league presented.

Senator Cook: What problems do you foresee with the establishment of the World Hockey League Association [*sic*]?

Clarence Campbell: The first thing is very obvious, the contention which will arise for talents, not only those players who are currently signed with us under option to their member clubs, but also, of course, the amateurs [who] are perfectly open. We have provided the supply of talent through our subsidization of the sport and they [the WHA] are going to benefit from it, I assume, to the extent to which they acquire those players, and they will be perfectly entitled to acquire them. We place no obstacles in their way of any kind.

Later, however, he testified to the exact contrary. His testimony sounded like a threat to the ears of owners of WHA franchises, but, then again, they all knew it was coming.

Clarence Campbell: [The legality of signings] would probably be tested in several places as to whether or not players will be able to jump [leagues]. They may not be enjoined from doing so.

Senator Cook: You don't look forward to handling that on a player-by-player basis?

Clarence Campbell: Yes. That will be on a player-by-player basis. Individual players will decide that.

Senator Cook: In a civil action!

Clarence Campbell: Yes, a civil action.

"Civil actions" was going to be more accurate. Later:

Clarence Campbell: One thing is sure and that is: That the pattern which [the WHA principals] have laid out for themselves, and salaries which they have declared publicly they are offering, there is no way they can maintain themselves without a schedule of prices that is equivalent to ours. And I know that they are very likely to be able to do that . . .

Senator Cook: Until the signing of Bobby Hull yesterday, what was the total remuneration—

Clarence Campbell: What was the total what?

Senator Cook: Two and a half million dollars . . .

Clarence Campbell: Two and a half.

Senator Cook: Until that signing, in your memory, Mr. Campbell, what was the highest price contract ever paid to a hockey player to secure his services?

Clarence Campbell: Oh, I don't remember any hockey player being signed for the acquisition of his services by anyone for more than . . . I don't remember any player ever being transferred from club to club for in excess of a hundred thousand dollars.

This was, of course, a well-timed stutter, because Campbell knew that Orr was making $200,000 and Hull had been in six figures with the Black Hawks. The league president neatly jumped from the sums players were "signed" for to the money paid out for players who were "transferred." Suffice to say, in Campbell's time, no player of any great significance, no one on the magnitude of an Orr or a Hull, was sold from one NHL team to another—those flogged were much smaller fish. The senator from the great state of Kentucky didn't pick up on

Campbell's evasion. The exchange continued and Campbell reached the payoff:

> *Senator Cook:* Boy, you have come a long way in a hurry, haven't you?
>
> *Clarence Campbell:* I want to point out, or to give some additional strength to the position that we require the preservation of the reserve clause more on the account of the requirement, our player requirement, which has to be based on the cost of developing a player. In other words, if a player were free to take advantage, either of his initial signing, and the number of years in the minor leagues, and a fairly substantial salary, and they are fairly substantial now by former standards, or by ones under which I grew up, then the gross inequity of the situation where he could just walk off and say, it was nice of you to have provided me with an apprenticeship to get to the National Hockey League, and now thanks very much, I think I will go and play for the Jersey Devils or someone else, somebody else in the same league. To me this would simply—the only effect this is going to have is that people will not expend the money to do this development work and the sport as a whole will deteriorate as a result of it.

Campbell was sitting at a table across from Senator Cook in the committee room. At that point, though, he could have dropped to bended knee. He was pleading and praying for "the preservation of the reserve clause."

Clarence Campbell was a man of an earlier, simpler time. So too was the reserve clause a carry-over from another era.

Campbell would retire from the league presidency in 1977. The reserve clause was going to be retired much sooner than that.

• • •

Just as Clarence Campbell's testimony in the U.S. Senate detailed the NHL position, a nostalgic soliloquy from Don Regan fully captures the collapse of the NHL's reserve clause and the WHA's smiting of the established league in U.S. courts. Regan was a complete counterpoint to Campbell. The league president was a man who carried himself as if he had been born swathed in a tweed diaper, while Regan, the WHA's general counsel, was a jock who was cut from the UCLA Bruins hoop team by John Wooden but ended up an All-American in volleyball. Campbell came off, at his sunniest moment, grim as a pallbearer, while Regan has always been endlessly bemused. Four decades later, in his Newport Beach law office, nothing seemed to give him greater amusement than recounting his WHA experience. It would be years before the WHA could compete with the NHL's best on the ice, but the newcomers, led by the callow and ceaselessly ironic Regan, routed Campbell, Wirtz and company in the courts.

It began with a light-bulb moment. "One of the first things I had Harvey [Wineberg] do was give me a copy of Bobby Hull's contract [with the Black Hawks]," Regan said. "I read it and one of things that makes it all so momentous . . . it wasn't a contract. I couldn't believe it. One of my friends from law school was a senior partner at a major law firm in Southern California and I sent it to him and a couple of others. I asked them to read this document that Bobby Hull signed. They all came back and said the same thing that I did: 'That's not a contract.'

"The standard NHL contract was set up by Alan Eagleson, not the most farsighted guy. For reasons known only to him, though you can draw inferences, he fought us all the way, even though another league was really in the best interests of his players, driving their salaries up."

Testifying at the same Senate committee hearings, Eagleson said that the NHLPA was "generally satisfied with its relation-ship with the owners of the NHL" and that he was "satisfied that the owners are acting in good faith." Regan said Eagleson missed—or was willing to overlook—a hole in the reserve clause that a student in first-year contract law shouldn't have missed. Regan: "The reason why [the standard NHL contract] wasn't a contract—this is the *Reader's Digest* version—it had all the things you've seen in a player's contract but at the very end it said that—in this case, 'Bobby Hull agrees to play for the Black Hawks next year on the same terms as this year's contract except for the salary which is to be negotiated.' In any legal sense everything in a contract has to be definite and certain. So the part [pertaining to] this year is valid but next year is invalid."

On the basis of that invalidating vagueness, the WHA was able to sign all sorts of players who had previously played in the NHL. The agreement to play another year for the same team going forward at a yet-to-be-determined salary was unen-forceable. If the salary wasn't spelled out, then the exclusivity clause was null and void. There's no provision in contract law for "we'll iron out those details when we get there."

As Campbell promised at the Senate hearing, the NHL went to war not on one front but every one possible. The NHL's full-scale legal assault accomplished nothing except providing proof of the truth and wisdom of A.J. Liebling's assessment of the Second City: "Chicago is unique," Liebling wrote. "It's the only completely corrupt city in the world." Regan recalled: "The NHL sued us in all twelve cities [where the WHA was establishing franchises]. We had their suit knocked out of court in eleven of the twelve cities. Everywhere except Chicago. I was in Chicago and—this is the fun part—I was walking into the court with the lawyer Harvey [Wineberg] retained and there was a little guy walking behind us. I said, 'Who's that guy?' 'That's our appellate lawyer.' 'Our appellate lawyer? But we haven't even been to trial yet.' 'You don't understand. This is Chicago. This is Wirtz's judge. We're going to lose this case. We're supposed to lose it. We have to be ready to appeal right away.' And that's what happened. We were sued in twelve cities and we won in eleven of them. They were suing us on the basis that we were violating their reserve clause. All the judges would stand up and—it was the same deal as I described—they said: 'That's not a valid reserve clause,' then they threw it out of court. We lost in Chicago but the decision was reversed on appeal."

With its limited arsenal, the WHA's strategy was a single strike. "Among the more cogent decisions I ever made, I said, 'If they're suing us, why don't we sue them on anti-trust grounds?'" Regan said. "In theory they're trying to keep us out of business. A lot of big companies will sue little companies on any grounds they can come up with—they figure they can keep the smaller competitor out of business and bankrupt them with legal fees. That's what the NHL was trying to do to us. They had twelve lawsuits in twelve different cities. The lawsuits were exactly the same—fortunately for us the NHL had photocopied all the complaints and the complaints were identical right down to the typos in them. So I went to my friend with the big law firm here and we tried to determine the most likely plaintiff's anti-trust jurisdiction to sue the NHL.

We picked Philadelphia because its federal court and appellate court were supposed to be favorable jurisdictions [for plaintiffs in anti-trust]. We also picked a lawyer named Cohen who was the smartest SOB I have ever met. I got the credit but he was something else. There was just the two of us and we sued the entire NHL and all of its teams in Philadelphia. The NHL had eleven lawyers on their side of the room. The NHL even brought in Edward Bennett Williams, who was probably the most effective lawyer in the history of the United States. He arrived in the middle of a hearing and stood up to start arguing with the judge. He said, 'Your honor, I'm not familiar with the facts and I haven't really studied the law yet.' I stood up and said, 'Your honor, if Mr. Williams isn't familiar with the case and hasn't studied the law perhaps he should just sit down.'"

Regan and his friends out in California had identified the right jurisdiction and happened to end up in the court of the ideal jurist for their case: Judge A. Leon Higginbotham Jr. Other judges might have slapped down Regan for his impudence with Williams, a living legend. Not Higginbotham. "The judge laughed all over the place and told [Williams] to sit down," Regan said. "Williams chased me down later on and said, 'Boy, no one ever did that to me in a court of law.'

"Judge Higginbotham was really practical. He saw that the NHL was trying to bigfoot us. They were as arrogant as Bill Wirtz in Chicago. They did really sloppy legal work—not what you'd expect of the giant coming after Jack. The judge knew exactly what they were doing and it backfired.

"The NHL kept trying to get continuances. Judge Higginbotham said, 'Be here at 8 a.m., Saturday.' Judge Higginbotham said, 'Look, I have trials with guys on death row. I've got serious things here. Do your work and be here.' The way they filed the lawsuits, they had a hard time overcoming it. It wouldn't have gone on for seventeen days if they didn't have a lot of facts to bring up but they had a losing case. I don't know if Doofus No. 1 and Doofus No. 2 would have won our case, but Cohen was a brilliant guy."

Clarence Campbell sat in the gallery and looked straight ahead with a funereal aspect. The NHL's business had changed barely a whit since he wore a striped shirt and blew a whistle. And then two wise-guy lawyers who knew nothing at all about the game turned it inside out. All that money that the NHL had thrown into player development, for naught. The league's lifeblood had turned into legal bloodshed.

"Campbell could see what we did: all the lawyers for the defense arguing among themselves because they knew they were losing the case. The lawyers were the best from one of the biggest firms in the country, Covington and Burling. I can safely say they've done better legal work in other areas. Their side could see Judge Higginbotham was going our way. It wasn't a hundred percent versus zero percent, but we, in all humility, weren't that bad and we had the facts on our side."

"The NHL is merely sustaining the fate which monopolists must face when they can no longer continue their prior total dominance of the market," Higginbotham wrote. And no longer, as the judge found for the plaintiffs. Clarence Campbell and the NHL had come a long way in a hurry . . . and lost at every turn, embarrassingly.

By striking down the NHL's position, Higginbotham had struck a blow for the WHA. And, according to Gordon Hylton, a law professor specializing in sport's legal history at Marquette University, Hull's contract established far-reaching precedents. "Hull's 1972 contract was a milestone in the history of North American sports," Professor Hylton said. "In scale it ranks with

Joe Namath's $400,000 contract with the Jets in the AFL and Catfish Hunter's 1975 $3.75-million contract with the Yankees as early landmarks in the history of the financial landscape of sports. And it certainly had a broader and more dramatic impact on player salaries across a sport. In truth, though, the contract itself was unlike those [previously used] in sports—Hull was the first athlete signed to a contract that would be, in word and spirit, closer to one that a Hollywood star would sign. Before and after his contract, others were signing contracts standard for their time. Hull's, though, was for 'personal services.' It was a contract not simply for performance but everything beyond the arena. In that sense it was forward thinking, way ahead of its time."

Hull wasn't being paid to take slapshots and he didn't just want a stall in the dressing room. As a playing coach, he had some creative control but, more than that, he would be the de facto voice of the organization. His contract was like the old-time movie contracts in that movie stars didn't sign on for individual films but rather for a term exclusively with a studio—Hull wasn't playing the game but rather selling the league. The contract anticipated where the business of sports was heading—players weren't just sweat and muscle but images to sell behind, tools of marketing.

Whether this occurred to Hull is hard to say. Likely he cared most, if not entirely, that he was out from under the Wirtzes, with a million dollars in his pocket.

• • •

Judge Higginbotham's ruling changed the business of hockey and in fact the business of sport overnight. The next summer,

NHL players would enjoy leverage that they could never have imagined. Jim Pappin's example was instructive. "Before [that ruling] I'd go into the GM's office and hope to walk out of there with a five-thousand dollar pay raise," Pappin said. "The next summer [1973] the team's first offer was to double my salary."

Judge Higginbotham's ruling was reported in the sports pages of the day, though its importance was not properly understood. The developments in the Philadelphia court didn't get a lot of play against NFL games coming up on Sunday and the full schedule of NHL and NBA games. Yes, Bobby Hull was going to be allowed to play and some made the connection that all the defected NHL players could join their WHA teams without fear of injunctions forcing them to the sidelines and into court. But the real effects of the ruling wouldn't be plain until the next round of contract talks.

The Belleville *Intelligencer*, the paper that used to write up Bobby Hull when he was a youth-league phenom, gave a couple of inches to a wire story that briefly detailed the unshackling of the local hero. Another story in the *Intelligencer* wasn't picked up elsewhere: Canada Cement announced that it was closing down its operation in Point Anne. The story didn't go into detail about the reasons for the closure. In fact, the bay that Hull and his family and his friends used to skate on was too shallow for ships to haul out cement, and a rival plant had opened up on the other side of the bay that ships could access directly from Lake Ontario. The new plant was equipped with the latest precision equipment and technology lacking in Point Anne. Horses were still being used at the Point Anne plant when Robert Hull started there. Canada Cement had tried to keep up but had lost too much ground.

Robert Hull was out of work but it mostly stung his pride. He was already counting the days to retirement and could count on help from his kids if needed. Others with whom he worked, others whom his son had known growing up, weren't quite as fortunate. After the last day shift on October 31, 1972, "No Trespassing" signs went up at the gate that Robert Hull and his friends had walked through five and six times a week for 40 years. A skeleton crew inside the chain-link fences was taking inventory of any equipment that could be salvaged and planning the demolition of the plant. The general store closed. Houses went up for sale and would stay on the market for months and eventually years. The former Canada Cement workers moved away, looking for work. One by one the churches closed. Back in the '60s, some time after Bobby Hull had racked up his first 50-goal season, folks in Point Anne had put up a hand-painted wooden sign on the one road into town, proudly proclaiming that Point Anne was "the birthplace of the greatest hockey player in the world." Over the years the sign, like the folks in town, would be battered by blizzards and winds blowing in off the bay. Within a few months of the padlocks on the gates being snapped shut, Point Anne became a ghost town. No one bothered to touch up the sign when it showed signs of wear. No one would know if the sign had been taken down or if it had just fallen down, but one day it just wasn't there.

Point Anne was a town founded at the start of the 20th century but it had one foot squarely in the 19th. New times were beckoning. Point Anne had outlived its usefulness. It was as outdated as the notion that the man who signs your checks will always be there for you, will always look after you.

6

Exile on Portage
and Main Street

Imagine a coffee-table book dedicated to the career of Wayne Gretzky. Would it be an egregious omission if there wasn't a section dedicated to No. 99's brief stint in St. Louis? Not even a picture of The Great One skating beside Brett Hull, a marriage that lasted only one semi-glorious spring? It wouldn't set off howls of protest across hockey. It might raise eyebrows or draw a laugh, but nothing more than that.

If it were his seasons in Los Angeles that had been left out of Gretzky's life history, if there were no mention and no spread of photos focusing on his years with the Kings, it would be a more glaring oversight. Though he never had a chance to raise the Stanley Cup there, Gretzky did lead the team on his last run to the final, a loss to the Canadiens in 1993, breaking the hearts of Toronto Maple Leafs fans in the sixth and seventh games of a memorable

Western Conference final. He brought flash and celebrity to a mostly moribund franchise and fueled interest in a previously overlooked sport in the market, so much so that, a generation later, Los Angeles' grassroots youth hockey programs rival any in North America.

Of course, it would be unthinkable to put together a Gretzky career retrospective that overlooked his years in Edmonton where he started and those in New York where he finished. It wouldn't make any sense to overlook his best hockey and best years on the one hand and his time on the biggest stage on the other. It would be because of Edmonton and New York that you would produce a book at all.

Every stop along the way is to be found on the walls at Gretzky's but the coffee-table book that is on the table between Hull and me is very selective.

Not surprisingly there's not a page or image capturing Hull in action with the Hartford Whalers. That doesn't raise any flags. He played a few forgettable weeks with the club at the very end of his career but there might only be a handful of photos out there of that time and they might not rise to the quality of those on display on the glossy pages.

More surprisingly, only two pages are given over to Hull's time with the Winnipeg Jets. It almost seems like his hockey history ground very quickly to an end after he skated his last shift in a Black Hawks sweater at Madison Square Garden in April '72. That has put the noses of some of Hull's friends and fans in Winnipeg out of joint. When he chose Winnipeg, thousands gathered around him at Portage and Main, chests swelling with civic pride. They felt validated. They felt big enough and good enough for the very best. That so little real estate has been given over to the Jets in this book passes for a renunciation of Winnipeg. Circa November 2010 the city longs for the return of the NHL—it wouldn't matter if it were the franchise that was shipped off to bleed millions in Phoenix or another flat-lining Sun Belt club. At a time when the issue of relocation generates almost daily conversation, the people of Winnipeg are like the keenest students in the front row of seats, backs straight, hands raised and waving, desperate to get attention. At a time when a few words from Hull might mean something, it's as if he is spurning the city where, for a time, he was worshipped.

The wounds shouldn't cut that deep. The concentration on his years with the Black Hawks is strictly a commercial impulse. Chicago is a major North American market, a couple of tiers above Winnipeg. With a population of 2.7 million, Chicago is the third-largest American city. From bygone days it retains the handle of the Second City but on a Midwest axis, Winnipeg, at 633,451 in the 2006 census, is at best a runner-up. If the decision to give little play to Hull's Jets years has wounded pride, it's simply because Winnipeggers fail to make a distinction between people caring more and more people caring.

Another factor in the decision to focus on his time in Chicago is the surge of interest in the Black Hawks in recent years, especially after the team's Stanley Cup win in the spring of 2010. It's simply a clear-eyed rather than nostalgic reading of the greater hockey world. The Black Hawks are at or near the top of the NHL, a power restored. The WHA is no more. The Jets, Nordiques and Whalers are more than a decade gone from Winnipeg, Quebec and Hartford. Edmonton has stuck around but all its glories are defined by its NHL triumphs and particularly those of the guy whose name is attached to the restaurant Hull and I are sitting in. When people speak of the Oilers, they speak of Gretzky, Messier, Kurri and Coffey or maybe more recent players, but not Wild Bill Hunter.

As it turns out, Hull is more willing to talk about his time in Winnipeg than to put it down on the pages of the coffee-table book. When I suggest to him that he might have played on better teams in Chicago but none more important than the Jets of the mid-70s, he corrects me.

"Our best teams in Winnipeg could have played with anybody in hockey at the time," he says. "And we did. I played with the best linemates I ever had and we had some other talented guys. We played and we entertained. I'm really proud of that—we gave the fans a lot of entertainment, which is the most important thing of all."

I float the idea of the Jets as the most influential team of their era. Most pundits and experts have conceded that the Jets would be in tough head-to-head against the late '70s Canadiens, but they'd at least have made it more interesting than most of Montreal's NHL rivals did. And Glen Sather has said that he looked to Hull's Jets teams when he came up with a vision of Gretzky's Oilers. Hull smiles when I say that pro hockey looked one way before the Jets and another after.

"Those were some special teams," he says. "If only more people had a chance to see us."

• • •

Back in the summer and fall of '72 the Rolling Stones were touring behind *Exile on Main St.*, at the time an album widely trashed by critics. *Exile* was recorded when the Rolling Stones were effectively in exile. Mick Jagger and company had been taxed out of England and sought safe haven in the last place someone would think as a money-saver, France. They had been screwed over by a manager who swindled them out of the rights to, fittingly at one level, "(I Can't Get No) Satisfaction." The band was far removed from the axis of the music establishment—France had no rock 'n' roll history. The Stones weren't working with state-of-the-art studio equipment but rather recording in the basement of Keith Richards' *pied-à-terre*. There was no master plan, no schedule, just band members and their friends dropping in to get drunk, crank heroin and occasionally play. No one could make out the words— ultimately cover versions would, Jagger insisted, feature mangled lyrics. And, of course, out of the dislocation, discontent, revolt, primitivism, disorganization and self-abuse came a work that, on four decades of re-assessment, has become regarded not only as the band's masterpiece but arguably the greatest rock 'n' roll album of all time.

It was a moment of collective genius: none of the principals knew it at the time and, really, no one recognized it immediately after the fact. A few couldn't even remember it. It wasn't planned or shaped or even produced. It just happened at an unlikely intersection of talent, inspiration and dumb luck. Actually, "it happened" doesn't fully capture it, because it actually happened to them, something bigger than them, something they could never really explain. It shouldn't have turned out the way it did. It should have been the disaster it looked like at a quick glance. Instead, it soared. Everything the band would do thereafter, however good and occasionally great, suffered by comparison. All attempts to recapture that moment were never as good as that short time when they didn't control it but rather gave themselves up to it.

Bobby Hull was never a Rolling Stones type of guy. When he broke into the NHL, Elvis was everybody's idea of living dangerously. The Rolling Stones were nothing that he ever played on his transistor radio on the steps of Belleville Collegiate. Still, Winnipeg was Hull's *Exile*. His time with the Jets played out in the aftermath of a dispute with a guy who had hustled the best years out of him. It played out hundreds of miles off the professional hockey axis. It played out not in a historic building that had been the scene of great hockey moments but rather Winnipeg Arena, which possessed the aesthetic of a cinder-block aircraft hangar. The team wasn't poorly organized as much as improvised, with Ben Hatskin's friends dropping by and the owner finding some role for them to play even if their professional credentials were lacking—not an assembly of the best and the brightest, just those who were around. The team was an opportunity for some who were leaving behind their own burnt bridges in the established league, lesser names than Hull but his kindred spirits. Some weren't questing for excellence so much as looking for a good time—the Black Hawks had gone at it "hard" off the ice, as Frank Orr noted, but some of the Jets went at it harder. And, of course, this dislocation, discontent, revolt, primitivism, disorganization and self-abuse eventually produced a team that was better than those Hull played on in Chicago and a line that was indisputably the most spectacular of its era.

Ben Hatskin was going to fall painfully short of his master plan. He had hoped to kick down the NHL's door and force a merger but that was going to prove to be more complicated than the jukebox dodge. His personal folly had unintended by-products, however, foremost among them a team that was like no other in the mid-70s. At a time when the NHL continued to be parochial—the Philadelphia Flyers winning their Stanley Cups with an all-Canadian lineup—the Jets looked to the horizon for talent. Philadelphia's goon show had others shaping their teams in that mold, but the Jets bucked the fashions and their greatest successes were based on skill and speed and intelligence—watching the two you'd be left with the impression that you weren't watching different teams or different leagues but rather different sports. Polar opposites, at the Flyers' end war and at the Jets' end art. It would be, like *Exile*, a moment of collective genius: none of the principals knew it going in or maybe fully appreciated it until it was gone. Like *Exile*, an inexplicable experience just happened at an unlikely intersection of talent, inspiration and dumb luck. Said Peter Sullivan, who was going to walk into the middle of it: "Bobby Hull had a vision of a way to play the game that would focus on skill and speed and entertain fans. He loved the game and believed in it. And maybe the team that came out of his vision wasn't the best ever but it might have been the most important one."

● ● ●

The WHA in theory looked far better than the real-life, on-ice product at the launch. Following the Jets' lead (but without the pooled money from other franchises), owners signed stars but with ridiculously mixed results. The Philadelphia Blazers tried to crash the Flyers' market and signed Derek Sanderson away from the Boston Bruins, casting him in the role of an alternative-league rebel star like Joe Namath's with the New York Jets in the AFL's early days. To sign Sanderson, the Blazers made him the world's most highly paid athlete—on paper, anyway, and for about 15 minutes, the time it took him to waste a fortune. The Quebec Nordiques went in exactly the opposite direction and brought in the Canadiens legend Maurice Richard as a coach. For fans, seeing him behind the Nordiques' bench was like filing by Lenin's tomb, fascinating but awful—in fact Lenin's tomb might have been more action-packed. Richard lasted two games before packing it in.

Aside from Hull, the Jets looked like most of the WHA clubs. Their lineup featured three types of players. The first were established NHLers who took on bigger roles with the Jets than they had with their old clubs. They were collecting money and, what's more, offered an opportunity. They jumped as a career move. Christian Bordeleau, who was going to center Hull, fit that profile. Others had their troubles at their last stops and needed a fresh start. Veteran goaltender Joe Daley was "disillusioned" in Detroit and told the Wings that he had played his last game for them before signing with Winnipeg. Then there was the plurality: career minor-leaguers who could get a good payday, which described Norm Beaudin.

Hull had often been underwhelmed by the surrounding talent on his Black Hawks team—or at least bemoaned the players at the bottom of the roster. But when he started skating in the Jets' training camp, he could look around as hard as he wanted and he'd see no one possessing the skill of Stan Mikita, no blueline unit that could match Pat Stapleton and Bill White, no netminder you'd mention in the same breath as Tony Esposito.

Hull had always been a group of one as talent with Chicago—Mikita was a legit Hall of Famer but a lesser one to be sure. With the Jets there was a precipitous drop down to the next player. "I'm not going to sugarcoat it," goaltender Daley said. "We were a line, a pair of defensemen and a goaltender above a good AHL team. Bobby, Christian and Norm were an NHL-quality first line and we had a couple of defensemen who could play but not star in the NHL, and Ernie Wakely and I were NHL goaltenders. After that, it was the American Hockey League or the old international league [in quality]."

When Hull stepped onto the ice for the Jets' first practice in their first training camp, he must have had a "we're not in Kansas anymore" moment. He was, in fact, in Kenora. And if the Jets' training camp was the logging town's biggest hockey event since its Thistles won the Stanley Cup in 1907, the town wasn't any promoter's idea of the ideal site for rolling out the next big thing. Instead of banging the drum the team was in virtual hiding. The team later moved on to do the last prep work at the Winnipeg Arena. In August, Hull had sat in the arena's stands and watched the best players in the world, competing in the Summit Series. In September, he was on the ice with a few players who might have struggled to make a decent minor-league club. Said one former teammate: "He never said so, but when he looked around he must have had buyer's remorse."

If the Jets looked like semi-pros at the bottom of the roster, they looked like rank amateurs in the front office. Hatskin hired friends and nephews and assigned them duties that he determined they were least under-qualified for. He hired a friend from his football days, Annis Stukus, to be the Jets' general manager even though he had no hockey background. "It was strictly on the basis that Stuke could sell ice to Eskimos and BS anybody and everybody," Joe Daley said. Hatskin hired Nick Micoski as Bench coach, which, given Hull's minimalist criteria, meant he stayed out of the star's way and acted as travel secretary when necessary. Later he'd bring in Hull's coach from his days in St. Catharines, Rudy Pilous, a Winnipeg native who was a decent enough junior coach in his prime but long past it. A few behind the scenes were effective—Billy Robinson, the director of player personnel, would do some excellent work beating the bushes looking for prospects and recruiting them into the fold. But the professionally competent were a minority. Hatskin was a jovial presence and he did come up with the million-dollar check (with the Simkins doing a lot of the lifting) but he didn't inspire confidence that he could make a business fly.

At the start of their first season, the Jets were operating at a considerable disadvantage: Hull couldn't play. The case was still playing out in Judge Higginbotham's court in Philadelphia. What should have been a glorious league debut when the Jets went to New York to open the WHA's first season was an opportunity denied by the court—Hull was reduced to sitting in a chair beside the Jets bench and signing autographs. In fact, his best moment in the game was an autograph signing. A boy came down to Winnipeg's bench early in the game and asked Hull for an autograph, which he happily signed, but an usher was annoyed and frog-marched the kid back to his seat to the boos of the crowd. After the first intermission, Hull walked up into the stands and escorted the boy down into his seat next to the team where he watched the rest of the game. The crowd cheered but the league couldn't get by on Hull's goodwill alone.

When the Jets were on the road, Hull flew into town a day in advance to do interviews and signings. It was spelled out in his personal-services contract, but he took an almost proprietary interest in the league—he wanted it to work. After Sanderson signed his deal with the Blazers, he reported to training camp out of shape and seemingly disinclined to put out for his $2.65-million contract. When the Blazers came to Winnipeg early in the season, Hull blasted him, saying that he owed the fans and his teammates an honest effort.

"Bobby told him, 'They're coming to see you play. Don't you have any pride?'" Daley said. Sanderson, whose career was swirling in the bowl, paid no heed—the Jets gave Hull a million-dollar check and the Blazers gave Sanderson a million-dollar buyout after he played in only eight games.

Again, it seemed fair to expect Hull to lead the Jets—he was their coach but served in no capacity as a travel secretary. It also seemed fair to get as much promotion value out of him as possible. That he was trying to motivate Sanderson, and was annoyed that he couldn't, revealed his mindset. "For Bobby, the league's success was his success," said Ab McDonald, the Jets' first captain. "[But] there wasn't anything he could do about it until he hit the ice."

At 36, McDonald was likely the Jets' second most accomplished player behind his former Chicago teammate. With Hull absent, traveling ahead of the team, McDonald filled a leadership void. "I organized it so that everybody, veterans, rookies, had to go out after games and other times, mandatory attendance," McDonald said. "We hit it off. We were sort of a family."

Hull received full status as a family member with Judge Higginbotham's ruling in Philadelphia in early November, but he had something less than an immediate impact: an assist in a 3–2 loss in Quebec and another the next night in a win over the woeful Ottawa Nationals. More than rust held him back. "I think he could have played a lot better and enjoyed himself a lot more but Bobby was living with all that pressure," McDonald said. "I knew Bobby pretty well. He was a good teammate but I don't know that anyone ever took on as much as he did. We all tried to go out in the community and

(AP Photo)

When Bobby Hull joined the Chicago Black Hawks at age 18 in October 1957, he had been married once and never before been outside the province of Ontario. He had played in a high school football game the day before he was called up to the team.

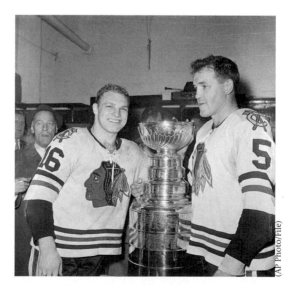

(AP Photo/File)

When the 22-year-old Hull led the Black Hawks to the Stanley Cup in April '61, it seemed to be the start of a glorious run for a young emerging team. Though Hull and his Chicago teammates made it to the final only twice over the next decade and lost two seven-game series against Montreal.

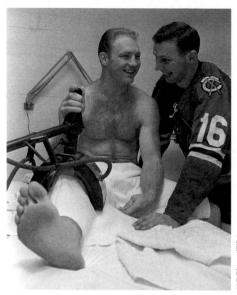

Sitting on a trainer's table next to his brother Dennis, Bobby Hull is undergoing treatment for an injured right knee. Teammates maintain that no player in league history ever endured more physical punishment and pain than did Hull.

Bobby Hull played the role of goaltender while his sons Blake, age five, Bobby Jr., six and Brett, three (left to right) take turns trying to put the puck past him at the Black Hawks' Christmas party. His wife Joanne watches from the side of the net. Hull often brought his sons to Hawks' practice but the Wirtzes banned children from workouts after his messy contract dispute.

Bobby Hull didn't fight often during his career but he did fight many heavyweights, including Montreal's John Ferguson, the NHL's toughest customer. In this fight in 1968, Hull was taking issue with a high stick from Ferguson that cut him for five stitches. Hull and Ferguson were the bitterest of rivals, but Ferguson would end up as general manager in Winnipeg when Hull was attempting his comeback in the late '70s.

Hull's former teammates maintain that the referees let opponents get away with murder when they tried to shut down Hull. Here, Detroit's Ron Harris submarines Hull in a game from January, 1970. Gordie Howe, right, never had to put up with any hard shadowing because of a fearsome disposition. Opponents took liberties because Hull rarely played dirty.

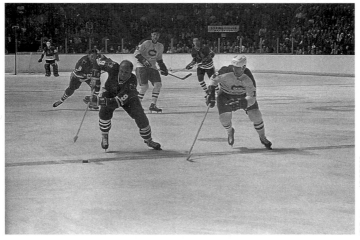

Bobby Hull carries the puck into the Montreal zone and Rejean Houle, right, gives chase. In the 1971 Stanley Cup final, Houle, a rookie with a nickname of Peanut, drew the assignment of shutting down the most prolific scorer the game had ever seen. Peter Mahovlich, center, also played a big role on the Canadiens' checking line.

On June 27, 1972, Hull sent shockwaves through hockey when he signed a $2.75-million contract with the Winnipeg Jets of the fledgling World Hockey Association. Here, he steps off a jet in Winnipeg with an outsized $1-million cheque, his signing bonus. Joanne and their sons are disembarking just ahead of Ben Hatskin, the founder of the Jets.

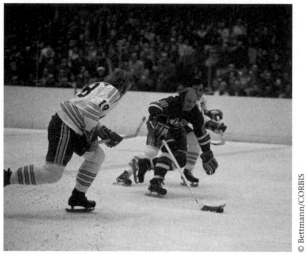

Hull returned to Chicago as a member of the Jets in December 1972. Here he splits Chicago Cougar defencemen Ron Anderson, left, and Larry Mavety in the first period at the International Ampitheatre. Later in the game Hull would savagely beat down former Black Hawk teammate Reggie Fleming.

Hull was the only WHA player who played for Canada in the 1976 Canada Cup. Though he was by far the oldest player in the Canadian line-up, he led the team in goals scored. His play, however, was over-shadowed by the heroics of Bobby Orr.

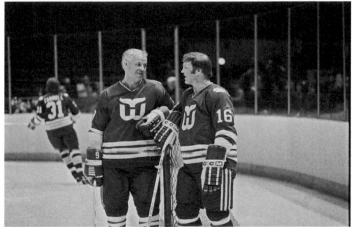

After the WHA and NHL merged in 1979, Hull attempted a comeback with the Winnipeg Jets, but after struggling and some controversy, he was traded to Hartford in February 1980. Hull, here talking to Whalers teammate Gordie Howe, had minimal impact with Hartford. Teammates said that Howe "owned" the Whalers' room.

Hull's nemesis in his years in Chicago was the team's president Bill Wirtz, a.k.a. Dollar Bill, right. Though Hull did participate in the retirement of his number at Chicago Stadium in December 1983, he kept his distance from the club until Wirtz's death in September 2007.

(AP Photo/M. Spencer Green)

Hull waves to fans at a rally in downtown Chicago in June 2010 after the Blackhawks won their first Stanley Cup in 39 years. Shortly after Bill Wirtz's death, his son Rocky Wirtz brought in Hull to be one of the franchise's ambassadors.

(AP Photo/Nam Y. Huh)

Hull has signed so many free autographs over the years that he has driven down the price-point for his signed photographs and collectibles. Here he signs autographs at Harry Caray's Tavern in Chicago in June 2010.

do things for the team. I was coming home to Winnipeg to end my career and I actually enjoyed doing that. But the demands on Bobby, so much more travel—a lot more time to be 'on' and not be able to rest or relax—it cost him in a lot of ways."

It's impossible to calculate that cost and it might not seem that his performance fell off. The Jets made it to the WHA final before losing to the New England Whalers—"the best and deepest team in the league," Daley said. Though only playing 63 games of a 78-game schedule, Hull led the team in goals (51), tied with Beaudin for the Jets' lead in points (103), was named to the WHA's First All-Star team and was awarded the Gary L. Davidson/Gordie Howe Trophy as the league's most valuable player. But no one, not Hull, not the most ardent booster of the WHA, would claim the exchange rate on those numbers was on par with the same in the NHL. It might seem unfair to pick on Beaudin but he was coming off a 33-goal, 66-point season with Cleveland in the AHL season before joining Christian Bordeleau and Hull on "the Luxury Line." Bordeleau had 21 goals in his best NHL season, 47 in year one with the Jets. "We were the Luxury Line all right: Chris and I had the luxury of playing with a legend," Beaudin said. Among those NHL veterans named to the WHA First All-Star team, only Hull and J.C. Tremblay had won any equivalent honors, first or second team, in the established league. The WHA First All-Star right-winger, Danny Lawson of Philadelphia, had scored 61 goals with the Blazers but the season previous, in 78 games with Buffalo, scored his NHL career high of 10.

While the Jets fell short of a title, Hull's former team played their way to a rematch against Montreal in the Stanley Cup final. The series wasn't quite as tense as the '71 final—the Black

Hawks fell to the Canadiens in six games. "Bobby could have been the difference in that final," Cliff Koroll said. "We really didn't have a dramatically different team other than losing Bobby. Everything was in place except for our losing him."

Hull's exile was not just a step away but a giant step down. It seemed like he'd never see the heights again.

• • •

Hull had been virtually the whole story in the WHA in its first season and the league was desperately in need of a boost to sustain interest the next winter. "Bobby Hull" could get fans into the arena, but "Bobby Hull Again" might not have been enough to get them back. At age 45, Gordie Howe was lured out of retirement, the incentive being an opportunity to play with his two sons, 18-year-old Mark and 20-year-old Marty, both fresh out of junior hockey. Howe and Hull: they had been the subject of the great debate about the game's best player in the early and mid-60s. By the spring of '74, Howe forced even Hull's backers to re-assess.

The NHL owners mocked the rival league when the Howes signed on with the Houston Aeros. The rhetorical question: how watered down is the competition if a 45-year-old can survive in it? Howe didn't survive, however. He thrived. He defined the league to an even greater extent than Hull had in the WHA's debut year. It was anything but a nostalgia tour. Sentiment didn't factor into it. Howe's season points total, 100, edged Hull's 95. That, however, was the only place where Hull came close. Howe led Houston to the regular-season title—the Aeros were clearly the WHA's best team and Howe *père* was their best player. In the playoffs Howe and his team were even more impressive than they had been over the winter, winning 12 of 14 games en route to the second WHA title. In that playoff run was a four-game sweep of the Jets in the opening round.

For Hull and the Jets it was an embarrassing end to a season fraught with problems. The team finished in fourth place in the Western Conference, five games under .500. Hull's 53 goals were impressive enough but the glass slippers fell off the feet of the other members of the Luxury Line— Christian Bordeleau fell from 101 points in the debut season to 75 in year two, Norm Beaudin from 103 to 55. At 37, Ab McDonald still provided leadership behind the scenes, but he had squeezed all the juice out of the lemon, scoring only 12 goals in 70 games. Joe Daley was giving up a goal more a game on average. "Compared to last year, we didn't have the same spirit," Hull said at season's end. True of the team, even more true of the team's star.

Hull's role wore on him, on and off the ice. It wore on him emotionally. Over that second season he developed an ulcer. A divide started to develop and it was to be expected given the time he had to spend on league affairs rather than going bowling on the team's family outings. Interviewed at the time Joe Daley said that Hull "wants to be one of us but he's in management." No one would go further because, as the Jets' personnel director said, the first player to openly criticize Hull "will be gone in a week." He was spokesman for a league that was getting hammered by the media in NHL markets. The Black Hawks' party line was that they had no interest in getting Hull back to his former club. "He's not playing major-league hockey anymore," said the team's PR man, Don Murphy, a thuggish ex-boxer who was a carry-over from the Wirtz's ring operation. Ted Lindsay, Old Scarface, Hull's former teammate in Chicago and no friend of the NHL establishment when he was trying to start up the players' association, was drinking Clarence Campbell's Kool-Aid and called the WHA "a graveyard for aging stars." Hull was enraged. "That Lindsay always created trouble," Hull told *Sport Magazine*. "People like him, people who go around saying those things, are like the long-haired goons who get on TV and yell something . . . just for publicity. And people without minds believe that stuff."

His role also wore on him physically. Long-haired goons in the WHA ran him with impunity. He had been targeted for tough treatment in the NHL but it was far worse when he was in against the marginal talents on WHA rosters. In the NHL the Philadelphia Flyers were making Gong Show hockey the fashion in the game and WHA teams, with the exception of Winnipeg, were picking up on the trend. Shots in the face or to the back of the head were routine. If Hull had the puck along the boards, he had to quickly pan the ice, looking for a kid or career minor-leaguer who was going to take a run at him. He was considered the big score for all the league's tough guys and they were legion: John Arbour in Minnesota; John Schella in Houston; Dave Hutchison and future NHL vice president Colin Campbell in Vancouver.

Every mulleted muttonhead in the league wanted a piece of Hull and, with no tough guy in the Winnipeg lineup, he was flying without protection. Duke Asmundson led the Jets in penalty minutes with 85, but he was no enforcer and every other team in the Western Conference had a player with twice Asmundson's total. With 673 minutes in penalties, the Jets were the least penalized team in the league; the next most civil team, the Toronto Toros, had 871 PIMs. The league's most penalized team, the Edmonton Oilers, had 600 more minutes in the penalty box than Winnipeg, and every other team in the West had over 1,000 PIMs. "Other players didn't care that he was Bobby Hull," Joe Daley said. "They didn't give a shit what he was doing for the league or how much more they were making because he put his name behind the WHA. He had to have his head on a swivel all game because a lot of goons were taking liberties with him. You could see the difference with Gordie when he signed with the Aeros. They wouldn't think of doing to Gordie what they did with Bobby. It wasn't that they had to take it easy on an old guy. If they tried to take liberties with him, Howe would have had his stick in their eyebrows. That's the way it always was with him."

The only one who might have felt more beaten up than Hull was Ben Hatskin. The debut season had been a celebration. Public goodwill had flooded the intersection of Portage and Main in June '72 and the team was knee-deep in it for the ensuing season. By season two, the goodwill was drying up and the novelty wearing off. Hatskin had been bold, operating on gut instincts and wishful thinking in the startup but he couldn't avoid the math: the Jets were a money-losing proposition. In its configuration back in the '70s, Winnipeg Arena seated about 10,000. For many games in the first two seasons, the arena was half full by the announced attendance numbers. In the first year, average attendance in the regular season had been 6,032; in the next, 6,483, trending in the right direction but not far enough and not fast enough. Those small gains didn't offset a bad arena lease that Hatskin was saddled with and couldn't renegotiate.

The big picture was even gloomier. The *raison d'être* of the league, a merger with the NHL, wasn't on the horizon. Several of the teams were losing money faster than the Jets. The optics could hardly have been worse—the New York franchise, which changed its name from the Raiders to the Golden Blades, was tossed out of Madison Square Garden for non-payment on rent and had to move to New Jersey. If the WHA couldn't fly in the biggest of all markets, there was no chance of a national television deal to boost the league's profile and, more importantly to Hatskin, franchises' revenues. "The Simkin family had patience but it was finite, not infinite," said a high-placed member of the group that would eventually bail out the franchise. "The Simkins probably saw the writing on the wall before Ben did. When no one potential owner stepped forward, that's when the idea of a public ownership or trust started to get floated."

It was an unholy mess of a season. Finances were going to force Hatskin to the sidelines. Hull's self-imposed exile from the NHL was looking ever more misbegotten. Two initiatives, one of them a big play by the league, the other a seemingly smaller bit of work, were in the works behind the scenes. One of them would offer a chance for Hull to fall back in love with the game, a chance to make beautiful music.

7

Not Disgraced

Maybe it's just the luck of the draw, maybe it's the fact that the part-owner of the restaurant never played beside a famous name who learned the game with Red Army or Dynamo, but there's seemingly no Soviet or Russian content in the memorabilia at Wayne Gretzky's. No Jofa helmet that Valery Kharlamov or Igor Larionov wore. No signed photo or stick from Slava Fetisov. Walking into Gretzky's is an experience in hockey history but not the whole of hockey history, not if you're trying to capture many of the greatest players of the '60s, '70s and '80s. In recent years the Hockey Hall of Fame has given an appropriate nod to the other superpower in bygone days—some would say, the superpower. It took a little while for hockey's hall to give the stars of the Soviet world and Olympic championship teams their due. Bobby Hull would tell you it took too long.

"I always loved the game the way the Russians and the Europeans played it," Hull says. *"I really learned to play the game early in my career when one year I went to Europe and played a bunch of exhibition games with the Rangers. The crowds were very respectful. The players were too. And their game emphasized all the right things, unlike the game we were playing in the sixties and seventies. The idea of sending someone out to just shut you down or try to run you . . . they wouldn't do anything like that. They tried to play their game and beat you fair and square."*

I ask Hull how he would feel if he had never had a chance to play against the Soviets in the '70s.

"I'm satisfied with my career, happy with it, proud of it . . . but it would feel incomplete if I didn't have a chance to play against Valery Kharlamov, Alexander Yakushev, Boris Mikhailov, Vladislav Tretiak . . ."

His voice grows louder with each passing name. He holds up his fist and pops out a thick finger for every star of the Soviets in the '70s. He works his way through five on his right hand, then on his left and back to the right. Right through to the bottom of the roster. I'd ask him who Tretiak's backup was but I don't know and I doubt it would stump him.

• • •

The WHA was already at a point of crisis going into its third season. More of the same wasn't the answer. The league needed a game-changer, a big moment to shore up its legitimacy. The Summit Series against the Soviet Union had enhanced the NHL's brand. WHA commissioner Gary Davidson followed the NHL's lead and pitched Hockey Canada on a series pitting the best of the maverick league against the Soviets. Hockey Canada signed off on it and the Soviets named their price. It was a risky gambit for the WHA. A poor showing would have cemented the perception of the WHA as a minor league. The Soviets sent a representative squad, wiser for the experience gained in the Summit Series. The mainstays from '72 returned, including Valery Kharlamov, Boris Mikhailov, Alexander Maltsev, Alexander Yakushev and Vladislav Tretiak.

The WHA talked a good fight. Before the opening game in Quebec, Edmonton owner Wild Bill Hunter described the WHAers as "the finest team that has ever represented Canada in international competition." To the hockey-going public, it sounded like a punch line. Team Canada '72 had been instantly elevated to the ranks of greatness with its impossibly narrow series victory and, if you looked at it coldly, despite some dreadful moments and a few very ordinary talents.

By the WHA's third season, its teams were much the same as they had been in the launch: NHL quality at the very top of the roster and minor leaguers filling out the lineup sheet. That fact, however, mattered little in putting together a single roster for a short series like a showdown with the Soviets. In the media, few pundits gave the WHA stars much of a chance of salvaging respect. Still, Hull, unofficially the team spokesman, talked up the WHA's chances at the training camp in Edmonton that opened 16 days before Game 1 in Quebec: "I don't think I've ever been to a camp with a better group of guys with a better attitude," Hull said. The consensus was that Hull had better leave his bridge in if he wanted to whistle in the dark.

In retrospect, the WHA team might not have been better than Team Canada in '72 but Hull and company were definitely better prepared—fact is, given the overconfidence of the

NHL players going in, it would have been hard for the WHA to send a team that was less prepared than the Summit Series winners. And perception wasn't quite the reality with regard to the talent that the WHA had on hand. The '74 squad had three key players back from '72: Paul Henderson, Frank Mahovlich and Pat Stapleton. Hull was one of three players who would have played in the Summit Series if it had been open to those who had signed on with the WHA, the other two being defenseman J.C. Tremblay and goaltender Gerry Cheevers. If Gordie Howe hadn't retired from the Detroit Red Wings in the spring of '71, he too would have been invited to the Summit Series. The '74 squad also had useful, middle-of-the-roster players with Stanley Cup experience: Rejean Houle, Hull's shadow from the '71 final, and Ralph Backstrom, who, game in and game out, turned out to be the best two-way forward.

A few players on the WHA squad were a little indignant about the attention on Hull. "It was all about Bobby Hull and he didn't mind it that way," one said. That was harsh. Hull could hardly be blamed for the spotlight falling on him. His was the most compelling story from the WHA side going into the series because of his rescinded invitation two years earlier. And no one faced any greater pressure than Hull. The conventional wisdom (or, at least, the official line) in the NHL was that his game had fallen off dramatically. Many thought that Hull, at age 35, was losing it, that he had gone soft.

This was just one of many opinions that required revision after a Soviet–WHA series.

Over the course of eight games against the Soviets, Hull emerged as the defining player for the WHA team and was challenged only by Valery Kharlamov as the player of the tournament. Hull's speed and power bought him open ice and he bulled through checks to fire his slapshot through traffic.

Not that he or his teammates, going on, knew how it was going to turn out. Hull admitted before the opening game in Quebec that he had "never been tighter" in the minutes before stepping on the ice. Hull was not alone in apprehension and even dread. On the eve of the opener Gordie Howe said: "I only hope we're not disgraced."

It never looked like it. Not even for a shift.

Gordie Howe, wearing No. 9, was out for the opening face-off with Backstrom and Mahovlich matched against the Soviets' top line of Kharlamov, Mikhailov and Vladimir Petrov. And the WHA unit, featuring three players all older than any in the Soviet lineup, took them to school. Howe quickly established his menace and Backstrom made smart use of the wingers. The Soviets had all the advantages in speed but the veteran NHLers made the puck do most of the work. Hull wore No. 16, deferring to Howe, and the two legends from the previous decade combined on a glorious power-play goal that gave the WHA a 2–1 lead midway through the second period. Before he hit the blueline, Hull dumped the puck into the corner and Howe tenderized a Soviet defenseman with a flurry of old-school sticks and elbows. Howe fed the puck to Mike Walton, who in turn sent it on to Hull, who blew in from the left point and hammered the puck in stride at the face-off dot. Tretiak never saw it and he was swinging at a blur, tumbling backward into the net.

With little more than eight minutes left in the third period, the WHA was trailing 3–2 and Hull scored again. Andre Lacroix dug the puck out of the corner and Hull one-timed a shot from the dot on his off wing to tie the game. A couple of shifts later

Hull narrowly missed picking up a hat trick and the winning goal in his first game wearing the Maple Leaf. In a virtual replay of Hull's first goal, Howe won a battle for the puck in the corner and hit Hull with a pass as he poured in on the Soviet goal. The shot caromed wide.

The final score, 3-all, fairly represented the balance of play, but the WHA thought they might have had the game won. And on the last shift of the game, Howe, looking fresher than anyone on the ice and twice as mean, viciously slashed Mikhailov, grabbed the puck and sent Mahovlich in alone on Tretiak. Mahovlich had the Soviet goaltender down and beaten with a deke but he lost control of the puck at the edge of the crease.

Hull and Kharlamov were named the outstanding players for their respective teams. Hull expressed a sincere respect for the Soviet players, saying that he had watched them in practice and admired their speed and skill. The game was enough to lead people to believe that the 1972 Summit Series would have looked very different if Wirtz and Campbell hadn't shut out Hull and the other WHA players. If Canadian hockey fans had any doubt, there'd be none after the fourth game in the series at the Pacific Coliseum in Vancouver.

In one explosive stretch in Game 4, Hull scored three goals over a five-minute stretch in the first period. A goal on three consecutive shifts. The game opened again with Howe and his son Mark hammering the Soviets in the dirty areas along the boards. That seemed to buy the WHA players a lot of room on the ice. As Howie Meeker noted on the CTV telecast: "You can play pretty good hockey when you're not going to get hit." Hull's three goals showed the full range of his game: the first a blast from the point on the power-play; the second a solo rush up the middle of the ice, splitting the Soviet blueliners

and rifling a wrist shot; and the third, a shot from the slot top
shelf on Tretiak's stick-side. Along with a goal from Mahovlich,
the WHA went from 2–1 down to a 5–2 lead. Andre Lacroix,
who fed Hull the puck on the third goal, retrieved it from the
net and handed it to Hull who took it over to the WHA bench.
Hull almost had a fourth goal on a couple of occasions over
the course of the game. The Soviets rallied to tie the game with
two goals in the last five minutes but still, for Hull, it was an
impressive performance. He displayed finish and pure scoring
instinct that would have made him the lead forward for Team
Canada in '72. At the end of the game Hull and Yakushev were
named their teams' players of the game, but while the Soviet
skated out to accept his award, Hull did not. From Game 1 on,
he was playing through a knee-ligament strain and was getting
treatment for the injury. He also had his left hand in an ice
bucket to bring down bruising from a slash.

• • •

As all expected, some of the most heated battles in the Soviet
capital were waged in an end room at the hotel where the
Canadians were staying. Screaming matches between Bobby
and Joanne made the showdowns on the ice seem like
sessions at the bridge club. A line that has been credited to
several players, reporters and even Ben Hatskin: "If he takes
that out on the ice, we should be okay." There's even a little
window onto the strain behind the scenes, thanks to a documentary of the series backed by Hockey Canada. In one scene
showing the players and their wives shopping for souvenirs in
Moscow, Joanne holds up what looks like a small folk-music
instrument, a small pipe. Hull takes one look at it, shakes his

head in the negative and then rolls his eyes, looking disgusted. At another point, which couldn't have been included in the family-friendly cut of the documentary, Joanne and other wives and their husbands boarded a bus for a tour of Moscow but Bobby was held up by a crowd of autograph seekers. The bus was idling for a few minutes but none of the players wanted to say anything to Hull about getting it over with. Joanne was not reticent, though. She went to the door of the bus and dropped a couple of F-bombs in full voice. Hull was the WHA's unofficial goodwill ambassador but now even Muscovites were getting an idea of the tensions inside the embassy.

• • •

What if? It's the tantalizing question that can be asked so often about Bobby Hull's career. The what-if question leads to a sequence of consequences that fall in a line like so many dominoes.

What if Jacques Lemaire's long shot in 1971 doesn't beat Tony Esposito? Topple the dominoes: the Black Hawks win the Cup, which spurs Bobby Hull to sign a generous contract to stay in Chicago and go on to be the dominant player in Canada's victory in the Summit Series, achieving an unprecedented superstardom and, at the same time, putting millions more in the pockets of NHL owners. Of course it's all conjecture but it's easy to imagine that the goal that drifted out of the gloamin' had immense, even industry-shaping magnitude.

Hull and the WHA came to another what-if when the series went back to the U.S.S.R., each team with a win and two games ending in ties. Again, it came down to a single play, one that breached the time-space continuum.

The Soviets narrowly won Games 5 and 6 in Moscow and needed just a tie to clinch the series in Game 7. A win in the seventh contest followed by another in the eighth would give the WHA a draw. Before the game defenseman Rick Ley was booed viciously—the Soviet hockey bosses were calling for him to be jailed for assault when he suckered Valery Kharlamov after Game 6. The home crowd also booed Gordie Howe who had Soviets cowering when they were within a stick length of him. The only WHA player they cheered was Hull. The first half of the series had been a shining example of sportsmanship, but play went over to the dark side in Moscow. Hull, though, was the scoring leader for the visiting team and had yet to take a penalty. His popularity also stemmed from the circulation of hockey films on Moscow's black market. Just as the Beatles' albums were traded stealthily among rock 'n' roll fans, so too were highlights of '71 playoffs, including Chicago's loss to the Canadiens in Game 7. They too knew all about Hull denting the crossbar behind Ken Dryden with the Stanley Cup on the line.

In the last two minutes of the critical Game 7, it was tied 4-all and the puck was frozen in the Soviet end with 1:32 left in the game. The issue for the visiting team was the clock. The whistle blew at 1:32 but the clock ran down to 1:28, a bit of home cooking by the off-ice officials. Gerry Cheevers was livid. He had the best view of the seconds ticking away on the game clock. The goaltender skated the length of the ice, shouting at the referee, a Canadian named Tom Brown. WHA coach Billy Harris also took up the cause. The WHA players chased Brown all over the ice. The timekeeper advised Brown that seconds couldn't be added to the scoreboard clock so the referee told him to wait two seconds after the next face-off and to flip the switch at that point. As it turned out, four seconds would have been enough to send the WHA into Game 8 with a shot at squaring the series.

In the last minute, with Cheevers on the bench in favor of a sixth skater, the WHA stormed the Soviet goal. In the very last seconds, Henderson chased the puck down in the corner and found Hull in the face-off circle. Hull fired the puck through a tangle of skates and sticks and it was by Tretiak. The red light went on. Improbably, so did the green light. Arenas everywhere are wired so that the goal judge can't turn on the red light if the game has ended and the green light has fired up first— but everywhere, it seems, didn't include Moscow's Luzhniki Ice Palace in 1974. Replays showed that Hull's goal went in at the stroke when the digital 0:01 went to 0:00. Adding to the confusion: the horns should have sounded but didn't. There's no knowing if something was lost in translation and the time-keeper did wait the two seconds that Brown had asked for. What we know is that if those four lost seconds had been added back, Hull's "goal" would not need quotation marks. And maybe that would have spurred the WHA to win Game 8 and split their series with the mighty Soviets, earning the credibility that the WHA needed for mainstream acceptance. What if. If only.

With little to play for, the WHA lost the final game 3–2. Hull led tournament scorers with seven goals and two assists in the eight games. If anyone thought that Anatoli Tarasov was laying it on thick when he said that Hull would have been worth one or two goals a game against the Soviets in '72, the notion was put to rest. At 35 and playing hurt, Hull was a threat on every shift. "In my opinion the Canadian team was just as strong as the National Hockey League team we saw in 1972," Soviet hockey boss Boris Kulagin said. "I understand they are already talking in Canada about the need to form a combined NHL and WHA team for future series." That was only a couple of seasons in the offing, although the degree to which the two leagues were combined would be the bare minimum: it was going to be Hull, and only Hull, with players from the league he had walked away from. It would be Hull's last great turn for all to see.

8

"Kid, you go over to the other side"

There's no point asking Bobby Hull if his enthusiasm waned at any point in his career. He wouldn't admit it. It was always about enter-taining fans, being accountable to teammates, and, in Winnipeg anyway, giving good value for a contract offered in good faith. If I asked him if it was ever a chore to come to the rink, it would chill the conversation. When talking about playing the game, he accentuates the positive. "I'd do it all again" is his refrain and there's no guess-ing how many times a day he says it.

Still, it's hard to imagine that Hull was much looking forward to doing it again when he reported to the Jets' training camp in the fall of '74. It had to feel anticlimactic after the series against the Soviets. He would have had trouble seeing the positive in returning to Winnipeg after the team's negative outcome in the spring of '74 and he had to be worried about the business of the Jets franchise and the league as a whole. Yet, listening to Bobby Hull talk about the time after the WHA's series against the Soviets, it's clear that he fell back in love with the game.

"You could see the future of the game," he says. "I knew it right away, literally just in a couple of minutes."

Hull's hockey life played out in arenas in front of thousands and on television broadcasts in front of millions. And yet a watershed moment, the one that restored his love of the game and raised his own to new heights, played out unseen. An empty arena but for a couple of dozen players. All but three of them would never earn a dime from the game. Those three, however, would redefine and even re-invent the game.

"It was really magic," Hull says.

• • •

The big story in Winnipeg after Hull's second season with the Jets played out off the ice. Some worried that Winnipeg Arena might stay dark all winter. Ben Hatskin had hit the wall. The Simkins wanted out. The word was put out but no one in the city's business community was rushing to buy them out. Anyone with the gelt to underwrite the team knew that he'd be buying fool's gold. The Jets were a point of civic pride but a financial mess. Lieutenant-governor Jack McKeag was an unlikely white knight for the franchise. McKeag dropped the puck at the ceremonial face-off before the Jets' first game at Winnipeg Arena but he had no big interest in or knowledge of hockey. McKeag and Bob Graham, a gas executive, made the push for community ownership of the Jets and they, along with 50 other Winnipeggers, became the team's patrons. Hatskin and the Simkins maintained that they could have

fetched more for the Jets if they'd sold the franchise to someone intending to move it to a bigger market, but said they were
willing to take a bit of a haircut to keep the Jets in Winnipeg.
The "Group of 52" devised a hydra-headed deal that required
the city underwriting a $300,000 loan, which passed through
council, and a $600,000 loan from the province, which died
in the legislature. The Group of 52 took the extraordinary step
of soliciting public support. The "Save the Jets" campaign had
the aspect of a charity drive and ended with a telethon with
members of the booster club working the phones, taking the
pledges of fans. Hull appeared on the screen. He had gone
from the WHA's promoter to the league's defender and now
was reduced to soliciting donations. The ultimate testament
to Winnipeg's love of hockey: the telethon, with a target of
$600,000, raised $629,502.51.

• • •

The Jets were still in business, but barely so, and there seemed
to be little reason for optimism going into the season. Hatskin
was out but he hadn't ever really defined the franchise—Hull
had, and his influence was as large as ever. The team was
nominally owned by the Group of 52 but the Jets still rose and
fell with Hull's way and whim.

The Group of 52 hired Rudy Pilous as coach. Pilous had
been Hull's coach in St. Catharines and in Chicago in the early
'60s—in fact, Pilous's name was engraved on the Stanley Cup
right beside Hull's. Pilous was a veteran hockey man and some
might have thought that he was handpicked to mollify Hull.
If that was the intention, it was wrong-minded at best. A couple of years after the Stanley Cup victory, Hull had a leading

role in insurrection by the Black Hawks, a dressing-room revolt that led to Pilous's firing. When the Jets brought in Pilous, Hull said all the right things. "I've learned my lesson," Hull said. "I was wrong in the past." He might have even believed that to be true. Still, even if this difficult bit of history wasn't fully behind them, Pilous was an improvement on Nick Micoski. Added value: Pilous had grown up in Winnipeg. Under Hatskin, the team had exercised a personal bias, favoring Friends of Ben. With community ownership it seemed that a provincial bias was more appropriate. The Group of 52 had tapped one of their own to take the coaching load off Hull's shoulders.

It didn't work. Not quite.

In fairness, it would have been a challenge to any coach. Pilous wasn't familiar with the players on his roster and around the league. Even Jets veterans were asking, "Who are these guys?" The team opened the season with 10 new players in the lineup. In midseason Pilous would be kicked upstairs and Hull would assume the coach's duties again, in name at least. Pilous was the tried and true, but what Hull and the Jets needed was something new.

• • •

Bad things usually happen when plans are poorly conceived. Best-laid plans often result in good outcomes. Magic can only come about by accident.

Going into his third season in Winnipeg, Bobby Hull needed a tonic to restore his game and, more importantly, his will to play it. The series against the U.S.S.R. had re-ignited his competitive fire but it would have been too much to expect it to carry over through the entire season. It was one thing to play in front of capacity crowds in games broadcast nationally with a chance to take a place in hockey history, and another to play the Mariners in an almost vacant San Diego International Sports Arena. It was one thing to play with a team representing the country and another to play for an organization that survived thanks to a telethon.

Dr. Gerry Wilson stumbled upon the tonic that Hull desperately needed. Dr. Wilson knew about elite hockey. Bob Pulford, the former Toronto Maple Leafs center back in the '60s, called Dr. Wilson the best junior he ever played against. The course of Dr. Wilson's life might have gone in another direction if injuries hadn't wrecked his career. In fact, it was his too-frequent trips to the hospital and all the surgeries that spurred his interest in medicine and ultimately led him to med school. In the early '70s, Dr. Wilson worked with the Jets in their first season but then landed a fellowship that took him to Stockholm for a year for a sports-medicine research project. The research was dedicated to conditioning for the development of hockey players. He was assigned a research assistant: Anders Hedberg, a full-time student who moonlighted with the Djurgarden hockey team. In fact, in the papers and guide that later came out of the research project, Hedberg takes a star pictorial role, doing various plyometric box jumps and other extreme calisthenics that were ground-breaking at the time but *de rigueur* 20 years later.

Dr. Wilson knew a lot about hockey but nothing about Swedish hockey and he went to see Hedberg play in Stockholm. Borje Salming and Inge Hammarstrom had joined the Leafs and Thommie Bergmann was in his first season with Detroit and stereotypes of Swedish players still prevailed—too soft to play the North American game. Dr. Wilson's attitude wasn't too far removed from the conventional wisdom until he saw Hedberg in a Swedish Elite League game. He was a near-immediate convert to the belief that Hedberg could play in the NHL and WHA. Dr. Wilson passed on an informal scouting report about Hedberg to Billy Robinson, the Jets' personnel director.

In later years, it would be widely reported that Dr. Wilson had discovered Hedberg. It was something less than that. He had shown up on the radar before the Jets and the WHA opened for business. "I first played for Sweden at the Izvestia tournament in late '69, when I was eighteen," Hedberg said. "After that I got a call from the Vancouver Canucks. I really didn't consider it because I wanted to finish my schooling and was planning to become a phys-ed teacher."

When Robinson went over to Sweden to scout and recruit Hedberg, the Toronto Maple Leafs were on the trail as well. Borje Salming was showing the elite skills on the Toronto blue-line that would lead him to the Hockey Hall of Fame. The Maple Leafs were going to put Hedberg on their negotiation list and eventually make him an offer larger than the one Robinson was authorized to put on the table.

It was in part Dr. Wilson's connection to the Jets that had Hedberg leaning toward Winnipeg. The other major factor was that the Jets were going to be in a position to offer a contract to Ulf Nilsson, a center with AIK who had played with Hedberg on the Swedish team that took a silver at the world championships. Robinson was able to sign both, along with Lars-Erik Sjoberg, a squat but skilled defenseman, another player not in the North American conventional mode.

Hull had been the seal of approval when management recruited pros to jump from the NHL and the pro minors. Billy Robinson tried to use Hull's presence as an incentive with the

Swedes but it had no impact on their decision to sign. "I didn't know who Bobby Hull was or even who the Canadian players on the team in '72 were," Hedberg said. "I had never seen an NHL game. I just thought it would be a fun place to play and a good time for the three of us."

● ● ●

In late summer of '74 the three Swedes took the ice with Hull at St. James Civic Centre Arena in Winnipeg. They joined in a skate with the University of Manitoba varsity, an informal session without coaches, players going through drills. Hedberg lined up for a line rush at his customary position, left wing, and was standing behind Hull along the boards. Hull looked at him and spoke to him for the first time.

"Kid, you go over to the other side," Hull told him.

"I didn't even know that Bobby Hull played left wing," Hedberg said. "I had never played right wing in my career. A little center, but almost always on the left. I was a left-handed shot and someone left-handed playing the off-wing was very rare in those days. But I was new—I still felt like I was a guest. So I skated over to the other side and Ulf was in the middle."

The three scored on their first trip down the ice. Then the next. Then the one after.

"I had never had the feeling before," Hedberg said. "And wherever I went, it never happened again. It was instant chemistry. We didn't know each other. There should have been a learning curve, you think. We never had played with a Canadian player or in the small rink. I was out of position. It was summer—we were fit but it wasn't like we had our timing in midseason. But it worked. It was like the radar was on. We scored every rush—against college players, I guess we should have. But I knew and Ulf knew that this was something special."

"I asked Anders after, 'What's Bobby thinking?'" Nilsson said.

They had no way of knowing. Hull didn't say much to the two—actually he didn't say anything during the skate with the exception of telling the "kid" to go over to the other side. Neither did Hull skate with them for a few weeks after—he went off to join the WHA team for its series against the Soviets. The two Swedes weren't sure if they'd play together or with Hull. The Jets were still an unknown to them.

What they didn't know was that Hull was putting the word out. "When he got back to camp, before he skated with us, Bobby told us, 'You should see these guys,'" Joe Daley said.

It turned out that Hull had made calls after the skate with the college players. "These Swedes are fuckin' unbelievable," he told Dr. Wilson.

The three skated together from the opening of training camp, through exhibitions, and then took the ice against the Blazers in Vancouver. Effectively, the line was like a small team of comic-book superheroes, each bringing a super-power. Though lacking the long, lank blond locks, Hull was, as ever, Superman, the strength of the troika. Hedberg was The Flash, pouring down his right wing with electric speed, forcing defensemen to scramble. Not a physical force in any particular way, Nilsson was Brainiac 5, distributing the puck with an intelligence bordering on genius. "We complemented each other perfectly," Hedberg said.

Just as superheroes never look the worse for wear one frame to the next, the Hot Line seemed immune to fatigue. "You couldn't put a checking line against them," said Hull's erstwhile shadow, Rejean Houle, who had moved on to the Quebec Nordiques of the WHA. "If you tried, they would just keep on going, staying out on the ice for two or three minutes, wearing you down."

"It probably couldn't have worked if we had been North American players, especially at our age," Hedberg said. "Young players could have been intimidated playing beside a hero they worshipped when they were growing up. They would defer to him or try to play Bobby's game rather than their own. We didn't look at it that way."

Hull's goal scoring soared. In his first season skating with the Swedes he racked up 77 goals in 78 games, the highest season number over the course of his career. He won the Gary Davidson Trophy as the WHA's most valuable player. Hedberg missed 13 games with injuries but still scored 53 goals and won the Lou Kaplan Trophy as the WHA's rookie of the year.

The line's success wasn't anything that you could have measured by scoring summaries or other statistics. In fact, in the Swedes' first season, the Houston Aeros won their second consecutive championship and the Jets finished out of the playoffs, five points behind the Phoenix Roadrunners for the last playoff position. But they made the game beautiful. "I came in their second season together," Peter Sullivan said. "In the one game in Phoenix they scored the best goal I ever saw, fifteen passes, bing-bing-bing. It made your head spin to watch it. The crowd went crazy. The Phoenix players stood up on the bench and were banging their sticks. I remember saying [to other Winnipeg players], 'That was amazing.' They said, 'It's been like that since day one.'"

In their third season the Jets were making personnel moves left and right. Trading Hull's original center with the Jets, Chris Bordeleau, to Quebec constituted a minor move, given

Nilsson's arrival. They junked the old-school approaches to team-building, signing but later dumping journeyman tough guy Howie Young. Young's toughness wasn't much use—he just slowed down the game. Ditto defenseman Larry Hillman, who would play out the season and later become coach, but wasn't much service to Winnipeg in the last season of his long career—the game the young Jets were playing little resembled the '67 Leafs, a Stanley Cup–winning team flecked with liver spots. Winnipeg was not just going younger but in a different direction entirely.

There were bound to be hiccups. The WHA's leading knuckleheads who had gone after Hull (albeit with caution) in previous seasons, now homed in on his Swedish linemates with abandon. Worse, if Hull had little protection against the goons, Hedberg and Nilsson had none at all—they were victims of a slow-to-evolve culture of the '70s dressing room, full of resentment toward Europeans coming in and taking the jobs of Canadians, teammates from past seasons, friends. "Even the refs had it in for us, letting guys get away with murder going after us, when they would have called penalties if it had been anyone else on the end of it," Ulf Nilsson said. Hedberg added: "We thought that we were going to have to learn to fight after our first season [in the WHA]."

The Jets talked them out of taking boxing lessons or doing anything rash. Hull's was the loudest voice telling them to stay with their game. "Bobby was so supportive," Nilsson said. "He said, 'Don't change.'"

● ● ●

Despite missing the playoffs the previous spring, the Jets believed that they were on the cusp of something special when they reported for training camp in the fall of '75—that the chemistry that developed between Hedberg, Nilsson and Hull was going to carry over to the rest of the team. It was something that the players understood even if management didn't quite get it—to Rudy Pilous's mind, the team missed the playoffs not despite the efforts of Hedberg, Nilsson and Sjoberg but because of them. He thought the team was too European to compete with WHA teams that couldn't muster three players who touched them for skill. Fact is, the rookie seasons of Hedberg and Nilsson had been a disappointment—in terms of making the playoffs—almost entirely because of a dearth of talent at the bottom of the roster. They were undone by CanCon.

Thankfully, Bill Robinson tuned out Pilous, who would have readily cast the Jets in the mold of the NHL's brawling Philadelphia Flyers and the lesser WHA clubs. Dr. Wilson was installed as the chairman of the Jets' international-relations committee—for an outfit with a public–private ownership group this was an appropriately bureaucratic-sounding designation for bird dog and fixer. Robinson and Dr. Wilson ran 180 degrees counter to Pilous's philosophy and signed one solid Swedish center, Mats Lindh, and one superior right-winger, Willy Lindstrom. Though the Jets picked up some muscle per the general manager's request, the best Canadian recruit was a skilled forward buried in Montreal's system: Peter Sullivan, who was coming off a 44-goal, 104-point season with the Nova Scotia Voyageurs of the American Hockey League. As a role-playing forward, the Jets brought in Bill Lesuk, a Winnipeg native who had bounced around the NHL for a few seasons and was unlucky enough to get moved out of Philadelphia just before the Flyers' run to their Stanley Cups.

Pilous wasn't the only skeptic about the composition of the Jets' roster. Said team president Bob Graham on the signing of former NHL coach of the year Bobby Kromm to work the bench: "This is considered a difficult coaching job because of the unique make-up of our team." Hard to imagine that the All-Star Swedes and an utterly content 77-goal scorer would be high maintenance, but for Graham and Pilous and others there was no thinking out of the box, no getting beyond the NHL's orthodoxy. When the Jets went to Europe for their training camp in September '75, they impressively beat the Swedish national team—impressively in retrospect, anyway, if not to the minds of Pilous *et al*.

If the Swedish national team couldn't beat the Jets in a contest of skill, the dregs of the WHA couldn't and wouldn't bother trying. Instead they tried to intimidate the European players, Hedberg and Nilsson most of all. "What Anders and Ulf did took a lot of guts," said Hull.

Hull boiled over a couple of months into the 1975–76 season. He sat out a road game against the soon-to-be-out-of-Denver Spurs as a protest of referees' reluctance to enforce the rules and coaches condoning and encouraging what he'd later describe as "brutality and savagery." Although he was too familiar with the rule-breakers himself, he didn't sit out the game from self-interest. It was strictly to bring attention to his teammates' plight. "It's time we took some action," Hull said. "If something isn't done soon, it will ruin the game for all of us."

No one was spared Hull's vitriol. "It's becoming a disaster," he said. "The idiot owners, the incompetent coaches, the inept players are dragging the game into the mud. They're destroying it with their senseless violence. You talk to some of these idiots at the top and they say, 'It's the nature of the game. It always has been that way and always will be.' They're full of bull. It's worse than it ever has been and it's going to end up ruining hockey. They ought to take all these incompetents, these idiot owners, coaches and players and put them in their own league so they can kill each other."

The protest lasted just the one game, a routine win for the Jets. Hull would later say that he didn't continue to sit out because it "didn't have any effect." Still, for a man who cultivated a relentlessly optimistic image, who had expressed only his love of the game, whose credo was the title of his autobiography, *Hockey Is My Game*, Hull sounded like a man who could walk away from it all and not look back. "The game is no pleasure anymore," he concluded. "It's an ordeal."

Despite the gloom, Hull had rich experiences in the offing and, in some way, they might stand as crowning achievements. He'd also have ordeals that would test him and punish him far worse than the rough treatment suffered stoically by Hedberg and Nilsson.

• • •

If you ask members of the Jets of the mid-70s, only a few will point to their Avco Cup championships as watershed moments. Hull never has, really. It's simply a function of the lack of drama. In Hull's two championships with Winnipeg, the Jets thoroughly dominated in the post-season. They were playing one game and everyone else something less. In '76 the team that Pilous thought was too European to succeed in North America won 12 of 13 games through three series and emphatically swept the defending champion Aeros in the final, winning Game 4 9–1 in front of the capacity crowd at Winnipeg Arena.

After losing in Quebec in Game 7 of the '77 final, the Jets rebounded in spring of '78 winning eight of nine play-off games, beating New England in the final. The latter was bittersweet. Hedberg and Nilsson were heading to the New York Rangers the next season. "Ulf and I asked Bobby if we should go when the Rangers made us the offers," Hedberg said. "We felt that we owed it to him to ask. He couldn't have been more supportive. He told us that we had to do what was best for our careers and the feeling was that the WHA was on very shaky ground. Bobby's game was starting to slide too. We all knew it. Bobby couldn't go to New York but he told us that didn't and shouldn't stop us."

Given that Hull was cruelly denied a chance to play for Team Canada in '72, it's fitting that his two greatest games in the twilight would be played against the Soviets.

• • •

Hockey historians concede that the edition of Team Canada that won the 1976 Canada Cup was the most dominant hockey team ever assembled. Members of that team don't disagree. "It was far superior to the '72 team," said Bobby Clarke, a member of both teams. "It was better than any team that came later." Only future Hall of Famers needed to apply and all needed to fight for minutes. Some franchise players were left at home.

Thirty-five years out, a few images endure. The most vivid was Bobby Orr, hobbling on one leg and winning the player of the tournament award. "The bravest thing I ever saw in the game," said Clarke, who was the captain of Team

Canada '76. "Bobby could barely walk in the morning and he'd get to the arena four hours before the face-off so that he could play. He suffered big time, never said a word and was our best player."

The Canada Cup brought together stars of the teams that owned the NHL in the '70s: Boston, Montreal and Philadelphia. They made up a full two-thirds of the roster and represented the name value. The biggest names in the league were able to set aside their usual hostilities for a common cause. "In '72 there were guys who thought they were doing the country a favor and didn't want to give up their summer hockey schools for a few weeks," Clarke said. "In '76, everyone was committed. There were no attitudes."

(That's not quite the way Al MacNeil described it. MacNeil, Boston's Don Cherry and Winnipeg's Bobby Kromm were assistants to head coach Scotty Bowman, who was coming off his second Stanley Cup with the Canadiens. "We needed four coaches to keep all the egos in line," MacNeil said.)

The balance of the roster was largely drawn from players who hadn't been quite ready to make an impact in '72: Darryl Sittler, Lanny McDonald, Gil Perreault, Denis Potvin and Marcel Dionne.

And there was Hull.

Unlike the Summit Series, the Canada Cup was open to WHA players. The NHL couldn't flex its muscle after the power-play that shut out the WHA players four years before—Hockey Canada wasn't going to get hoodwinked again. In fact, the tournament needed the contributions of WHA players to keep some sense of competitive balance on both sides—shutting out Hedberg, Nilsson, Sjoberg and Lindstrom would have left Team Sweden completely devalued.

Hull was the only WHA player on the Canadian team and there was nary a complaint about the fact—which stands as a good measure of the falling status of the rival league going into its fifth season. For casual fans all these years later his name would not be top of mind when trying to list the players on the Canadian roster. And it's true even for some who played in the series. Clarke, for one, worked his way through the lines and only came around to Hull toward the end.

"As the tournament played out, some guys, like Esposito and Hull, had less of an impact and got less ice time," Clarke said. "[Coach Scotty] Bowman didn't owe anybody ice time. Everyone went in knowing that they were going to get a fair chance—if you could help the team win, you were going to get ice time. Hull would have been an impact player in '72, clearly, but the younger guys had passed him by '76."

Clarke seems harsh in his assessment of Hull's play.

Team Canada '76 was a once-in-a-lifetime assembly of talent but the tournament was anticlimactic. The final was expected to be another installment in the rivalry between Canada and the U.S.S.R.; instead, it was the Czechoslovaks who upset Canada in the round-robin and advanced to the best two-out-of-three final. The consensus as the tournament played out was that the Soviets had brought less than their best team—Alexander Maltsev was their lead player and Vladislav Tretiak was again in goal, but the likes of Kharlamov, Yakushev and Mikhailov were absent, their omission not explained but presumed to be victims of an internal power struggle.

Though the Soviets were something less than the force they had been in '72 and '74, they were still a threat. Most fans wouldn't today know that Canada had one must-win (or, more precisely, one must-win-or-tie) game in the tournament: at the end of the round-robin against the U.S.S.R. If you went by that single game, Clarke mischaracterized Hull's role. In fact, in that pivotal and tense contest, Hull was a defining player for Canada.

Even at this late stage of the tournament, Bowman was shuffling lines. Some combinations stayed mostly intact through the game—Clarke between his Philadelphia teammates Bill Barber and Reggie Leach, Bob Gainey with Peter Mahovlich coupled a shutdown unit, Steve Shutt and Guy Lafleur on opposite wings. Hull was one piece that Bowman moved around, looking for the right mix.

Hull was on a makeshift line, with his center from the '65 Hawks team that went to the Stanley Cup final, Esposito, and Marcel Dionne, usually a center but taking the spot on right wing. Five minutes into the game, still scoreless, Hull powered wide down his wing, passed a blueliner and forced Maltsev into taking a tripping penalty, giving Canada its first power-play of the game. Hull didn't stay on for the first power-play, but came out later in a stoppage and was playing alongside Perreault and Lafleur when Perreault opened the scoring—he deflected a point shot from Potvin past Tretiak.

As the game wore on, it was Esposito and not Hull whose ice time was diminished—Esposito had been at his career peak in the early '70s but by '76 he couldn't keep up with the pace set by his younger Canadian teammates and the second-tier Soviets. The years hadn't been kind to him. Hull, on the other hand, was moved to Perreault's left. If Hedberg and Nilsson benefited from not knowing their linemate-to-be in Winnipeg, Perreault was elevated by his knowledge of Hull. "It was amazing to get a chance to play with Bobby," Perreault said. "I had a chance to play against him before he left [for the WHA].

He was someone I watched growing up. Look, when he signed with the WHA, my next contract went from thirty thousand to a hundred and twenty-five thousand. Everybody on that team owed Bobby. He made all our lives better. And here he was, thirty-six or thirty-seven, and he still worked hard every shift, every practice. He pushed you and he pushed me in a way that I don't know that I ever had been before."

The Soviets tied the game midway through the first period—Vikulov being credited with the goal when in fact Alexandrov had scored. That set the stage for Hull again. Before the first intermission he scored what would be the winning goal and evoked the Hull of the mid-60s, when he was the biggest name in the sport. With the Canadians pinning the Soviets in their end, Perreault had the puck behind Tretiak's net and threaded it to Hull on the left wing. Hull one-timed the puck at the face-off dot, leaning into it, his stick a bowed blur. The puck went right through Tretiak, leaving him reeling backward. Hull was swarmed by his teammates, smiling tooth-lessly and ferociously chewing gum.

Hull had other highlight-reel moments. Passing to Perreault, sending him in alone on Tretiak for a chance that would have produced a goal if the puck had sat down for the center. Drawing defenders over to his left wing and buying open ice for Perreault. Taking another pass from Perreault in a virtual replay of his go-ahead goal and one-timing it, only to have it ricochet painfully off a Soviet defender's leg. Chasing down a young Soviet forward and breaking up a three-on-two when Canada was still clinging to a one-goal lead. Hull wasn't the same player that he had been in '71. He was thicker and a step slower, to be sure, but he compensated and adapted. Rather than relying on his speed to look after his defensive

responsibilities, he intuited opponents' plays in formation—
he made the break back to pick up his man a beat faster.

Hull finished the Canada Cup with five goals, the most
of any Canadian player, one ahead of his sometime linemate
Perreault and tied for the overall tournament lead with Milan
Novy of the Czechoslovaks and the Soviet's Viktor Zhluktov.
In the pivotal game of the tournament, where a loss would
have left Canada out of the final, Hull combined with Perreault
not only for the most important goal but also more quality
scoring chances than any other wing–center combination—
this despite fewer power-play shifts than the likes of Lafleur
and Shutt.

If Clarke was harsh in his assessment of Hull, Denis Potvin
was effusive with praise. Potvin wrote a memoir of his experience for *Canadian Magazine* that appeared in the fall of '76. He
paid tribute to his teammates at the end of the piece but saved
special mention for Hull. Potvin wrote: "Thirty-seven years old
and playing like a kid, and such a nice guy who liked everybody and was liked by everybody. They call him the Golden Jet
and he really is, he has an aura about him. He really is golden."

• • •

The WHA–Soviets series in '74 failed to provide a great game
between the two powers in the sport, one contest still talked
about. The same is true of the Canada Cup in '76—few people,
even devoted fans, could tell you the score or remember a play
from the pivotal contest that knocked the Soviets out of the
tournament. There is, however, one game between Canadian
and Soviet teams that still sparks discussion among hockey
fans—they remember details from it, recall where they were

when they watched it played. It came outside of a tournament but it was an exhibition in name only.

A huge audience watched the Montreal Canadiens play Moscow Red Army to a 3-all draw at the Forum on New Year's Eve 1975. After the '74 series with the WHA, the Soviets began sending club teams on tours of North America, taking on teams in the NHL and WHA. The motive for the Soviets was ostensibly a good-of-the-game proposition but it was really driven by the pursuit of hard currency. The Canadiens–Red Army game came when Montreal was emerging as the dominant NHL team of the era and one of the greatest of all time. For suspense, that game stands by itself. For individual excellence, however, one game eclipsed them all: the Jets' 5–3 victory over the Soviet national team at the Winnipeg Arena on January 5, 1978. Bobby Hull put on a performance that stands as the greatest for a Canadian in any game of consequence against the Soviet or Russian teams. It's a game that hockey fans still talk about but only in Winnipeg, because no one saw it beyond the reach of the television signal of CKND, the Global TV affiliate that broadcast games locally.

The Jets had gone into the four-game series against the Soviets with some well-founded confidence. The previous winter, in 1976, they had taken the Soviet nationals to the wall at the Izvestia tournament in Moscow. In the Izvestia the Jets fell behind 5–1 but stormed back with three goals in the third period to reduce the Soviets to the narrowest of leads. Though the Jets lost in Moscow 6–4, they took confidence away from the game. Hull scored twice and it seemed that he was still basking in the afterglow of the Canada Cup. "We proved the Soviets don't walk on water," coach Bobby Kromm told Reyn Davis of the *Winnipeg Free Press*.

The next three shots that the Jets would get at the Soviets felt like both teams were walking, or at least skating, on water. The game was played in the most unlikely venue ever to host a major international event and on an equally unlikely surface: a frozen-over indoor Olympic swimming pool in Japan. The previous year, in the Izvestia, the Jets would have liked a neutral site. As neutral hockey sites go, Tokyo would have to be the most neutral imaginable. "I don't know what the fans could have seen, the stands were so far back," Bill Lesuk said. "It was hard on the ice for us to see them in the warm-up. And all game there wasn't a sound. It was like a concert recital or something. You called for the puck and it echoed around the stadium."

The Jets had scheduled a four-game series with the Soviets, the first three in Japan and the final game at Winnipeg. The Soviets swept all three games, the first two competitive fare, the third a 5–1 rout on New Year's Day, 1978.

When the Jets flew back to Winnipeg, a 24-hour marathon with stopovers, the team crossed the international date line and Hull celebrated his January 2 birthday twice in the air. Three nights later, despite the grinding schedule and jet lag, Hull summoned up a performance equal to any in his career, at this point more than two decades after his debut with the Black Hawks. The Jets' 5–3 victory over the Soviet national team was indisputably the last great moment of Hull's career. Hull had a hat trick and Nilsson the other two goals. "They had to take Mikhailov, Kharlamov and Maltsev, their first line, off the Hot Line," Daley said. "The Russians might have been the second-best line in the game at that time but they could stay with Hull, Nilsson and Hedberg."

His first goal was a Hull of old. He stepped into a shot from the left wing, taking a windup like John Daly's, beyond

180 degrees, maybe closer to 270, from the point of full extension to contact with the puck. Tretiak was overpowered—he couldn't pick up the puck and was standing stone still.

His second goal was a carbon copy of his key goal against the Soviets in the Canada Cup. Reprising the role of Gil Perreault in the Canada Cup game, Nilsson set up along the boards, buying time, getting defenders to overcommit, while Hull skated into open space. His one-time wrist shot beat Tretiak cleanly.

His third goal wasn't a work of art like the others, more opportunistic than classic. It belonged to no era but it was desperately needed. In the third period the Soviets rallied from a 4–0 deficit to get within a goal of the Jets. Hull fought through checks to pounce on a loose puck in front of the Soviets' net and buried it in the last minute.

"It was the most amazing thing that I ever saw," Hedberg said. "Here's a player, just days after his thirty-ninth birthday, who takes over the game. We were unhappy with how we played in Japan—we had played much better in Moscow and honestly I think we cared more about [the Izvestia] than we did exhibitions in a swimming hall. We wanted to be the first club team to beat the Soviet nationals, we wanted to do it in our arena and we wanted Bobby to have a great moment. We got all three of them."

"It's a game that should be up there with the Red Army–Canadiens game and it would have been if people saw it," Joe Daley said. "Nobody did. If that game had been on *Hockey Night in Canada* they'd still be talking about it. Fans saw it in the arena and on local TV in Winnipeg, but you couldn't find it anywhere else."

It was Hull's moment. It wasn't quite his swan song. The Jets would win another Avco Cup that spring and he again would be skating with Nilsson and Hedberg to a champion-ship. Everyone knew, however, that the Hull of the '60s or even of the early '70s was now only occasionally seen. And if his game could be drawn out by Nilsson and Hedberg, it could be drawn out no longer after the season's end. His linemates signed with the New York Rangers for the 1978–79 season. His world was about to fall apart. The almost-secret glory of the victory over the Soviets was going to give way to public scandal.

9

A True Gentleman at the Rink

Near the end of our three-hour conversation at Gretzky's, Bobby Hull looks down at my data recorder like a cockroach was creeping across our table. "You're going to clean this up, right?" he says.

When we first sat down I asked him if it was okay to record our talk. He agreed. Everything was on the record.

I nod assent. I will clean up what it is libelous, what is unfairly, even grossly inflammatory. If I don't, the lawyers will. Not as clean as his story was rendered in the '60s and through the mid-70s, when he was portrayed as the sainted hero, the good family man. That wasn't "cleaned up." It was a sanitized fiction.

Sitting in the booth across from me, Hull has been almost entirely unguarded. Only once has he been circumspect: when he said that Billy Reay had the wrong players on the ice in Game 7 of the '71 final, "two guys who hadn't even played in the playoffs before the final." When I asked the obvious follow-up, "Precisely who were those two?" Hull looked at the data recorder. "No, no, you got something going on there," he said.

It's amazing that a man who has lived half a century in the media's klieg lights thinks that an interview on the record, with a data recorder running, would be "cleaned up." Or that a writer would select details of the conversation that would fit him like a tailored suit and buff his image. That, however, is exactly what Hull expects. That was what he expected when he broke into the league, what he could count on back in the late '50s and '60s.

• • •

From the dawn of the century through to the 1970s, members of the press corps and later broadcasters saw their job as reporting the scores and heroics of the men who played the games. They weren't stenographers. They generated interest for the teams and the leagues—and, in turn, themselves—by weaving sweeping narratives and casting the pro athletes as heroes in them. Heroes drove sports leagues as a business like matinee idols were the foundation of the movie studios. Heroes were good for business. It was Babe Ruth hitting home runs for kids in hospital beds or Red Grange galloping ahead of the field or Rocket Richard's dark fire. As a child of the midcentury, Bobby Hull knew only of sports icons without flaws or foibles, stars whose successes seemed to be the by-product of unimpeachable character as much as athletic gifts. Out in Belleville Hull used to duck out of high-school classes to listen to the Yankees in the World Series on his transistor radio. The defining hero of his teenage years was Mickey Mantle, The Mick, the good-looking Yankees outfielder who, in his worst possible moment, might have said "aw-shucks" but nothing stronger. At least, nothing that you'd have known from reading stories about him in the newspapers and magazines, or from listening to games on the radio or watching broadcasts on television. Former *New York Times* sports columnist Robert Lipsyte suggested that sportswriters were delivering what was expected and desired. The public, he wrote, is "primarily interested in the affirmation of their faiths and prejudices, which are invariably based on previous erroneous reports." The famous names were expected to be heroic in the arena and on the field and their heroism was expected to carry over to their lives away from the game—they were supposed to deserve their athletic gifts and good fortune.

The buffing of the image of star athletes wasn't a purely cynical exercise on the part of the media. It could even be considered sympathetic. The reporters rode the same trains as the players. Their wages were about the same as the players. They'd socialize with them. They did unto the players what they would have wanted for their own. Albert Schweitzer called the quiet conscience the invention of the Devil but, for sports reporters, erring on the side of discretion was an expression of kinship and an occupational necessity. As Robert Lipsyte once described the attitude of the press corps: "We're all of the carnival and the rubes [the readers] are out there."

When Bobby Hull left St. Catharines for good back in the fall of '57, the media rendered him a hero in the mold of the young Mantle: Hull was an unfailingly modest, earnest and unaffected kid from the country. He possessed a confidence, a social intelligence that served him in good stead with media and the public.

As far as most of those in the media knew, he was nothing more than that. Over the years, the perceptions of him behind the scenes changed. His story became better known. That he was a ladies' man. That he had been married, fathered at least one child and divorced while in his teens. That he could be rough and profane. The press corps grew to know Bobby Hull better but his original image stuck. Joanne Hull told Michael Farber of the Montreal *Gazette* in 1980: "He was a true gentleman at the rink. I don't know if it was good that he carried that appearance all the time. At home he had to let his hair down. So he kept the public image of being a golden angel and I think it was unfortunate [that] sometimes the children and I paid for it."

• • •

Hull was far from the only hockey star protected by reporters. Every team seemed to have a story that was hushed up. Some of them entered into the game's lore, handed down from one generation of sportswriters to the next at the arena, a little color added, past their best-before dates for publication and still enough to put a libel lawyer's kids through an Ivy League college.

One tale, frequently retold everywhere but on the printed page, dated back to the '50s and featured a Hall of Famer, a paragon of virtue, and his wife, who was open to the affections of others. One of the others, evidently, was a well-known professional wrestler who booked appointments with the star's missus when the team was on the road. The player's problem became the team's—broken-hearted, the player went into a terrible slump and so did the team. When the root cause of his slump was identified by his teammates, a quorum paid a visit to the wrestler and beat him within an inch of his life. The wrestler didn't call the police and risk his wife getting wind of his fooling around.

Even more troublesome was a player who missed games supposedly because he had suffered an undisclosed injury in a household accident. "It turned out that his wife had stabbed him with a pair of scissors," said Jim Kernaghan, who covered for the *Toronto Star* back in the '60s and '70s. "There was what we knew and then there was what we could write. We had to be able to prove it or verify it and it would have to be able to get by the lawyers. We couldn't."

Lawyers were a consideration but not the only one. Often the main motivation was access: burn a player and you'd risk losing not just him but the entire team.

Hull was at the very front rank of players in the '60s and he was also the very front rank of those who needed protection. He needed it because his commercial viability was riding on his image as a clean-living family man. His team and league needed it because the game's narrative was a pitched battle between noble warriors. It was a trade the reporters and broadcasters were willing to keep—they would get access, maybe even exclusives, from the players and teams that needed stuff kept on the down-low.

Today, if a bunch of players go out clubbing, they're Twittered and video flashes on YouTube and it shows up on Page Six of the *New York Post* the next morning. There's no hushing or covering it up—it plays out in real time. Hull and the Hawks had cover. The Hawks, as Frank Orr said, "went at it hard." By accounts of those who were along for the ride, though Hull wasn't the heaviest drinker he was the one who landed in more jackpots.

One reporter used to tell the story of an incident he witnessed in a parking lot beside a Montreal bar after a Hawks–Canadiens game back in the '60s. Hull walked out of the club with a woman who was not his wife and chased down Gump Worsley. The Canadiens' goaltender had just sat down behind the steering wheel and was looking for his keys.

"Don't go home, Gump," Hull yelled. "Let's go get laid."

Worsley was mortified. His wife was in the passenger seat.

"The stories were out there," Red Fisher of the Montreal *Gazette* said. "He liked to drink. He got ugly when he was drinking. He fooled around. But there was nothing we could do with that."

"I really think it was the tenor of the times," Jim Kernaghan said. "His marital troubles were known and discussed by the players and the media. With something like that, though, unless criminal charges were filed, we wouldn't write about it."

• • •

Decades later, Hull's former teammates continue to protect him. Start making calls, start asking questions about the private Hull and there's the circling of wagons. Hull's friends report back to him and assure him that they've stonewalled anyone snooping around. When one reporter started research on a Hull book back in the '80s, he made a call to Ron Murphy, Hull's roomie with the Black Hawks. If anyone had a good reading on the mating habits of Bobby Hull, it was Ron Murphy. Just a couple of questions set off sirens and prompted a panicked hangup.

Those who didn't rattle would deny that anything was going on or knowledge thereof. Pappin's example is instructive. He admitted that he had seen the Hulls argue when they would go out as couples after games for a few drinks. He claimed that it wasn't serious—in his version, the Hulls were a happy if scrappy couple in spite of abundant evidence to the contrary. He and others professed to have been in the dark about the deeper troubles in the Hulls' marriage or to discount later accounts as exaggerated.

Vic Grant, a veteran newsman in Winnipeg who worked the Jets beat for the *Free Press* and later in radio, didn't buy the idea of players having their heads in the sand. Though it wasn't reported in the papers or over the air, Grant said the story of the Hulls' marriage was a matter of common knowledge in Winnipeg. "There were incidents in public . . . well, I was incredulous about what I saw between him and Joanne," Grant said. "They were yelling at each other at airports. He'd tell her to go fuck herself and she'd turn around and do the same. It wasn't just the team and the reporters who were around. There would be dozens of people around. No doubt the word got around the city, although a lot of people thought of Joanne as the evil temptress just because of Bobby's image. And we all knew that the trouble wasn't Joanne. It was Bobby Hull. If what he did to Joanne played out today, Tiger Woods would look like a saint by comparison."

Grant said that Hull's cruelty extended beyond Joanne to his sons and, again, the public saw another Bobby Hull around local rinks. "The one boy that I knew fairly well was Bobby Jr., the oldest," Grant said. "Bobby Jr. played on a team with the sons of some of the other players. He wasn't the best. He was a good kid but he wasn't the smartest kid. He didn't stand out in any particular way. Bobby taunted him. He basically told Bobby Jr. that he wasn't good enough and he didn't mind who was around when he said it.

"I didn't have a lot of admiration for Bobby Hull because I saw what the public didn't see. Just like his teammates did.

He was a hard man to admire and I doubt many of his team-mates did, even if they would never admit it."

When Bobby Hull broke into the NHL the media portrayed all its stars as solid family men, upright heroes like you'd find in an old-fashioned boys' novel. Hull embraced the image of faithful husband and good father. He made public appearances with Joanne, an arm trophy inevitably cast as the dutiful and worshipful spouse. He worked their sons into commercials to buff that image. It was all a patent lie. It was off-limits to the media until it went to court and, by that point, it was out of the sports reporters' hands: it was news, not sports. News-side picked it up and ran with it and told stories that many people in Winnipeg suspected or already knew. It was not a criminal trial, but not many criminal trials would offend the sensibilities like Hull vs. Hull.

10

Hull vs. Hull

Bobby Hull doesn't tell the joke that's always attributed to him. "Joanne made me a millionaire," he'd say and then pause for the rimshot line: "When I met her I had three million." There's no knowing if he came up with it himself or cribbed it from a sportswriter or stand-up comic. There's no way of knowing that he actually said it. Still, it's the line that everybody knows, a personal trademark. "She made me a millionaire" is to Bobby Hull what "I get no respect" was to Rodney Dangerfield or "Take my wife . . . please" was to Henny Youngman: the plaint of a sad sack. "She made me a millionaire" is distilled self-deprecation, leaving the impression that he was always unsinkable, that he kept his good humor through hard times when, in fact, for so long he was angry and indignant.

The three million: the joke overstates the case. When Bobby met Joanne McKay in 1959, he was in his third year in the NHL and his total career earnings were not even six figures. When the joke is told he paints her as a gold-digger, one of the garden-variety trophy wives of professional athletes who see their man as the shortest route to the good life. At a glance she might have fit the profile. She was a skater in an ice show, not a lead skater, not a name. Her livelihood was tied to her good looks and a willingness to stand out in the cold in scant dress. The arc of their relationship, a rush to the altar three months after they met, would make many even more suspicious of her intent. She was 24 and he was 21. Both were coming out of failed first attempts at marriage. She was worldly in a way that he was still a townie in the clover.

Joanne might have been many things but a gold-digger doesn't fit. By her account their marriage started in humble conditions, unimaginable for an NHL rookie today but not uncommon in the early '60s when many NHL salaries were in the four digits. "He was making only eighty-five hundred the year we married, twelve thousand the next," Joanne told Michael Farber of the Montreal Gazette in 1980.

Bobby Hull puts a bit of a gloss on most things, almost all of the time. He's always has had an intuitive, impeccably calibrated sense of spin. "He plays the room," said Ted Forman, who used to advise Jets players, though not Hull, on financial matters back in the '70s. "He always knows the stories that they want to hear." When Hull appeared in Chicago a few days before to promote the book he is signing at Gretzky's, he told fans that he "should never have left" the Black Hawks. Back in the summer, when he appeared with Anders Hedberg and Ulf Nilsson at a Jets reunion in Winnipeg, he called his time in Winnipeg "the best years of my life." An absolute emphasis on the positive: these mutually exclusive ideas are never called into question because he has an accurate read of his audiences—though a few friends and fans in Winnipeg will be a little ticked that "the best years" get barely a parenthetical treatment in the book that is otherwise devoted to his Chicago glories. "I'm really pissed off and I'll tell him that when I see him," Ulf Nilsson said. "I don't think our line is recognized for what impact or influence we had. Bobby leaves it out of his book and tells people that he should have stayed in Chicago. If Bobby doesn't recognize it, nobody will. Anders and I added years to his career. Why wouldn't he want to talk about us? Because the Blackhawks are signing his checks?"

Toronto is neutral ground and so there are a few shades of gray and the hyperbole is drawn down a notch. There was good and bad in Chicago and Winnipeg.

In Chicago, Winnipeg or anywhere else, like Gretzky's, Hull skates carefully around the subject of family, about good times and bad times away from the arena. He is loud and proud about Brett, the middle of five children he had with Joanne. "The greatest shooter in NHL history," he says, like it's his crown to hand down. He presents his current situation as one of utmost domestic stability: "Been with the same lady for thirty years . . . live in a gated place in Florida." Hull frequently works that lady, Debbie, his wife since 1984, into conversation, though usually portraying himself as a hen-pecked Dagwood, a grounded Jet. Hull was once charged with battery and assault in a domestic dispute with Debbie and though the charges were dropped he pleaded guilty to assaulting a police officer in the incident. At the time, there was a lot of eye-rolling and here-we-go-agains, but Hull and his missus seem to have moved past it.

His resentment about Joanne is another matter. Hull doesn't bother with gloss or revision. His anger endures even though their marriage is more than three decades in the rear-view mirror. One line captures his anger.

"She still uses my name," he says.

That much is true. On Facebook she lists herself as Joanne McKay Hull Robinson, hometown Los Angeles.

Thirty years later it still galls him. Another standard line he offered back in the '80s was not funny at all but evoked the existential despair that he plunged into when his playing career and marriage ended. "I have nothing left, just my sanity, my health and my memories," he said. These he would present as his only wholly owned assets at the end of his marriage to Joanne. His name did not appear on that very short list. Hull? As far as the name goes, it has turned out to be joint custody.

There's no understanding the end of Hull's career without plumbing his domestic life. They're entwined. To understand the former, you have to dive into the latter.

• • •

Flash back to New Year's 1977. The Winnipeg Jets were stumbling in midseason. They had played so poorly that coach Bobby Kromm carved them in the press. As far as Kromm was concerned, Bobby Hull wasn't above reproach. The coach was so frustrated with his team's play that he broke up the Hull–Nilsson–Hedberg line. The players, Hull among them, bristled. They wouldn't deny that they were slumping. Hull even described December 1976 as "the worst month of my career," owing to lingering issues with a wrist injury suffered in the preseason. The players didn't like the fact that Kromm had aired his grievances so publicly, Kromm lost the room.

The Jets' general manager, Rudy Pilous, had two courses of action: he could back his coach or take the players' side. He chose the latter, taking the exceptional measure of sending

Kromm up to the press box while he coached the team for a couple of games. Effectively, Pilous gave his coach a suspension and kept him dangling. In his fifth year in Winnipeg, Bobby Hull was well established as the show and everyone else relegated to players in support. It has occasionally been this way in sports and sometimes in hockey but never more so than with the Jets in '77. Hull had been part of a nine-man group that had bought out the Group of 52, the community organization that had stepped into Ben Hatskin's breach and stewarded the team through its best times. The new group of owners was headed by lawyer Barry Shenkarow and Michael Gobuty, a high-flying heir to a leather and fur business in the city. Never before had a player owned a piece of a pro sports team and it was a considerable chunk. For $430,000, Hull had taken on a one-ninth share of the team, all owners having equal pieces of the franchise. The equality did not extend beyond the boardroom, however. Not surprisingly, two sets of rules evolved in the Jets' dressing room: a very short one for Hull and another for everyone else, including the coach. Hull would take practices off. He'd leave the team for what he said were business meetings though many winked knowingly about the type of business that had him skipping out on the team. There was no hope of coaching the Jets if you lost Bobby Hull. Rudy Pilous had Kromm's job dangling by a thread and Bobby Hull had the scissors.

Hull could have returned fire at Kromm privately. Instead, he played it as a joke. After practice on January 2, his 38th birthday, Hull, unbidden, stood up in the dressing room and read a poem to the players within earshot of Kromm and reporters. He didn't name the coach but there was no doubt about Kromm being his intended audience. It was taunting trash-talk set to rhyme.

The Indispensible Man

by Saxon White Kessinger, 1959

Sometime when you're feeling important

Sometime when your ego is in bloom

*Sometime you think that only you are the best qualified in the
room*

Sometime when you think your going will leave an unfilled hole

Try this simple exercise and see how it humbles your soul

Take a bucket and fill it with water

Plunge your hand in it up to the wrist

Pull it out and the hole that's remaining

Is the measure of how much you'll be missed

You may splash all you like as you enter

But stop and you'll find in a minute

That it looks much the same as before

The moral of this quaint example is just do the best that you can

Be proud of yourself but remember

There is no "indispensible man"

Hull had made his point. Kromm was restored to his job
behind the bench, but he was chastened, his gripes muted.
Hull had made him a laughingstock.

There was never anything ironic about Bobby Hull's personal style. He was basically as straightforward and unsubtle
as his slapshot. But the poem he read was richly ironic, inten-
tionally and unintentionally so. Hull was effectively saying that
there was no indispensible man—except him. He had been

indispensible in getting the league off the ground and even in its fifth season he remained its biggest star. He was indispensible everywhere—except in the Hull household where his wife had concluded, days before, that their marriage was winding down.

"The Indispensible Man" was more grade school than Shakespearean, but Hull's reading of it was drenched in hubris, enough to fuel a collection of tragedies. Hull had a joke at Kromm's expense but the real payoff was at Hull's. Joanne had decided to dispense with her husband. Their marriage didn't end there. It took a strange turn—in fact, many of them.

● ● ●

It's a 36-page document, one page less than the contract that he signed with the WHA and the Jets. Its first page looks like a conventional set of instructions for the disassembly of a marriage.

IN THE QUEEN'S BENCH

BETWEEN: JOANNE HULL

Petitioner

and

ROBERT MARVIN HULL, LOIS CANTIN and CLAUDIA ALLEN

Respondents

AND BETWEEN: ROBERT MARVIN HULL

Petitioner by Counter-Petition

and

JOANNE HULL and ███████████████████████,*
Respondents by Counter-Petition

Tucked away in the top right-hand corner, though, is one notation that jumps off the 30-year-old page:

Counsel: A.A. Rich, QC, Cheryl Hall for Joanne Hull
Robert Marvin Hull appeared in person

There's a line about the man who represents himself having a fool for a client. Never in the world of sport and possibly a court house has anyone provided a better example than Bobby Hull's appearing in divorce court in Winnipeg. With millions on the line, all his worldly possessions and the well-being of his kids, he chose to represent himself. It was a bad situation for many, not the least his children, but Bobby Hull was seemingly intent on making the absolute worst of it. Why? Distrust is a good place to start. "Bobby hates lawyers," said a friend from his days in Winnipeg. "Dealing with them was a necessary evil to get the deal done to come to the WHA. I guess he didn't think it was necessary [in the divorce]." And there was no small amount of hubris attached as well. He was convinced that his invincibility on the ice would translate to a court of law. His celebrity had gained him special favor for two decades, so he inferred that at the very least it would grant him a fair shake before a judge.

---

*Another party was named along with Joanne Hull as a respondent in Bobby Hull's counter-petition for divorce. The court heard no testimony and nothing was entered into evidence regarding the counter-petition. Hull's counter-petition was later dropped.

Hull gave Joanne too much credit with his "millionaire" line. She alone didn't cause him to crash and burn. His judgment or lack thereof was perhaps just as significant a factor in turning his fortune into a pyre. He could easily absolve her and blame himself.

• • •

The judgment started plainly enough, a listing of facts at the time of the case going to court, June 1980. Joanne and the three youngest Hull kids, Brett, Bart and Michelle, were living in "the matrimonial home," a house that the Hulls had purchased in Vancouver in 1978. Bobby Hull's apparent good faith was established in hearings before the matter went to trial. "The father has expressed his intention to continue to care for all his children," the judgment stated. "He has free access to them as may be mutually agreed upon by both parties."

All of this painted a far rosier picture than the details that followed, evidence given at the trial. Embedded in the judgment is the outline of a bizarre relationship. Joanne had testified that she and Bobby had not cohabited as man and wife since December 1976 and yet she also testified that they were still living together at their home, 401 Bower Boulevard in Winnipeg, when she filed her divorce petition in early June 1977. The judge, Justice Louis Deniset, seemed to be incredulous at what happened next. "The parties continued to have marital relations," the judge wrote. "They ate together, made trips together, went out socially together, appeared in public together, acted as parents of a family unit. They carried on as a married couple even after he left 401 Bower in November 1977."

In hockey terms, Bobby Hull was giving it his all to the very last shift and even beyond in a losing game, knowing that he was about to be put on waivers. He had been served with divorce papers and he kept up the image of the family man. Maybe he even believed it. Or that somehow everything would turn out all right. You're only left to ask: What could he have been thinking?

The judge described the Hulls' relationship as "an 'on and off' affair for quite some time." That understates it unless you'd presume that "quite some time" would date back to the '60s. The judgment notes that Joanne had filed for divorce in 1970 and later reconciled. Although the judgment didn't make note of the details, the nanny who worked for the Hulls at the time witnessed firsthand the cause of the divorce filing, "She came back from Hawaii where they were shooting Bob for Jantzen [men's wear] advertising," the nanny said. "He'd been physical with her. She came home with a big black eye. We took pictures of it."

"I took a real beating there," Joanne told ESPN in a documentary in 2001. "He just picked me up, threw me over his shoulder, took me in a room and proceeded to just knock the heck out of me. He took my shoe with a steel heel and proceeded to hit me in the head [with it]. I was just covered in blood. I can remember him holding me over the balcony and I thought, 'This is the end.'"

They separated on that occasion and the nanny went with Joanne to California to look after the boys. Hull's negotiating of a working truce was as bald and brash as the man himself. As the nanny described it, they were going to "get back together once she agreed that he was in charge. He said to her, 'you don't do the things I want . . . and if I say I want something, you should do it.'"

It wasn't just one storm but many that blew through the Hull household. On many occasions, before and after the Hawaii incident, the Hulls' marriage had been on the brink. "One time Joanne told me to call the police on him," the nanny said. "When I picked up the phone, he ripped it out of the wall. I said, 'Go ahead and hit me. That will make a nice headline.' He laughed and dropped it. Another time I called the police and they came [though] they didn't charge him with anything. They really didn't help at all—just sort of were standing around making jokes with Bob. Joanne didn't stay at home that night but I had to stay there to look after the boys. I was terrified, but the strange thing was, the next morning, he was sheepish."

The nanny's account is of a piece with Joanne's. "I did call the police many times. I remember him yanking the phone out of the wall [with one hand] and in the other hand he had a handful of my hair."

Joanne's willingness to put up with Hull's abuse and philandering must have seemed limitless. "He was a womanizer," Joanne told ESPN in 2001. "I asked him, 'Have there been any recently?' He said, 'You'll never know how many.'"

And through all this, Joanne stayed on. You're left wondering: What could she have been thinking?

• • •

Flash back to October 1978. By Joanne's account she and Bobby had not been living as man and wife for 22 months—debatable, depending on your definitions. The paper trail leaves no room for interpretation: she had him served with divorce papers 15 months before. And yet it seems neither was sure that the marriage was over or even winding down. They were making plans. Their daughter, Michelle, had shown promise as a figure skater and Joanne took an active role in putting her on the right career track. She determined that the coaching Michelle received in Winnipeg wouldn't be up to the standards of coaching in Vancouver. This one time, it seems, Bobby Hull was willing to compromise, to follow Joanne's lead. They sold their house in the Tuxedo neighborhood in Winnipeg and bought a new home in Vancouver. He still had his obligations with the Jets and he held on to his cattle interests in Manitoba, Illinois and Ontario. That meant that Hull was going to have to set up his own *pied-à-terre* in Winnipeg during the season and commute back to Vancouver. He was going to have a lot of time on his own—not the best recipe for any marriage, never mind one that had been so troubled for so long, yet they thought it would work.

You're left wondering: What could they have been thinking?

• • •

When Bobby Hull reported for training camp at the start of the 1978–79 season, there was little talk about him being in the twilight of his career and nothing at all of retirement. The presumption was that he'd be able to continue on into his 40s, just as Gordie Howe had. After all, at the start of that calendar year, he had racked up the hat trick against the Soviets at the Winnipeg Arena. He was coming off a season of 46 goals and 71 assists in 77 games. Maybe he wasn't a match for his former self, his Hart Trophy seasons of the mid-60s, but in training camp it looked like he still had a lot of game left in him. Anders Hedberg and Ulf Nilsson had signed with the

New York Rangers but it looked like the fall-off on Hull's line might not be dramatic—he was skating beside two other Swedish imports, Kent Nilsson, one of the most skilled players ever in the game, and Willy Lindstrom. Hull's recast line wasn't the only change in the Jets' lineup: they had landed several members of the Houston Aeros after the franchise folded. And with Indianapolis certain to fold before Christmas, the Jets' owners figured that they were going to land the teenager who had signed with the Racers, Wayne Gretzky.

The Jets stumbled out of the blocks at the start of the 1978–79 season, but that wasn't reason enough to worry. There was one sign, mostly unnoticed, that something was amiss: the Jets were trailing the New England Whalers 4–3 in the last minute of the third period and Larry Hillman pulled Ernie Wakely for six skaters, none of them Bobby Hull. When Kent Nilsson, the star ascendant, scored he was on the ice with Barry Long, Bill Lesuk, Peter Sullivan, Morris Lukowich and Rich Preston. Hull wasn't one of Hillman's six best that night. Still, the omission was nothing that really raised alarms.

Nobody thought too much of it when Hull skipped a practice in the second week of the season either. The official line from the team was that he was in Toronto, fulfilling an endorsement deal with a leather company, presumably linked to his friend and fellow Jets owner Michael Gobuty's Victoria Leather business. But then Hull missed another practice. And then a game. And then another. Hull's absence just hung out there, an uncomfortable subject for the Jets' front office and his teammates. A rumor circulated that Hull was unhappy with the Jets' divided and dissension-ridden dressing room. A full week passed before the Jets announced that they were giving Hull an indefinite leave, citing "personal matters." It stretched over 12 days and Hull missed five games. He didn't bother going to the arena over that time. On November 1, Gobuty "categorically denied" that Hull was retiring or even considering retiring. The next day Gobuty was front, center and unaccompanied when he announced that Bobby Hull had in fact advised his friend of his immediate retirement.

• • •

The *Winnipeg Free Press* headline, "Heart not in game, Hull retires," took Hull's explanation at face value. At a glance, it seemed a credible reason to hang up his skates. There's no predicting when a star athlete comes to the realization that he just doesn't want to go through it all or can't perform the way that he wants to. Some retire suddenly, like Wayne Gretzky did in the spring of '99, effectively giving two games' notice. Some have retirement forced on them by injury, like Bobby Orr, or illness, like Mario Lemieux. Some go out with a well-orchestrated farewell tour lasting an entire season. And some, very few, leave with a deserved sense of closure, like Jean Beliveau's raising the Stanley Cup in '71.

Hull's retirement was nothing like any of those.

Back in the WHA's startup he had traveled ahead of the team to bang the drum in the media. He embraced the role of ambassador, talking up the league. Those days were long gone. The media rushed to Winnipeg Arena to ask him about his decision to retire but Hull wasn't there. He wasn't available for interviews over the phone. A guy who craved the spotlight had decided to go underground. The team issued a statement from Hull but it was written by a member of the public-relations staff who somehow channeled Hull: "I have always said that

I would play hockey as long as I continued to enjoy the game. However for personal reasons I have not been able to devote my full attention to the game and therefore in fairness to my teammates and management, I feel this is the right decision for all parties."

Over the summer there had been rumbles about the Rangers bringing Hull in to reunite Nilsson and Hedberg but the statement from the team, issued in the first-person, was unequivocal: "If I ever play again it will be with the Winnipeg Jets. Obviously the decision to hang up my skates was not an easy one, so it would be ludicrous for anyone to suggest that I am contemplating playing with another team . . ."

Nobody, it seemed, had seen it coming.

Not Hull's teammates. "I would have preferred to see Bobby skate out to center ice to bid farewell," said Joe Daley, the last of the original Jets. "To retire this way seems so wrong. He provided hundreds of us with a place to play, the chance to earn a living. Seven years ago all we had was Bobby. He was the league, the franchise and we were just a bunch of guys tagging along."

Not those in Hull's inner circle. Harvey Wineberg was contacted on a vacation in Florida and said that he knew nothing about the retirement of his most famous client. "I haven't spoken to Bobby for several days," Wineberg said.

Gobuty and other Jets executives floated the idea that, having hung up the blades, Hull might increase his one-ninth share in the team. The idea of Hull getting more deeply invested in the team did not come to pass.

Everyone behind the scenes knew exactly why Hull had been away from the team and why he had announced his retirement. Everybody knew that it was Joanne and the marriage.

The only one who even faintly alluded to it at the press conference was the man who had brought Hull to Winnipeg in the first place. Ben Hatskin, the CEO, told reporters that he thought, wishfully, Hull would come back. "He has the physique to play hockey forever," Hatskin said. "I think he loves the game. One of these days he has to take control of himself and maybe by Christmas he'll be back."

"Control of himself": those were the key words. Many athletes undergo a midlife crisis, the middle-age crazy, after they walk away from their sports. Not Bobby Hull. No, he was in the middle of his. He had, as Hatskin noted, lost control of himself.

According to the testimony in the divorce court and the judgment that was handed down, Joanne had held out hope for salvaging the marriage all that time after she had filed for divorce. But then, just after the start of the 1978–79 season, she caught Bobby in a lie, caught him cheating. Maybe he presumed that he could get away with it or that if caught he wouldn't have to pay the price because he never had before. Maybe he presumed that Joanne was just bluffing. You have to suppose that if being served with divorce papers didn't chill him nothing was ever going to.

Bobby Hull was a slave to two diverging things: his routine and his impulses. Joanne and family were the routine, the foundation of his ability to perform on the ice. Other women were the impulses, the entitlement that accompanied his hard-won accomplishments.

In bidding Hull farewell upon the announcement of his retirement, Reyn Davis wrote in the *Free Press*: "You're a champion in every household in the country because you stand for excellence as an athlete, commitment as a citizen, a model of good health and an example of fair play."

Joanne Hull didn't see it that way. Bobby was no longer the champion of the Hull household in Vancouver.

Hull was scarce in Winnipeg after he walked away from the Jets in November. He moved into a house outside the city that he shared with his companion of the moment, Claudia Allen, the estranged wife of a Winnipeg dentist. Joanne's paperwork was grinding through the courts. She was granted spousal support and child support. She'd later testify that money rarely came on time, if at all.

One who believed that Hull's marital breakup wasn't the pivotal factor in his walking away from the Jets was Vic Grant. "If domestic trouble was going to cause him to retire he would have retired a long time before," Grant said. "It's not like this happened overnight."

● ● ●

Hull's retirement was the big news of the day, so much so that it overshadowed other franchise-shaking developments with the Jets. Hull was heading out the door at the very moment that his nemesis on the ice, John Ferguson, was walking in. Although Ferguson had successfully scalped Ulf Nilsson and Anders Hedberg from the Jets just months before, his time as the Rangers' general manager had come to an abrupt end. Gulf and Western bought the team and swept Ferguson and others out to the sidewalk with a broom. Hull's anger toward Ferguson had not subsided since Game 7 in the '71 Cup final and, with Ferguson's retirement after that series, Hull never had a chance to get back at him. It's hard to know if Ferguson's arrival in Winnipeg had anything to do at all with Hull's retirement— most inside say that it didn't. But the Jets' ownership group had been in touch with Ferguson about coming in as general manager long before Hull's decision to retire. And if he was dead-set against Ferguson coming in, Hull's vote was only one of nine. If Hull had stayed on it would have made for an awkward situation: Hull being one of Ferguson's bosses and one of his players. The old fires still burned.

Hull and Ferguson had been very different players: Hull blossoming as a star in the NHL as a teenager, Ferguson toiling in the minors for four seasons before breaking into the Canadiens' lineup at age 25. Beyond their careers and games, Hull and Ferguson were very different men. What cattle-ranching was to Hull, horse-playing was to Ferguson—in fact, back in '71, during the Stanley Cup final, Ferguson's thorough-bred picks were a daily feature in the *Gazette*'s sports section. What infidelity was to Hull, monogamy was to Ferguson. When Ferguson married Joan in his early 20s he wasn't an NHL star—it might have looked like he'd never make the NHL. He didn't look forward to road trips for their extracurricular opportunities the way Hull did—in fact, when he landed management and scouting jobs he took his wife on the road with him. Hull came from a sprawling family and his father spent countless hours on the ice with his worshipful son, while Ferguson was an only child raised by a single mother and never knew his father. Even on appearances, they could scarcely have been more different, Hull with his leading-man good looks and Ferguson with features like a club fighter's.

With Hull out, with the Jets struggling, it looked like Ferguson was brought in as the housekeeper, not to win that season but to oversee the transition if and when the WHA was able to negotiate a merger with the NHL. Ferguson was a monster on the ice and could be a seriously tough guy in a jam off the ice but with that exception he was the soul of decency. He could rage about a call in a game but didn't take out his troubles on others when he left the arena. It was as if he understood that he could never aspire to Jean Beliveau's talent on the ice but he tried to match his good friend in class and respect.

Even though he had retired with Beliveau after Game 7 of the '71 Stanley Cup final, Ferguson was still trying to shake his on-ice reputation in the late '70s. He was still the Canadiens' policeman even though he had gone on to be Harry Sinden's assistant coach with Team Canada in the '72 Summit Series and served as coach and later general manager of the Rangers beginning in 1975. He was still the fighter even though he really was only fighting for respect as a hockey man, even though he had put together the Rangers team that would go to the Stanley Cup final at the end of the season when he was fired.

Hull's retiring and Ferguson's hiring might have looked like steps backward for the Jets but, in fact, they presaged the last glorious run for the team and the league. And if Ferguson seemed an unlikely angel for the franchise, the same could have been said of the man he hired to coach the team: Tommy McVie. "The little general," Joe Daley called him.

McVie's resume was singularly unimpressive. He played 18 seasons in the minors and, despite expansion opening the floodgates to many of his teammates, not a single NHL game. He missed out on any sort of financial windfall from the launch of the WHA. By the time Hull was making his debut with the Winnipeg Jets, McVie was in his last full pro season with the Johnstown Jets. His one shot at the NHL had been as a coach but he was saddled with an awful team in Washington— just the sort of team that made the WHA more attractive than

an NHL expansion franchise to potential investors. In his best
and last season with the Capitals, his team finished 17 games
under .500. He was typecast as a coach you could bring in for
a rebuilding project rather than getting an emerging team over
the top.

Ferguson and McVie had been friends going back to their
youth, playing lacrosse and hockey together in Vancouver.
In the fall of '78 McVie was out of work for the first time
in 24 years but Ferguson let him know that he'd have a
job in Winnipeg—just as soon as Ferguson was installed as
Winnipeg's general manager. It couldn't come fast enough
for McVie. "I spent six months sitting on my porch yelling
at the mailman," McVie said. Ferguson let Larry Hillman go
in February '79 and brought McVie in as coach for the last
19 regular-season games.

Just as Hull's retirement had drowned out word of Ferguson's
arrival in Winnipeg, so too was McVie's hiring buried by bigger
news. While McVie was still learning the names of his players,
the NHL board of governors met to figure out what to do with
the WHA. Through the mid-70s a majority of the governors
had dug in and opposed a merger, believing that they could
wait out the WHA. By March '79 the idea of a merger gained
traction—protest groups in Edmonton and Winnipeg threatened to boycott products of corporations that owned NHL franchises or were associated with them. On March 22, 1979, the
vision of Ben Hatskin, Bill Hunter and the California lawyers
finally came to pass when the board voted to bring four WHA
franchises—Winnipeg, Edmonton, Quebec and New England—
into the fold that fall. The WHA was playing out the string.

At that point the farewell season looked like it was going
to be an inauspicious one for the WHA's cornerstone franchise.

The Jets were in fourth place at the time of the merger's announcement. Still, they would go on to win their third and most unlikely Avco Cup.

"I got real lucky," McVie said. "When I came in, we weren't as bad as our record might have led you to believe. We had some guys who were really only starting to break through as players, like Rich Preston and Morris Lukowich. What really hurt that team, though, was losing [Lars-Erik] Sjoberg. He came back late in the season from a severed Achilles tendon. I don't know how he did it—it was one of the bravest things that I ever saw. We were one team without him but as good as anyone with him, just a fantastic player. By the time of the merger—after that injury—I don't think the NHL saw what he could have done."

McVie's Jets weren't Bobby Hull's Jets. They weren't the high-flying hybrid that borrowed liberally from the Euro style. There was abundant irony in the fact that the Jets, so long just Bobby Hull's supporting cast, forged their own identities once the marquee name was out of the room. They were a better team without him than they had been with him, at least at age 39 and with his private life in a state of upheaval. "I don't think they won because they wanted to show everybody that they were more than Bobby Hull, but it wasn't a coincidence that they finally broke through when he walked away," McVie said.

"I'm convinced that Hull's leaving the team and the divorce met with a relief on the team that this distraction was gone," Vic Grant said.

The Jets' parade with the last Avco Cup rolled right through the intersection of Portage and Main and so the World Hockey Association effectively finished right where it started, where

Hull had stood in front of thousands with his oversized million-dollar check in May 1972.

• • •

While Bobby Hull's day in court loomed, he hired and fired lawyers who filed documents on his behalf. He was out of contact with his former teammates and many friends. He kept a low profile, presumably to lick his wounds and try to get his life back on the rails. A low profile, though, had never suited him before. When negotiations between the NHL and WHA finally produced an agreement that would bring the Jets, the Oilers, the Nordiques and the Whalers into the established league's fold in the fall of '79, Hull's competitive fires were re-ignited, or at least worked up to a good smolder.

Hull had always been a slave to his routines. The same meal, steak with asparagus and cheese sauce, and afternoon naps with Joanne on game days. The same cycle of chores on the farm during the summer. These, though, weren't the only routines. Hockey was as much a part of his routine. It gave his life structure. It gave him his identity. He wasn't Bobby Hull without it. He still had money to make, a contract with the Jets and bills to pay, some larger than he imagined. Joanne was chasing him for support payments set down by the court. Though his worst rival was the general manager and a stranger was the coach, Hull still had friendships in management, particularly with the lead man on the ownership group, Michael Gobuty.

In retrospect, Hull's comeback from retirement was inevitable.

It's tempting to say that comeback attempts never go well, but some do. None were more successful than that of the player to whom Hull had been most frequently compared back in the '60s, Gordie Howe.

Howe had come back at age 45 after two full years on the sidelines in what many at first thought was a publicity stunt. Howe's wasn't the lone comeback that restored a former star to previously enjoyed heights. Jacques Plante came out of a three-year retirement when the NHL first expanded; in the Indian summer of his career he won a Vezina Trophy with St. Louis and led the league in goals-against average with Toronto at age 42. Later, Guy Lafleur would come back three years after the Canadiens had nudged him out of the Forum. Each was motivated by a wish to go out on his own terms, to not be retired by their teams.

For a select few, Rocket Richard and Jean Beliveau among them, retirement gave them closure.

Bobby Hull didn't have anything resembling closure when he walked away from the Jets in November '78. He was used to being Bobby Hull, used to enjoying all the perks that went with being Bobby Hull. He had the attitude that he was somehow exempt from rules of athletic mortality and at some level physically he might have been. Where Hull was wrong was probably to be expected: he always fancied he was a businessman, that he set the terms and other people worked around them. He had, in fact, often been at the mercy of business. He had been under the Wirtzes' thumbs in Chicago. The Black Hawks' owners almost taunted him while taking advantage of him, humbled him when he gave up the gentleman-farmer gambit to come out of his first retirement. And though he set the terms with Ben Hatskin, a win on the micro scale, he had been at the mercy of the limited financial clout of the league. The under-capitalized owners couldn't really assemble a league that rivaled the NHL. They couldn't establish their brand or wield the clout to get a significant network television deal. The WHA had delivered on Hull's salary but fallen very short of its vision of a viable alternative to the NHL. Hull had been less of a player and more of a partner when he signed on and though that million-dollar check cleared, the business was in a state—franchises folding, players who had signed on with the new league winding their way back to the old one. The Jets lost Hull's linemates, Nilsson and Hedberg, to New York because the Rangers just had greater financial wherewithal. Hull didn't blame them for their defection.

For Hull, it was always every man for himself. Get the best deal for yourself. So when Hull decided to come back, he decided that he didn't owe the Jets anything and that he wanted to make his comeback where he started, with the Black Hawks in Chicago.

• • •

Topps' Bobby Hull card of 1979–80 is indisputably the most unusual artifact among the hundreds of collectibles generated and circulated over the course of Hull's career. Yes, even more unusual than a set of his false teeth that he left behind some-where and that ended up being put up for sale.

It wasn't the fact that the company had prepped a card for a retired player that made it unusual, though that was the case. Hull had been out of hockey for nine months when his cardboard likeness started rolling off the presses, to be wrapped in wax paper along with a stiff stick of bubble gum. No, it was a matter of lead time. A difficult aspect of the sports-card busi-ness is that it sometimes must sell not what was but rather what will be. The planners at the Topps company felt relatively sure that Hull was coming back. They presumed, however, that he would come back with the Black Hawks. They got it only half right. Thus does Topps' Hull card reprise the *Sports Illustrated* cover shot from the spring of '72—with a lank combover and sideburns down to his jaw, he was once again wearing Chicago's classic red sweater.

Topps had good reason to believe that Hull was going to play for the Black Hawks in the season following the merger. A condition of the merger was that the former WHA teams return defected players to the established NHL franchises that had held those players' rights. Those clubs would then submit a list of 15 protected players and the incoming teams could draft the leftovers. Thus Hull was going to be returned to Chicago. Topps worked on the assumption that the Black Hawks would protect Hull or, failing that, the former WHA clubs would, by gentlemen's agreement, not draft Hull out of respect for the player who had done so much to promote their defunct league.

Topps' misfortune was the same as Hull's. It just happened that his career rested in the hands of not one nemesis but two.

While Hull was off in Winnipeg Bill Wirtz had kicked Tommy Ivan upstairs and installed Bob Pulford as the Black Hawks' general manager. Pulford got along with very few people and with Hull not at all. The precise origins of their enmity are lost in the blur of years but it might have dated to a game at Maple Leaf Gardens back in '68, when Pulford had sliced Pat Stapleton a new seam running from his eyebrows to scalp. Hull and his Black Hawks teammates were livid. Whatever its origin the hard feelings forever endured. His standard line about Bob Pulford: "He couldn't lead a dog out of a thunderstorm with a T-bone steak."

John Ferguson was a menace on the ice but off the ice he was intense but sociable. He at least put on a good show of bygones being bygones in his dealings with Hull, no matter what the real tensions. In contrast, Pulford was mostly peace-keeping in his playing days but a dark and difficult character as an executive. To Hull's distress, Pulford didn't get along with Ferguson either and made no secret of it.

Hull was Chicago's to keep. Pulford only had to put Hull's name on the Black Hawks' list of 15 protected players. When Pulford submitted his list, he left Hull's name off it. The Chicago general manager decided to protect, among others, Alain Daigle, a forward who had scored 11 goals the previous season, and he decided to leave the franchise's all-time leading goal scorer exposed, there for claiming. Pulford's belief—or at least the rationale he later professed—was that Hull's age, his desire to play only in Chicago and his salary (still the $250,000 a year as stipulated in the contract signed in 1972) would scare off the incoming teams. It was a move that Pulford could not have made without Bill Wirtz's knowledge and approval.

Pulford also said he didn't believe Ferguson's talk about drafting Hull if the Black Hawks didn't protect him. "I guess our backs are against the wall now," Pulford said with an attempted straight face. In fact, his back was right where he wanted it: turned on Hull.

The Jets claimed Hull back from Chicago. Ferguson said his motivation was payback—not directed at Hull but at Pulford. He said Pulford had given his word that the Jets were going to be allowed to keep a young building-block forward, Terry Ruskowski, if he, Ferguson, didn't put a claim in for Hull. But Pulford wanted Ruskowski and claimed him. Ferguson felt burned. "We had a deal and then we didn't have a deal,"

Ferguson said. "The next thing you know they reclaim Hull and then reclaim [Ruskowski]. Well, you've heard of *The Sting*, the movie filmed in Chicago. Well, let us call this *Sting II*. We now are in a position to force these guys to deal. The names they were offering would have trouble playing road hockey. I didn't want a superstar. I just wanted an NHL body."

It was uncharted territory: the return of a superstar hinging on leverage for a middle-of-the-pack player. Hull was caught in a pissing contest between two general managers. If Pulford and Ferguson were talking trade that would bring Hull back to Chicago, it wasn't serious. "I tried to get back to Chicago for the final year of my hockey-playing life, but it wasn't to be because Pulford in Chicago and Ferguson in Winnipeg weren't going to let me have any joy in Chicago," Hull told the *Chicago Tribune* in 2008.

At the start of the 1979–80 season, Hull stayed on the sidelines. Those close to the situation had a sense that the story wasn't going to end in Chicago or Winnipeg. They had something approaching metaphysical certainty that it wasn't going to end pretty.

• • •

Tommy McVie warned people that the Jets were going to be in rough shape in their first NHL season. "I spent the summer trying to lower expectations," he said. "I knew the NHL was doing everything on their terms and they'd leave us nothing to play with. I told people that we were going to have a roster like an expansion team, not a championship team."

Hull was both an absence and a presence in Winnipeg. He worked out so that he'd be ready when he was traded.

He declined to commit to playing for the Jets. Rumors floated daily about teams that were interested in acquiring him. The New York Rangers topped the list and restoring Hull with Anders Hedberg and Ulf Nilsson would have been storybook stuff. But days and then weeks passed and no deal came out of any talks John Ferguson had with fellow general managers. Hull feared that the passage of time might make a deal less likely and concluded that he'd have to establish that he had some game left to heat up the market. He had resisted initial overtures to jump back into the Winnipeg lineup but by November he needed the team—in fact, the Jets were more useful to him than he was to the team. Again, it was a situation complicated by Hull's ownership of a piece of the team. The best interests of hockey operations stood in direct conflict with the self-interests of the team's most famous part-owner.

Hull was in the lineup for four mostly uneventful games in December, ostensibly playing his way back into shape, playing out of the spotlight until he was properly restored to his former glories. The real roll-out of Hull's comeback tour was the highest profile date possible. On December 15, 1979, the Jets were hosting the Stanley Cup champion Canadiens. *Hockey Night in Canada* was picking up Montreal's first-ever trip to Winnipeg and broadcasting the game nationally. To the people of Winnipeg it didn't matter that the Canadiens had beaten the Jets in their first-ever meeting 7–0 in the Forum a month before. It didn't matter that the Jets had won only nine of their first 30 games in the NHL. These were the Montreal Canadiens, arguably the most dominant hockey team of the era. Though there had been dramatic games in the WHA era and some amazing and skilled players, they had played out in the wilderness, broadcast locally when broadcast at all. This was Winnipeg's first truly national game since the Summit Series game, when Canada and the Soviets played to a 4-all tie with Bobby Hull watching helplessly from the stands. It was the biggest night in Winnipeg's hockey history and everyone was dressing up for the occasion, designating the evening as Tuxedo Night. Every last tux and tails in town was rented out for the occasion. It was an occasion all right, but they never suspected how it was going to play out.

When the teams came out for warm-ups and the television lights heated up, Hull was nowhere to be seen. When McVie handed in the Jets' lineup, he hadn't written in Hull's name. Hull might have been in the stands when the puck was dropped, but he was out of sight at the final buzzer. Fans and broadcasters were in the dark about his absence all night. No one knew what the Jets management and players knew: that Bobby Hull had already played his last game with the Winnipeg Jets. It hadn't been the plan but now it was unavoidable.

Just as he had been with his marriage, Hull was seemingly ambushed when he should have seen trouble looming. He should have known that his support from Ferguson and McVie was half-hearted at best. He should have known that they had reason to suspect that injuries and his layoff had hurt his game more than he knew. He should have known that anything less than stellar citizenship was not going to be suffered, that he wouldn't be forgiven even the most innocent mistakes. He paid the price for the first one he made.

The usual Saturday night game time was 8 p.m. but because *Hockey Night in Canada* was taking the game nationally the puck drop was bumped up an hour. Somehow, Bobby Hull had either never been told or had forgotten. Tommy McVie had a hard and fast rule: players had to be in the dressing room 90 minutes before game time. Hull didn't arrive until 6:30. McVie's rule carried a mandatory sentence with no room for bargaining: a player would be scratched from the lineup. So it was that, with all of his teammates around him, Hull was advised by McVie that he was out of the lineup and then went into his office, closing the door behind him.

Ferguson walked in a minute later. "What's going on?" Ferguson asked.

"Hull was late," McVie said. "He's not playing."

"Late?" Ferguson said. "But . . ."

"It has to be that way, Fergie," McVie said. "If I let him play I lose every player in that room."

Ferguson turned and started to walk away, getting as far as the doorknob before turning around.

"It's Bobby Hull, y'know," Ferguson said.

"I can't do it, you know that," McVie said.

Ferguson turned again and again only got as far as the door.

"We're gonna get killed on this," he said.

"I can't," McVie said.

One last time Ferguson started to walk away and turned back.

"Y'know he owns the fuckin' team," Ferguson said.

McVie just shook his head.

When Ferguson turned this time, he didn't reach for the doorknob but instead kicked at the door. If McVie's account is to be believed, Ferguson not only kicked the door off its hinges but actually put his foot through it in the process, impaled up to the ankle.

It was a comic moment from where Tommy McVie sat, but anything but in the Jets' dressing room.

"It's not my proudest moment," Bill Lesuk said. Bobby Clarke once described Lesuk as "the most honest teammate I ever played with," and throughout his years in Winnipeg he was the same. Years later the incident still bothered him.

"I should have stood up and said something [to McVie]. Bobby had always been the first one to go to bat for a teammate. If it had been someone else Bobby wouldn't have sat still for it. Maybe I was waiting for someone else to do it. Maybe it was just the shock of it. We're only in that dressing room because of what Bobby had done. We owed him. He had taken a big chance and we had all benefited from it. When he needed someone [to have his back] no one stepped up—and I didn't step up."

McVie's decision was fraught with risks. The team could have quit on him in a show of solidarity, but instead the Jets ran the Canadiens out of Winnipeg Arena. A bunch of journeymen upset a constellation of future Hockey Hall of Famers 6–2. Little detail was given about Hull's deletion from the lineup but over the next few days Ferguson and McVie made it clear that they wanted to go in a different direction. The team had played so well without him, why bring him back? Hull could continue to work out but only so that he'd be ready to move on if Ferguson could find a trading partner. That ended up taking almost two months.

● ● ●

A cynic would think that it had been mercenary on Joanne's part to have clung to a troubled marriage until her husband's mighty earning power was winding down, but the gold-digger profile never really fit the former Joanne McKay.

True, she was a spendthrift by many accounts. "Joanne definitely had expensive tastes—only the very best suited her. In Chicago she could go out and spend hundreds of dollars on antiques and then we'd have to figure out a way that Bob didn't find the receipts," the Hulls' former nanny said.

But when we think of gold-diggers, those who come to mind are landing in newfound wealth. Fact is, Joanne was only seeking to maintain the high-society lifestyle that she was accustomed to. The McKays were an old-money family and her spending habits predated her second marriage. Some in her high-society circle might have viewed her as having married beneath her. "I had a sense that Joanne's mother looked at Bob and his family as 'country bumpkins,'" the Hulls' former nanny said.

It wasn't just a matter of urban sophistication. Class was in play. Joanne's parents had underwritten her figure-skating lessons to the tune of thousands of dollars. Hull had started playing on Canada Cement's pad in Point Anne with rolled-up newspapers for shin pads. And at some level her husband's tastes never got very far out of the company town. He could see investing thousands at a time in his prize cattle, but not the antiques that she decorated the house with.

Financially, it seems, the Hulls were incompatible from the very beginning. "My parents should never have met," the Hulls' youngest son, Bart, said.

But the Hulls did meet, when Joanne went to Chicago Stadium to get her skates sharpened in the fall of 1960 and her path crossed with the Black Hawks' young star. They married within three months. She wouldn't have been the first woman to stay in an unhappy marriage for the sake of her children but that doesn't square with her accounts of her husband's abusive behavior and assaults.

The Hulls' former nanny, who was with Joanne after their separation and reconciliation in 1970, discounts the idea that Joanne stayed in the marriage all those years for the welfare of the kids. By the nanny's account, Hull wasn't physically abusive with the boys or Michelle but he was far from an ideal father. "It was just the fooling around," the nanny said. "He could be very harsh and critical. The breaking point for me was when he ordered Bobby Jr. to his room I went to talk to him and Bobby Jr. said, 'My father doesn't love me' . . . [he thought] that he and his brothers were what made the marriage unhappy. I couldn't take working there anymore. I felt like I was enabling Bob to be abusive to them."

How did Joanne and Bobby Hull stay together almost 20 years? It can be gleaned from Joanne's own words after the divorce was finalized. She described her former husband as "the best-looking man I had ever seen in my life." At the time she was already in a relationship with Harvey Robinson, a Vancouver accountant whom she married a couple of years later.

"People don't talk about [physical] attraction, that it was real," Bart Hull said.

The Hulls' former nanny seconds the idea. She recognized it when the boys were too young to fully appreciate it. "There was a sexual energy between them," the nanny said. "I remember them arguing and he put his hand between her legs. Her eyes just glazed over and five minutes later you could hear the bedsprings springing. He always stuck to his routine on game days and didn't want any change: steak, asparagus with cheese, salad and ice cream. Then from one to four he'd have his nap. He insisted on the house being quiet and he wanted Joanne to have a nap with him. After a while you could hear the bedsprings again."

The nanny said that it went beyond simple sexual attraction. "Joanne got back together with him because she didn't want anyone else to have him," the nanny said.

• • •

At another level, as strange as it sounds, Joanne sympathized with him. "Joanne told me that Bob had been raised in an abusive home, that his father was physically and emotionally abusive to his wife," the Hulls' former nanny said.

"I remember the stories of how his father treated his mother," Michelle Hull told ESPN. "[It] was exactly the way he treated my mother. He looked for a reason to hit my mom or hurt her in some way."

Twenty years after Robert Hull's death, stories of his abusive behavior, to his wife and to others, still circulate around what's left of Point Anne and the rest of Prince Edward County. "Robert Sr. was an angry man, not versed in the social graces, and he could be very cruel [to his family]," said Charlie Roebotham, a former teammate of Bobby Hull in Belleville in the early '50s. "It's hard to imagine but if he didn't like how Bobby was playing he wouldn't take him to Belleville to his games and Bobby would have to walk seven miles each way or skate across the Bay of Quinte that far. [Robert Sr.] got away with murder—it wouldn't happen today."

Hull's older sister Maxine had referred to her father's "abuse" in a Fox Sports' documentary series *Beyond the Glory*. And even Bobby Hull hinted at it in an interview with Ken Howard in an episode of *Greatest Sports Legends* in 1982, saying that his mother mitigated the "abuse" he was subjected to by his father.

Hull's friends from his boyhood remember him being desperate to please his father, fearful of him. They all thought Bobby's mother was a saint. That she would be a victim of Robert Sr.'s emotional and sometimes physical abuse wounded other family members and had to damage the first-born son. To some it might explain if not excuse Bobby Hull for a social compass that was askew.

• • •

Hull had asked Michael Gobuty and John Ferguson to trade him out of Winnipeg. Gobuty, a friend of Hull, was willing to say goodbye and Ferguson, once again the adversary, good riddance. Though he was in no position to be picky, Hull asked to be moved to a U.S.-based team for tax purposes. The Jets, however, discovered that there was almost no market whatsoever for Hull. They couldn't give him away. Teams weren't interested in picking him up for a playoff run for nothing more than the cost of his contract. It seemed that his tardiness for the Montreal game was going to end his season and probably his career.

Surprisingly, given that it had been Bobby Hull and the WHA and not the other way around, there was almost no public outcry about the star not playing for the Jets. "Winnipeggers never got over that Anders and Ulf left, more so than the winding down of Bobby Hull's time with the Jets," Vic Grant said. "His hockey life and his stationary position on the throne of hockey was maintained by Anders and Ulf. Without them he would have been gone long before he was."

In late February, the Jets were able to trade him to the Hartford Whalers, the only former WHA club that would make the playoffs in their first NHL season. The Whalers were able to acquire Hull for future considerations. Foremost among those considerations was their willingness to cover Hull's salary over the rest of the season.

"Bobby was a good citizen when he was here but it didn't really work out," said Howard Baldwin, then-owner of the Whalers. "He just didn't have the impact we hoped for."

Hull fit in no better in Hartford than he did in Winnipeg. "It was Gordie Howe's team," John Garrett, the Whalers' goaltender, said. "He had the respect of everyone. He owned the room. He had his sons on the team. And at that point, Hull wasn't as good as Gordie, even though Gordie was fifty."

The Whalers said all the right things in the beginning—after the expected array of jokes about geriatrics, given that the lineup featured not only Howe but also Dave Keon, age 40. "I think [Hull's] going to help us," Hartford coach Don Blackburn told the *Hockey News*. "He's enthusiastic about playing and that's going to carry over to our team. If he can play anywhere near like he has in the past, that's a great bonus for us."

And in the beginning Hull sent all the right messages. He was out on the ice by himself half an hour before practice started and stayed out after his teammates hit the showers. He picked up a couple of goals and four assists skating with the third-liners, Bernie Johnston and Dave Debol. It looked like baby steps might lead to better things. "He needs games," Blackburn said. "It's timing and a little sharpness here and there. I can only see an improvement as his condition improves."

Right before the Canadiens came to Hartford for a game that was critical to the Whalers' playoff hopes, Hull received word that Claudia Allen had been seriously injured in a traffic accident. He asked for and was granted leave from the team. Howard Baldwin described Hull as "distracted by his lady friend's traffic accident." In fact, in recovery, Allen was completely dependent on Hull, who had to carry her around the house. And Hull seethed because police decided to let the motorist at fault in the accident walk away without pressing charges.

Also complicating Hull's life and distracting him from hockey was his imminent divorce. When the Whalers came to Winnipeg, the presiding judge ordered Hull to come in for questioning by Joanne's lawyers. He also threatened Hull with contempt charges if he didn't make good on $6,000 in overdue support payments. Lawyers he had hired and fired were also lining up to get paid. Joanne and her lawyers were trying to figure out his assets and income that were off the books.

Hull's game went sideways and south on his return and in the playoffs the Canadiens swept the Whalers in the best-of-five opening round. His last NHL game was another loss to Montreal, utterly without drama or occasion.

Even before the playoffs the Whalers management had made a decision. They didn't want Hull back in the fall.

• • •

Kramer vs. Kramer, the Oscar-winning domestic tragedy, was still playing at the movies in Winnipeg when, across town, Hull vs. Hull started its four-day run. The Hulls' divorce was equal parts tragedy and farce: tragedy, because of the children involved; farce, because Bobby Hull seemingly thought he would get out from under an unfavorable decision simply by force of his celebrity.

Hull had met with several lawyers, five by the local newspapers' conservative estimate, more by friends' recollections. Some walked away after he didn't pay them. He fired others and all chased him for billable hours outstanding.

Two weeks before the case went to trial, the lawyer last up in the rotation, William Percy of the high-powered Winnipeg firm Thompson, Dorfman and Sweetman, told the judge that he wanted to remove himself from the case and petitioned the court to be relieved because of an unpaid bill of $9,911.71. It had been four months since Hull had made a payment. The judge ordered Percy to stay on to represent Bobby Hull and advised the lawyer that funds from the sale of a farm Hull owned would be directed to the firm. This apparently sent Hull over the edge. He told the judge that he had "lost confidence" in Percy. Hull overreached once more—not for the last time— and told the judge that he didn't want the lawyer. With the pressure mounting, he was unable to sustain any perspective, to get his mind around the idea that the lawyer's fees might be money well-spent, short-term pain for his long-term benefit.

• • •

Hull didn't act impulsively on all occasions during the proceedings. Hull's counter-petition for divorce charged Joanne with mental cruelty and adultery. At trial Hull decided to drop the charge of adultery, saying he didn't want to "drag any mud" into the courtroom. Hull had also applied for custody of Brett, 15, Bart, 11, and Michelle, nine, but at trial he dropped that application as well. "The children are with their mother," he told the court. "I'm not objecting to that at all. I don't feel they're in jeopardy of anything where they are."

Hull was effectively standing naked in front of Mr. Justice Deniset when the trial began. He worked from notes scribbled on a yellow legal pad borrowed from a law student working for Joanne's lawyer. For lawyers on the other side, it was pure comedy.

The best evidence of Hull's emotional state came after Arthur Rich, Joanne's lawyer, called her as a witness. It was anything but comedy. During his three-hour cross-examination of Joanne, Hull effectively stalked the witness box. Rich asked the judge to instruct Hull to step back from the box when cross-examining Joanne and Justice Deniset did, telling him to stay 20 feet away from the box. Newspaper accounts of the proceedings suggested that Hull crossed the line frequently and the judge had to repeat his instructions. Hull grew combative over the course of his cross-examination of Joanne. It was as if he were out only to settle scores and, yes, "drag up mud." He asked the same questions over and over again and the judge tired of it quickly. "She doesn't have to give you the answers that you would like to have," he told Hull. "You are bound by the answers she gives."

Hull's approach wasn't just belligerent. His line of questioning was counterproductive. He accused Joanne of "coolly and calculatedly" gathering evidence against him to use in proceedings, going through his pockets and hiring private investigators. If it had called into question her intent, it only highlighted the fact that her version of events was corroborated. He challenged her by saying that she "wouldn't have put up with all this abuse if I wasn't just a meal ticket." Joanne denied the allegation. Again, it might have been an emotional purging for Hull but with this line of questioning Hull effectively validated that there had been abuse.

Joanne's lawyer understood that Hull was digging himself deeper into a hole with every question. That didn't stop Rich from taking thinly veiled potshots at Hull's manhood and intelligence when he raised his objections. "This man has taken over and dominated this court . . . in such a fashion as to make a mockery of it," Rich said. "The man comes here today . . . and says 'poor me, I don't have a lawyer, help me.' Either this is a court of law or it isn't. He doesn't know any tactics other than those in the corners of a hockey rink." Justice Deniset noted that Hull was "good at those tactics." That drew a laugh from the gallery and even from Hull, who seemed to miss the larger point that those tactics hurt more than helped in a court of law. What won over fans was clearly making the judge lose patience.

In court Hull was a man who didn't know which net to shoot at, fought fights that weren't worth winning and bailed on some that would come back to hurt him. He spent only 10 minutes cross-examining a financial advisor called by Rich who put the Hulls' net worth at $1.15 million. He virtually conceded the point.

Rich almost taunted him in questions. When Hull tried to make his case, Rich goaded him with ease about his signing off on the move to Vancouver and his wife and children counting on his support for this joint decision.

> *Rich:* You had been supporting [Joanne] to that time, in any event, had you not? Had you not paid all the bills?
>
> *Hull:* Lavishly.
>
> *Rich:* Yes. So you not only paid for them but you were responsible for all the expenses up to the time she at least moved out to Vancouver, were you not?

Hull: I expect a husband is responsible up to a point, but a well has only so much water in it.

Rich did everything but pull the sweater over Hull's head. Joanne's lawyer knew that, even though it was hardly a fair fight at one level, the judge wasn't going to step in until Hull was punched out. Rich beat Hull into submission after Barry Shenkarow told the court that Hull's one-ninth share of the Jets was valued at $430,000, with the total value of the franchise set at $3.87 million.

Rich: Well, why don't you give her some money and settle the whole thing?
Hull: I'd love to.
Rich: Give her the Jets.
Hull: She can have them.

Hull had told the court that he intended to call Harvey Wineberg as a witness to give evidence about his finances. On the day that the judge anticipated Hull calling his accountant to the witness box, Hull told the court that he had fired Wineberg. Later, when Rich pushed Hull to provide hard numbers, Hull told the court that he had rehired Wineberg and that he needed his former and present accountant "to help recall" details of his finances. Then, on the day of the promised appearance, Hull said that Wineberg had "a medical problem" and was unable to attend—a development that went over with the judge like the dog eating Hull's homework. (Asked about his "firing" years later Wineberg said: "I have always been Bobby's accountant. At no time was I ever fired or released." He didn't recall illness preventing him from

testifying at the divorce trial of his most famous client.) The
lack of paperwork or testimony of an accountant left the judge
to conclude that "much of Mr. Hull's financial affairs in the
U.S.A. is unknown."

Rich piled on: "If this isn't a flagrant abuse of the court I
don't know what is . . . I wouldn't get up in the middle of a
hockey rink and try to play hockey . . . he shouldn't try to skate
in a court of law." He said to Justice Deniset: "I don't know
how you have the patience, my lord, I don't."

As it turned out, it was just a show of patience.

On the day when thousands lined up to watch the fight
between Sugar Ray Leonard and Roberto Duran on closed
circuit at the Winnipeg Arena, the final bell rang in the courtroom across town with 30 spectators in attendance. On June 20,
1980, three years after Joanne filed papers that were served
on Bobby, Justice Deniset granted the Hulls a divorce, effective immediately. He awarded Joanne custody of Brett, Bart
and Michelle, allowing Bobby "free and liberal" access to
the children. He reserved the right to address visitation at a
later date if Bobby was not provided free access to his three
youngest children. (There would be no later application, as
it turned out.) Justice Deniset told the parties that he would
withhold judgment on Joanne's claims for maintenance, support and equal division of property. He would take four months
to hand in his scorecard and the decision was fair to Joanne's
mind and robbery to her former husband's.

● ● ●

The judgment handed down by Justice Deniset barely disguised
his withering contempt for Hull. Predictably he punished Hull
for not bringing in Wineberg and not providing documents.

He evoked better times in Hull's life as way of washing down
the bitter medicine. "The court knows little of the financial affairs of Mr. Hull prior to his coming to Manitoba . . .
however we do know that he was already a businessman, deriv-
ing income, fame and advertising value from playing some of
the most superb hockey ever witnessed anywhere in the world.
He also had interest in farming, cattle operations and other
enterprises, such as public relations work and endorsation [sic]
of commercial products."

The judge noted that the Hull money machine acceler-
ated once he arrived in Winnipeg and hinted that he believed
Hull had sold himself short in his guesses about the values of
his assets. He took the numbers of Rich and Joanne as fact.
"Before he came to Winnipeg in 1972 he already had a size-
able income, and some cattle business which he was using as
a tax shelter and which he continued to use while residing
in Canada. Unfortunately we have little evidence about these
operations in the U.S.A. Mr. Hull did not give evidence regarding that. We know . . . that cattle operations in Canada and
the U.S.A. enabled him in part to avoid paying income tax
in Canada [while with the Jets], while he was receiving, on
average, over $250,000 a year. The income-tax authorities were
satisfied, he says. That may be, but it still leaves the court in
the dark regarding profits and losses of what must be a size-
able enterprise in the U.S.A. While this business is conducted
outside of Canada it is still his and the court has to take into
consideration all assets that he has."

The judge didn't stop there in expressing his skepticism.
"Mr. Hull said that he could not 'retain' dates, could not 'retain'
facts," the judge wrote. "When cross-examined on his cattle
operations, Mr. Hull was unfortunately vague, imprecise, when
not plainly and uneasily ignorant."

Then the judge threw in a short sentence that would have chilled Bobby Hull if he could have read between the lines.

"Inevitably some inferences will have to be drawn."

Much of the back half of the document was mundane accounting, the determination of necessary support for Joanne and the children: Hull was going to pick up the mortgage on the Vancouver home ($682.52 a month); child support ($200 to $700 a month for each child); and spousal support ($4,000 a month). "Mrs. Hull is used to a high standard of living," the judge wrote, acknowledging that it might have to be "lowered somewhat" when proceeds on division of property rolled in.

If Hull had been unaware of the high cost of being Bobby Hull, he was getting a crash course in it.

The first body blow was a determination of back support: a lump sum of $100,695.55. If it looked bad to Hull it was only going to seem worse. "Having regard to all I know of the assets of both parties I fix the amount that Mr. Hull will have to pay his wife at $460,000," above and beyond the back support.

The judge worked his way through the Hulls' known assets, item by item. The house in Vancouver. The farm on Big Island. Other properties. The judge drew inferences, as was his prerogative, but he also hewed close to Hull's word, to Hull's detriment. An offhand remark in Hull's testimony also came back to haunt him: "She can have the Jets." The judge wrote: "There will be a charge in favor of the wife against all of Mr. Hull's interest [sic] in his share of the Winnipeg Jets Hockey Club and this charge will remain until further order of the court or by release of her." (The judge was hardly prescient when he wrote: "Whether or not the franchise would be sold one day for 4 or more times its present value is unknown."

Fifteen years later, the franchise, losing buckets of money in the Winnipeg market, was sold on the market for $68 million U.S., upwards of $100 million Canadian.)

The payoff in the judgment came on the last page. "Counsel [for Mrs. Hull] tells me that over 1,000 hours in time was recorded, not including five days in trial, four days in examination-for-discovery, court attendances on a succession of motions, both defended and prosecuted. Mr. Hull's attitude and his considerable lack of cooperation were in large measure the cause of much expense. I fix the cost against Mr. Hull at $30,000 plus disbursements."

He wouldn't pay for his own lawyer but had to pay for hers.

• • •

Hull launched an appeal, possibly believing that it couldn't go worse than the trial had. Once burned, Hull retained a divorce lawyer from Toronto. Still, the grounds for appealing the ruling on division of assets was as tenuous as anything he had scribbled on the yellow legal pad. Hull's side made the case that Joanne shouldn't get half of their assets but rather a third because she contributed little to his commercial fame.

Joanne's lawyer, Maurice Alpin, challenged the court to "put a price tag on her contributions if you can" and then proceeded to list them. This included not just the standard domestic child-rearing responsibilities and chores but also rounding up cattle and harvesting bull semen—a notion that would have drawn laughs from those who knew how much she hated the farm.

Hull's lawyer tried to advance the case, with some foundation, of Joanne's shopping obsession, noting that she would buy 25 brassieres at a time. He also floated the possibility that Joanne had received hidden benefits from being the spouse of the hockey star, painting a picture of her walking into Gobuty's retail outlet and walking out with six fur coats, gratis.

When the appeals court rendered its decision in May '81, the outcome was even more one-sided than the trial. It was laughed out of court. The appeals judges seemed to be staging a contest to register the most colorful expression of outrage.

"You don't throw a bunch of garbage at us and ask us to decide what's right," Mr. Justice Joseph O'Sullivan told Hull's lawyer.

"It's a lot of baloney. How can you do anything but draw the adverse conclusion that Mr. Hull doesn't want to indicate what he has?" Mr. Justice Alfred Monnin said about the claim that Joanne contributed little.

Mr. Justice Gordon Hall should have been declared the winner because he understood Joanne's real value to the business of Bobby Hull. "She walked into the arena and was shown to the public. Why was she there? [If she weren't required to bolster his image], she would have been left at home to look after the household," Justice Hall said.

• • •

The Hockey Hall of Fame has an archive of important paperwork in the game's history but not the most important of all documents: a copy of Hull's contract with the Winnipeg Jets and the World Hockey Association. Nothing in the hall's files comes close to having that contract's impact on hockey and, in fact, all of sport. Yet it might not be the most important pile of paper in the hockey career and life of Bobby Hull. The divorce judgment handed down in Winnipeg might rank ahead of it, because it was the divorce that spelled the end of Bobby Hull's career. His attempts to come back after he was thrown out by Joanne never had a chance. It's easy to believe that age, and a couple of thousand games going back to junior, were catching up to him and he'll advance that story today. It's easy to claim that you could no longer compete against opponents winning trophies you had previously owned rather than admit to being outplayed by your former trophy wife. Easy to say you were shut down by stealthy shadows rather than a painful and public midlife crisis. Hull would be loath to admit it over the years but in the heat of the moment, he confessed. "There's no sense me playing and giving half of it [his salary] to someone who didn't deserve it," he told the *New York Times* in 1978.

He had played his greatest game when he lived a lie and once that lie was exposed his will and skill ebbed.

Even if Hull's career had ended before his first comeback attempt, it still would have been one of the most remarkable in the history of the game. Its end could only take so much away from his accomplishments. Yet the divorce tarnished his reputation. His life, as he publicly portrayed it, was by this point known to be a lie sustained for almost two decades. If it had been a less sordid divorce, it might have only been a footnote. But what everyone in the game at least sensed, and what many knew to be true, was aired out in court and subsequent coverage.

Effectively, his image died of exposure.

11

Staggered

By late afternoon at Gretzky's, Bobby Hull enthusiastically switches over to red wine. "I tell my wife, 'Red wine is good for you,' and she says, 'By the glass, not by the bottle,'" he says. I'm not altogether sure this is going to be a good thing for the interview. It comes at the risk of clouding memories that already might have been elusive.

I had heard Bobby Hull on radio the day before. The hosts of the drive-time show on the sports-talk radio station brought him in studio. Hull took questions from them, the usual stuff. He didn't bother trying to get the two names straight. He just stuck to "Pal" for both. At one point they asked Hull about his training in playing days and they asked him to compare it to the contemporary NHLer's regimen. "I never lifted weights," Hull said. "The only time I tried was at one of those things where there's a bunch of events . . ."

And here memory and words failed Hull. There was an awkward pause and then the hosts chimed in.

"A triathlon?" one asked.

"Yeah, that's it," Hull said, and carried on with his story. He talked about how he worked all summer on the farm and that was the source of his strength.

Of course it wasn't a triathlon. Weight-lifting has never been an event in the triathlon. What Hull was referring to was Superstars, a junk-sport novelty that was a staple of the ABC Sports schedule back in the '70s. Superstars pitted the biggest names from different games in a series of events to determine—in a way—the best all-around athlete.

When Hull competed on Superstars, he was the oldest competitor in the field. He gave a fairly respectable performance in his preliminary group, sixth in a field of 12 that included the eventual champion, American soccer player Kyle Rote Jr. Hull had one win, tying David Hemery for first in the half-mile bicycle race. He placed second in rowing, third in swimming, fourth in the 100-yard dash (ahead of John Havlicek, the Boston Celtics' fast-break greyhound). Hull ended up finishing one spot ahead of Denis Potvin and took home $2,450 for his exertions.

Athletes in the weight-lifting event had to raise the bar not from the floor but rather from a shoulder-high stand. Hull had a successful lift at 200 pounds, pressing it overhead. He had the worst form of anyone in the field: narrow grip, arched back, legs rigid. He didn't even draw a breath before the big push. Potvin made a successful lift at 220 but Hull's attempt went sideways and he begged off. Hull ended up fourth in the competition. Brian Oldfield, the world-record holder in the shot put, won barely taxing himself and would later set a Superstars record with a lift of more than 300 pounds. Potvin finished second and Hull fourth.

The Superstars *competition wasn't a life-defining event for all involved. For Hull, who had known two decades' worth of glories and disappointments, it was neither great nor awful enough to burn indelibly into his memory. It might have been surprising that the baby-boomer radio hosts wouldn't have known or had forgotten the* Superstars *program with the hints that Hull dropped and it was more problematic that they would think that weight-lifting was an event in a triathlon. It was a little jarring that Hull couldn't come up with the name of* Superstars, *but not so very significant.*

It wasn't as if Hull had forgotten that it was Jacques Lemaire who had fired the long shot that beat Tony Esposito in Game 7 back in '71 or that it was Henri Richard who had peeled by Keith Magnuson. It wasn't like he had forgotten the white 1960 Oldsmobile convertible with a black rag top that he bought with his Stanley Cup bonus, "A real muscle car . . . they could hear me coming miles away when I'd be driving to our place on Big Island."

Apparently the big things from the height of his career were still vivid. What struck me about the sequence on the radio show, though, was Hull's readiness to accept the hosts' suggestion that he had competed in a triathlon. It seemed like, with their prompting, he had recovered a false memory. Or it might have been a practiced behavior, that when lost for words or when losing his place, Hull would look for or solicit that prompting. That same sequence played out several times over our conversation. He lost his place, conversation stalled and he either asked for a word that would fit or waited for me to jump in.

I mention to Hull that I saw a TSN program that nominated the 10 "most skilled players of all time" and that he didn't get so much as an honorable mention. His linemate from the Canada Cup, Gil Perreault, was No. 5 on the list and deservedly so. One of his teammates from Winnipeg, Kent Nilsson, was just behind Perreault on the list, and that might have been fair, a comment on the talent that he squandered and a Hall of Fame career that had been within his reach.

I tell Hull he wasn't the only one passed over from his era. Rocket Richard and Stan Mikita didn't make the cut. Jean Beliveau did receive honorable mention, a bone thrown to Montreal fans— there had to be some skill on the teams that won all those Stanley Cups in the '50s, '60s and early '70s.

I tell Hull that the producers favored fancy stick-handling over all else, that they seemed to consider the ability to unleash a 100-m.p.h. slapshot in flight a matter of brute force. Hull shrugs it off. No words, just an expression that says "always misunderstood."

What bothered me the most about the TSN program, though, was the ranking of Alexei Kovalev at No. 4. Kovalev has always been an enigma. "He's a fourth-liner in Ottawa now," I say to Hull. "He's older now, but not as old as you when you scored a hat trick against the Soviets in Winnipeg." Again, no reaction other than a look that says "no denying it."

I fill in the rest of the top 10 for Hull. Orr, Lemieux and Gretzky at the top, Pavel Datsyuk at No. 10. Jaromir Jagr at No. 9. Pavel Bure at No. 8. Denis Savard at No. 7.

"Three Russian players in the all-time top 10 and I'm not sure that they'd be among the three most skilled Russians," I say to Hull. "Which Russian players that you faced should be in there? Kharlamov? Yakushev?"

Hull goes in another direction entirely.

"I told them that the Russians were going to be good back then," Hull says. "I knew that because it was the only . . ."

His words shut off like a faucet. Not even a letter drips off. The thought seems to disappear down the drain. A few uncomfortable seconds pass.

"What's the word I'm looking for?"

I try to fill in the blanks like it's a game show.

"Competition that they were pointing to?"

"No." An emphatic shake of his head. Not even close.

"Point of pride? Tool for propaganda?"

"No."

"Aspect of culture . . . of their society?"

These aren't the words he's looking for but he feels like he can run with it.

". . . the only aspect of their culture that showed their system worked."

At least five times over the course of our conversation Hull grinds to a dead halt in midsentence, as if the pause button had been pressed during a recording. A couple of times his face betrays a discomfort that would come from something more than just losing his train of thought. At the risk of being overly dramatic, he seems to lose where he is.

It wouldn't stand out if Hull were a circumspect character, if he were someone who had trouble saying anything at all. That's not the case. When he's on a comfortable topic he's voluble. And if he were uncomfortable with interviews or unpracticed in them, it would be likewise understandable. But he has given thousands of interviews over the years. The night before my meeting with Hull at Gretzky's I screened extended interviews with Hull in the '80s, with the actor Ken Howard in California and with Bobby Orr poolside in Florida. Hull was at ease, never stuck for a word like he is 30 years later.

Is it the drinks piling up? That has to be a contributing factor, but it already occurred a couple of times before he finished his two small drafts. Is it fatigue? Possibly. It goes beyond what those with septuagenarian friends or family would charitably categorize as "a senior's moment."

The other thing that jumped out in that radio interview was that Hull called the interviewers "Pal." It seems like a small point, but their names would have been on his itinerary. He would have been reminded of their names by his beleaguered publicist. Just five minutes before, at the top of the segment, they introduced themselves on-air. Just two names to remember but they became "Pal" by interview's end.

Sitting at the table, I don't expect to be anything more than "Pal," I suppose. I'm a face in the crowd. When Tom Bitove, one of the owners of Wayne Gretzky's, comes by our table, Hull can't remember my name or the media outlet I work for. Fine. But he can't come up with Bitove's name either, although they have met dozens of times. Names escaping, thoughts lost, short-term memory erased: I've seen it with my father, age 90. I could put it down to the vagaries of age but it was right there in the divorce papers from 30 years before, the judge saying that Hull's memory was very poor.

What causes these lapses? What unleashed those demons in his troubled family life? There's no knowing exactly what they are. There's no discounting the possibility that they are related. Sitting across from Hull, I keep coming back to what Jim Pappin said: that Hull had absorbed more punishment than any player in history.

• • •

Dr. Charles Tator sat in his office in the neurology wing of Toronto Western Hospital and had his pen and notepad out. He wasn't interviewing or examining a patient across the desk from him. He was in front of a computer screen, watching and listening to a gaunt man talking on his deathbed to his son who trained a video camera on him.

"How long have you been in here, Dad?"

"Two years," the father said. Each word was a strain. His voice was weak. He looked blankly beyond the camera, a thousand-yard stare into the darkness.

"What do you think about?"

"When I get out," the father said.

"When is that?" the son asked.

"I have no idea," the father said, followed by a long silence.

Dr. Tator wound the video back.

"What was your favorite place to play?" the son asked.

"Chicago," the father said.

"What did you like about the city?" the son asked.

"The people, the city," the father said.

The son kept prompting the father with a connected line of questions. In the fewest possible words, the father answered the questions but he was becoming fatigued and agitated even with one-word replies.

"What did you like about the people in Chicago?"

"Their comfort . . . they made it easy for me to make a living."

"What else?"

"Jobs . . . I was able to get a job. My future was good."

Later the son asked the father about his favorite moment.

"We won the Stanley Cup. I scored a goal in the last game of the season . . . of playoffs. They treated me real good."

"Who was your favorite player?"

A pause.

"Bobby Hull . . ." the father said.

Dr. Tator stopped and started the video as he took notes. "No helmets in those days," he said with a sigh.

Dr. Tator reviewed his notes. "He's had a stroke," Dr. Tator said. "You can see that his left arm doesn't move at all, that the left side of his face doesn't move either."

He restarted the video and reached a graphic scroll where the son listed incidents in his father's medical history. He had a stroke. He had suffered his third heart attack. He had a pacemaker. He was on dialysis every other day. His gallbladder had been removed. He could not walk or even move. The son didn't list the most obvious condition of all: his father's near-total memory loss. Over the course of a half-hour interview the old man offered just a few vague details and but two names, Bobby Hull's and Stan Mikita's.

"He is very concrete in his memory. It's not rich in detail," Dr. Tator said. "It's quite superficial, maybe even practiced. It was long-term memory. That's characteristic of Alzheimer's disease. In initial stages the person remembers all the old stuff. The ability to register recent memories disappears much earlier. Eventually you lose all memories, both in the deep and recent past."

The man on his deathbed had been a journeyman hockey player. His name had been engraved above Bobby Hull's and other teammates from the '61 Hawks but otherwise he was all but forgotten—he hadn't worked in the game in 30 years. He achieved in death greater fame than he had ever achieved in the arena.

• • •

Reg Fleming was known in his youth and up to his middle age as a tough guy in hockey. In the video Chris Fleming, his son, asked his father about his nickname, Mr. Clean. "Because

I used to clean up . . . in fights . . . beat up on people," he said haltingly.

The numbers bear that out. In his best-behaved season, as a teammate of Bobby Hull on the 1961–62 Black Hawks, he recorded 71 penalty minutes in 70 games. In his 10 other NHL campaigns, he averaged more than 140 penalty minutes per season. Hockey historians—actually hockey-fight historians— have compiled an approximate dance card for the one-time Mr. Clean. By dropyourgloves.com's numbers, Reg Fleming was involved in 104 fights in 900 games in the NHL and WHA. With dates, colorful description and sometimes vintage video, the webpage lists a generation of hockey's fiercest fighters as Fleming's opponents: Keith Magnuson, Bugsy Watson and Dan Maloney, among others. Fleming fought Montreal's undisputed heavyweight champion, John Ferguson, four times. The web-site's number accounts for Fleming's fights in the highest levels of pro hockey, but not those bouts in his seasons in junior hockey and the minor leagues. Across three years in junior and his first season in the minors, Fleming racked up 500 penalty minutes. He ended up in the low minors where records were either lost or never kept. By a conservative estimate, Fleming fought 50 more times than dropyourgloves.com's stats. The website's numbers might reflect half his career's fights.

Memories of scores of fights died with Fleming. In fact, they died some time before him. One that lives on is a fight Reg Fleming would rather not have waged.

The Winnipeg Jets came to Chicago to play the Cougars on December 22, 1972. It was Bobby Hull's first game in some-thing other than a Black Hawks sweater in the city where he had gained his fame. The Cougars won 3–2 and the game itself was nothing special. The most memorable moment survives in a minute-long video clip of a fight between Reg Fleming and the player he called his favorite teammate. It's as hard to watch as Chris Fleming's video in the hospital. If you go to dropyourgloves.com you can find more dramatic fights but none more decisive and, with Fleming's passing in 2009, none more haunting.

The sequence begins innocently enough. Hull was skating along the boards behind the net and one of the Cougars' defensemen was holding onto him, almost bear-hugging. The defenseman was outmatched, and what he was doing was more desperate than cheap. Hull didn't wait for the referee to call a penalty. The puck moved around the boards and, behind the play, Hull dropped his wrestling partner with a clinical, cynical elbow. The referee blew the whistle and Fleming skated over, as he had a hundred times before, to stick up for his teammate.

Fleming announced his intentions without words. He tried to cross-check Hull in the face. Hull blocked the incoming shaft of Fleming's stick with his forearm and then dropped his gloves. He pushed Fleming backward and pounced. Hull may have taken more physical punishment than anyone in the history of the game, but he was also quite capable of dishing it out. He fought infrequently, only 29 times across a 20-year career, but the guys he took on were more often than not some of the game's toughest, including Ferguson and Orland Kurtenbach, who might have been the most feared puncher in the league. In a *Canadian Magazine* story in the late '60s, George Chuvalo, the first boxer to go 15 rounds with Muhammad Ali, ranked Hull among the 10 best fighters in the NHL. Against Fleming, Hull looked like he would have given Chuvalo a fight.

Hull threw Fleming around like a bale of hay, twisting him down to the ice until he was on his knees. Hull rained blows down on the back of Fleming's head, the nape of his neck and un-helmeted temples. Hull had perfect leverage and punched away with full force. The linesmen jumped in, trying to peel Hull off Fleming. When the two were finally separated, Hull emerged, his comb-over asunder, and tried to skate around officials to get at his former teammate again before being escorted to the penalty box.

It might have seemed like an extraordinary event. It was more like a day at the office. After the game Hull and Fleming were just a few feet apart, staying with other players on the ice for 10 minutes, autographing programs for kids who passed them over the Plexiglas. Hull and Fleming reprised the roles of the sheepdog and Wile E. Coyote, the Looney Tunes characters who fought almost to the death and then came to a dead halt, punching the clock at the end of their shift.

When Reg Fleming challenged Hull he was past his peak but not close to the end of his career. He finished up in the low minors, playing until he was 42. If the video of Hull driving Fleming's head into the ice doesn't dispel the notion of these fights as mere sweater-tugging wrestling matches, Earl McRae's account of Fleming being beaten up with the Kenosha Flyers in the minors will.

"Harris slams him in the face with a right, a left, drives a right deep in to Fleming's belly," McRae wrote in "Requiem for Reggie," a story in *Canadian Magazine* in 1975. "Fleming gasps, doubles over and Harris slams his head back with an uppercut . . . Fleming swings blindly at Harris but Harris moves in, punches him furiously in the face and head and hurls him against the boards. Harris pulls Fleming's jersey over his head, tosses him to the ice, jumps on him and flails away . . . Fleming is helpless. It's brutal and sickening to watch and finally it's broken up . . . blood pouring down his battered face. He heads to the dressing room, alone, closes the door softly behind him, and sits on the bench . . . He turns back, closes his eyes for a few seconds. He opens them and looks at his hands, turning them slowly. They're trembling."

At that point Fleming had eaten thousands of punches, been knocked cold several times and had his bell rung many more. By then, when he was sucking up punches like a sponge absorbing a kitchen-counter spill, Mr. Clean couldn't be counted on to clean up.

After Fleming had been pounded, McRae sought him out in the dressing room. McRae wrote that Fleming spoke "haltingly" and that his words ran out in midsentence. "Sometimes . . . Sometimes I wish . . . I wish I could control myself just once. It's . . . it's the kids. I go home and they see the cuts and bruises and—"

Fleming struggled for words, as he would on his deathbed. As Hull did on the radio show and in the interview at Gretzky's.

• • •

When Reg Fleming died in 2009, his family donated his brain to Boston University's Center for the Study of Traumatic Encephalopathy. Neurologists and pathologists there determined that Fleming had suffered from chronic traumatic encephalopathy (CTE), a degenerative neurological condition brought on by concussions and head injuries. "This case also points out that individuals who suffer from CTE are often misdiagnosed during life and may be told that they are suffering from a psychiatric disorder, such as bipolar disease, or later in life, from Alzheimer's disease," Dr. Ann McKee, a neuropathologist at BU, told the *New York Times*.

Dr. Charles Tator is the leader of a team at Toronto Western Hospital that is pursuing a line of research like the BU group's, collecting the brains of athletes who have suffered head trauma and injuries. Several hockey players whose careers were impaired or ended by concussions have committed to donating their brains to Toronto Western. Dr. Tator prefaced any statement about CTE by saying that research into the condition is still in early stages. He also said that research is limited by the fact that it afflicts those who have had multiple head injuries. "Other than people who've been in several car accidents or workmen who have fallen off a ladder several times," he said, it is almost exclusively the territory of athletes, particularly football players, whose heads have been either targets or weapons or both. In the limited sample, however, researchers have identified symptoms associated with CTE: memory loss, aggression, confusion, depression, loss of impulse control and addiction. They also believe that CTE routinely triggers depression and, in the worst cases, homicide and suicide.

Dr. Tator said that the partial list of markers of CTE reads like the short-term effects of post-concussion syndrome. The immediate effects of a concussion also include dizziness, headaches and nausea, and all the symptoms of post-concussion syndrome are exacerbated by alcohol and what neurologists call "co-morbidities," conditions that amplify the effect of CTE. Often cases of CTE are diagnosed as Lou Gehrig's Disease, Alzheimer's, dementia and Parkinson's. To what degree CTE is the cause or by-product of these conditions remains a gray area in the research. In Fleming the co-morbidities were clear and documented: his stroke, his heart attacks, kidney failure and Parkinson's among other ailments. While the science of substance abuse and CTE is still emerging, like all science in the field, it's a safe bet that Fleming's alcoholism contributed to the acceleration and impact of his CTE. "Just by itself alcohol causes the brain to shrink," Dr. Tator said. Alcohol made his CTE symptoms worse; CTE fueled his alcoholism: alcohol and CTE are, as Dr. Tator described it, alternately "gasoline and fire, fire and gasoline . . . with potential short-term and long-term effects."

Chris Fleming said that his father's symptoms fit the CTE profile on almost every count. On behavior: "During and after his career he would have frequent violent outbursts," he said. "He'd get road rage—I saw him once get out of his car and smash another driver face-first against the hood. He was charged with assault in an airport for attacking a man with a baseball bat—the man had made the mistake of calling my father a bastard, and my father grew up never knowing his father. But it took less than that to set him off. Once, when I was playing football at a small college our team was penalized for fifteen yards for unsportsmanlike behavior when my father ran down out of the stands and onto the field and chased a referee." On cognitive function: "He had almost no short-term memory at all. He would forget what we had talked about five minutes before, even two minutes before. He would lose a thought in midsentence and just go silent."

● ● ●

Bobby Hull never missed a game because of a concussion. In newspaper and magazine accounts of his career back in the

'60s and '70s concussion is never mentioned. Yet, by current criteria, it's safe to bet that he suffered several, maybe upwards of a dozen, that went undiagnosed and untreated. "In the '50s and '60s, when I was in med school, we were told that you had to be knocked out to get a concussion," Dr. Tator said. "Now we know that a loss of consciousness takes place in one out of twenty concussions. And that was the basic rule into the 1970s. We automatically missed ninety-five percent of concussions."

Dr. Tator said the force needed to cause a concussion is approximately 100 Gs. "Susceptibility is very variable," he said. "Suffice to say that the force that's great enough to break a nose would in all likelihood result in a concussion. And in the case of someone who has suffered a concussion—who has reported it and is untreated [the recommended treatment is to remain inactive for a week at minimum and until symptom-free] it might not take any contact at all to cause a concussion. It could be something as seemingly minor as a hard shake or a whiplash effect. It took the profession forever to come to grips with that fact. In the '60s and '70s, players would go back into the same game when they had 'their bell rung.' And when they did this they were harming themselves, stressing their brains before they had fully recovered. Beyond that, they were putting themselves at mortal risk—we've seen instances in a variety of sports of athletes at various levels who have returned too quickly and suffered fatal brain injuries."

Bobby Hull has always joked that he has lost count of the times he suffered a broken nose. By the end of his career it didn't much resemble the one on his rookie card. He also suffered significant head injuries. The most famous: Toronto's Mike Pelyk leveled Hull with an elbow that broke Hull's jaw. Hull was back in the lineup within the week with his jaw wired shut and a helmet fitted with a facemask. A couple of games later, against the Canadiens in Montreal, John Ferguson flung Hull around in a brawl. By linesman Matt Pavelich's account, Ferguson gave Hull "a bad beating [then] pulled back and said, 'I'm not going to hit you anymore.'" At a time when, by Dr. Tator's reckoning, nothing more than a hard shake could have caused a concussion, Hull was trying to trade blows with the league's No. 1 enforcer. This was an extreme but not unique example of what would have been a strategy for teams taking on the Black Hawks or the Jets when Hull was wounded: when Hull was most vulnerable to a concussion or needed time for recovery, they would be most likely to take physical liberties with him.

"My father was and is ridiculously stubborn and he really doesn't have much use for doctors," Bart Hull said. "One time he suffered a fractured orbital bone, a real serious injury, and the doctors told him that he was going to be out of the lineup for weeks—that he would be taking real risks if he tried to get back in the lineup. He checked himself out and made his way to Detroit and played the next night."

● ● ●

Michelle Hull said that she "has had discussions with my family members about the concussions my dad may have suffered." A former elite figure skater, she believes she suffered undiagnosed concussions on at least two occasions in training. On the record, Michelle Hull won't offer any details of those conversations about her father's health, his possibly undiagnosed brain injuries or any chronic conditions, including CTE. Her accounts of her father's physical and emotional abuse of her mother given to ESPN's *SportsCentury* series caused hard feelings that, after more than a decade, haven't healed. She remains estranged from her father and her contact with her brothers is hit-and-miss, though she talks fairly regularly with Bart. A lawyer in the state of Washington, Michelle Hull works frequently with victims of domestic abuse. She expressed concern that lawyers for men accused of domestic crimes are mounting defenses that advance the theory of CTE as the root cause of their actions.

Bart Hull is more forthcoming. The fourth son of Bobby and Joanne, Bart played football at Boise State University and briefly in the CFL, and minor-league hockey with the Idaho Steelheads. Bart Hull is sure he suffered concussions during his own sports career. Likewise he's sure that his father suffered undiagnosed concussions during his playing career. Bart Hull believes, however, that those concussions did not impact his father's behavior during his playing career or in retirement. He also said that any injuries his father suffered have not impaired his cognitive functions. "When you talk to him he still remembers, still sharp as a tack," Bart Hull said. He does say that he and his brothers have detected "a tremble, a head wiggle" when they've seen their father in recent years and that it's a cause of concern. He suggests that this might be a reaction to medication that doctors have prescribed for his father's arrhythmia. He also suggests that it could be nothing more than his father "getting old."

It's easy to believe that your father is just getting old when he struggles for words. Dr. Charles Tator, however, noted that struggles in self-expression can be a significant marker for CTE. "Inability to assemble sentences, get the words out, both physically and mentally [are among] the accompaniments of CTE," Dr. Tator said. He suggested those who suffer from this sort of impairment can be aware of the problem and even develop strategies to avoid embarrassment, including avoiding the use of proper names or any discussion of past events that are cloudy in memory.

The nanny who worked for the Hulls in Chicago doesn't suggest that Bobby Hull has CTE or any other chronic brain injury. She will say, however, that his worst and most violent episodes came "after games when he was tired, or maybe frustrated and after drinking," which is consistent with Dr. Tator's description of the fire-and-gasoline relationship between CTE and alcohol. And she also will say that Hull was remorseful when sober later. "The next day, it seemed like he'd realize what he did and that it was wrong and he'd apologize, almost be embarrassed by what he did," the nanny said.

By the medical criteria of the '60s and '70s, Bobby Hull might have never suffered a concussion. He might never have been knocked out and thus he fell short of that era's diagnosis of concussion, a diagnosis that required a loss of consciousness. That's to say that he might never have suffered any concussion that rose to the level of the five percent of actual brain injuries that were diagnosed at the time. Given current criteria, however, it seems highly improbable that Bobby Hull didn't suffer concussions on the ice.

The science of CTE is still emerging. It may never be possible to determine what, if any, impact brain injuries might have played in the wrong turns of Bobby Hull's life. It's tempting to draw lines between memory loss as a symptom of CTE and a man who doesn't remember names or years or games. It's tempting to draw lines between a loss of impulse control as a symptom of CTE and a man who cheated on his marriage at every turn. It's tempting to draw lines between aggression as a symptom of CTE and a man who has pleaded guilty to a charge of assaulting a policeman and almost pounded Reg Fleming through the ice in Chicago. It's tempting to draw lines between depression as a symptom of CTE and a man who went into hiding after his divorce and was "the most depressed guy I have ever talked to," according to CBC Radio commentator Peter Gzowski. The lines, faint or not, would be drawn when the Hull siblings discussed the possibility that their father suffered concussions during his playing career.

It's clear that Reg Fleming and his loved ones paid an awful price for the brain injuries he suffered playing a game at a time when those injuries were neither diagnosed nor understood. That his life was ruined and shortened by those injuries is a tragedy. Other teammates and opponents might have suffered similar injuries, perhaps not as dramatically, perhaps not as frequently, and they might not have paid such a high price. They might be categorized as lesser tragedies, but tragedies nonetheless.

12

How Can We Repay Bobby Hull?

The afternoon is winding down at Gretzky's and the stack of Bobby Hull's coffee-table books has barely been disturbed. Two regulars on the memorabilia circuit arrive at the restaurant. They don't bother ordering anything. They don't bother buying a book. They have folders of cards, and a copy of Hull's book Hockey Is My Game *from 1967. They walk over to Hull's booth and Hull recognizes them from past stops at shows in Toronto—no names but he knows what they're there for and that they know the terms. Without being asked they drop a couple of $50 bills on the table and he autographs each item.*

"Cash is king," he says, tucking the money into his pants pocket. It's also the currency of memories.

A thirty-something mother in tight jeans shepherds her eight-year-old son to Hull's booth and, at her urging, he asks Hull for an autograph. How many thousands, maybe hundreds of thousands of times has he done this.

"Sure, Pal," Hull says. He takes the cap off a Sharpie.

"Do you play hockey, son?" he asks.

The kid nods yes.

"Well, if you work hard enough, you'll have a chance to get one of these," Hull says. He lifts his thick right hand and shows a gold ring with a face as big as a belt buckle.

"I wish I had two," he says. "It would have been nice to get that one in '71, but then again it would have been hard to leave the game with no championships."

If you go to page 53 of the coffee-table book you can see the ring that the Black Hawks gave Hull and teammates. There are three photos of it: one head-on, two others side views. The ring in those photos isn't the one that Hull is wearing at Gretzky's and showing off to the young boy. The one Hull is wearing has no diamonds or at least none that are bigger than a mosquito's navel.

The ring in the photos in the book—in fact, the same photos themselves—can be found online accompanied by this description:

"Two of the greatest athletes in Chicago sports history, Bobby Hull and Stan Mikita, made their first appearances in the Stanley Cup finals and each contributed to Chicago's ultimate victory. Hull shone in game one with a pair of goals including the game-winner in a 3–2 win, while a Mikita goal was the winner in game five. The Black Hawks then clinched their first Stanley Cup since 1938 with a 5–1 win in Detroit in game six. To mark the joyous occasion Chicago players later received stunning gold rings. Bobby Hull's precious memento features a gold Black Hawks Indian head logo surrounded by ten diamonds and the words that Chicago hockey fans waited so long to hear, 'Black Hawks World Champions'. One shank includes a 'C' and crossed tomahawks with '1960' above while the likeness of

Lord Stanley's coveted trophy and '1961' are on the other. Stamped 'Balfour 10K' on the inside band, the ring is size 12 1/2 and in excellent condition, showing just light wear. The magnificent keepsake is from the personal collection of Bobby Hull. His signed letter of authenticity will accompany this tantalizing rarity."

These photos and the details about its history first appeared on the Internet on the Classic Collections website in 2004. Classic Collections is not a sports-history site but rather home to a sports-auction business, sort of a lawn sale for the stars. The ring's status appears beside the photos.

Lot #1

Current bid: $71,328.00

Bids: 25

Status: Auction is Over

The ring is the first in a lot that numbers 149 items. The list includes: 59 pucks from his landmark goals (the third goals of all his NHL hat tricks except the first; the pucks from his 50th goals in the 1966–67, 1968–69, and 1971–72 seasons and others); 18 Northland sticks, again from personal landmark moments from the early '60s to 1976, including one autographed by Anders Hedberg and Ulf Nilsson and another by all his teammates from the 1976 Canada Cup; his two Avco Cup rings; and his Canada Cup trophy. The oldest item dates to his midteens: a wrist watch given to him by the Woodstock Warriors Junior B team in 1955. Much of the stuff is the stuff of lawn sales: beer steins, golf bags and even an ashtray. Among the items is the oversized million-dollar check presented to him by Ben Hatskin at the corner of Portage and Main—bidding for that check started at $500 and ended at $5,178.40, about five times *more than the vast majority of the pucks in the lot and twice the puck for his 1,000th NHL point, fair measures of the check's place in the game's modern lore.*

At the bottom of Bobby Hull's page are collectibles that aren't his but fell into his possession, including two trophies given to his brother Dennis and an autographed Henri Richard sweater from an old-timers game. Rounding out the attic-cluttering detritus is a puck that Blake Hull scored his 50th goal within an atom league in Chicago in 1971. You might imagine that it would be hard to put a price on a memory of your son's or daughter's best days.

The items fetched more than $300,000 before the auction house's commission.

In fairness to Hull, he's far from the only former star who has auctioned off his treasures on the Classic website. Jean Beliveau has auctioned off one of his Stanley Cup rings on the same site, although with all those he has earned as a player and executive with the Canadiens, he still has more than enough left to wear on every finger, leaving a couple to convert into cufflinks. (Beliveau also contributed memorabilia to an auction with proceeds going to his charity foundation.) Classic also auctioned off the sweater that Paul Henderson wore when he scored the winning goal in the final game of the Summit Series; however, the $1.275 million U.S. it fetched did not go to Henderson, who had given the sweater away to Team Canada's trainer.

Still, many have found Hull's memory-as-retail attitude off-putting. None more so than the Shriners and Knights of Columbus group in St. Catharines who, in 1998, brought Hull back to his junior-hockey roots as the head-table celebrity guest at a charity-fundraising dinner. Hull offered up a few of his wares from his heyday, items that fetched $2,900 in a silent auction. It sounds like a tidy sum for the sponsors of the charity night but it turned out to be

nothing more than a break-even for the organizers. By an agreement
with Hull, he kept 75 percent of the proceeds and they paid for the
expense of flying him in and putting him up. Thus the auction of
Hull's items was a net loss of $20 for the Shriners and the KOC,
though a couple of grand in cash for Hull. As noted by Peter Conradi
in the St. Catharines Standard, *Mikita didn't accept expenses or an*
appearance fee to attend. That's not to say that the organizers didn't
get any value at all from Hull's attendance—they were getting $75 a
head for the dinner and some would have come just to see him and
hear him rasp out a few one-liners. Still, the value might not have
been what it appeared to those at the dinner.

Sitting at Gretzky's, I'm struck by the thought that Hull seems
unattached to the stuff of memories. That he lets go without hesita-
tion. And yet he won't let go of the hardest feelings, the worst of times.

• • •

There had been painful losses along the way. Hull had always
been able to find dignity in the worst moment on the ice. He
stood up and fielded questions from Frank Selke Jr. on *Hockey*
Night in Canada after the Black Hawks lost Game 7 in the
Forum in 1965. He kept perspective the same way after the
other Game 7 loss to the Canadiens in '71, musing out loud
about running out of chances, wistful but dry-eyed. He had
swallowed bitter pills without becoming bitter.

Hull vs. Hull was a loss of a different sort. It wasn't a
game but rather an existential battle: his image, years in the
making, versus reality, years in the hiding. After the judgment
Hull didn't take questions from reporters on the steps of the
courthouse. He retreated to Prince Edward County, to a farm
that's a 10-minute drive from where he grew up. He went with

his companion at the time, Claudia Allen, still recovering from the injuries from her traffic accident. He went underground. Reporters came out to the farm looking for him. Once he had all kinds of time for reporters and took every opportunity to build his image. By the fall of '80 he had nothing to sell. Companies had dropped him as a spokesman and endorser. He was radioactive. The few times reporters got through to him he had little to say other than intimating he was flat-broke. Hull also told the *Winnipeg Free Press* that he was hoping to raise a few head of cattle on his parents' farm. "That's if I have any money left after the just law gets through with me," he added.

Work in the media would have been enough to tide Hull over and he did show up on *Hockey Night in Canada* for a time. It was short-lived and painful. He was not comfortable enough with the work to make a second career out of it. Analyzing plays on air, he wouldn't use players' names, just their numbers.

In this time in the wilderness Hull would drive into Picton with cowshit on his boots to pick up a case of beer. Once, every visit warranted the organization of a parade route, but in the months after the divorce was finalized he just tried to get through it with the minimum humbling. He was shut out by some of his family members—they had never cared for Joanne, considered her snooty and "too city" but that didn't mitigate what he had done, bringing scandal on himself and, by extension, their family. Among those who had no time for him was his father. In the early '80s Hull snapped when he was asked about him and maintained that their relationship was "fine." By the accounts of those who knew them, it was broken. The man who shaped Bobby Hull's game was no longer proud of his handiwork, the child he had carried around in a blanket, telling people that he had in his hand "the next NHLer."

He was now shamed by the player that he made—shamed even though the son had done many of the same things as the father. The only difference is that Joanne fought back and made the private horror a matter of public fact.

Hull was completely absent from his sons' and daughter's lives by the time he was done in Hartford. The three youngest were on the other side of the country with their mother. Bobby Jr. started the 1980–81 hockey season with the Cornwall Royals in the Ontario junior league. It was Bobby Jr.'s second season and he scored nine goals in the Royals' first 21 games. His father saw none of them even though Cornwall is only a three-hour drive from Prince Edward County. The talented Cornwall team featured future Hall of Famer Dale Hawerchuk and would win the Memorial Cup that year. Bobby Jr. left the team and went out to Winnipeg to play for a junior team there, though his father thought he should have stayed. "He won't listen to me either," he told a reporter.

• • •

There was nothing but burnt bridges behind Bobby Hull by the summer of '81. The good times in Chicago and Winnipeg were overshadowed by things gone wrong in his stints there. He was always proud of his ability to fend for himself, but in Chicago he had been at the mercy of the Wirtzes, effectively helpless. He was always craving the spotlight, a stage worthy of his talents, but in Winnipeg he had played some of the greatest hockey of the decade out of sight. Things had ended badly in Chicago. Things had ended badly in Winnipeg. Things had started and ended badly in Hartford. His playing career had so often been storybook stuff but there hadn't been a last chapter that tied up all the themes. He hadn't really retired. He had just stopped playing.

There was nothing left for Hull but to try one last time. He wouldn't accept his exile. He called the Rangers and talked their general manager, Craig Patrick, into giving him a chance to go to their training camp without a contract, hoping to win a place on the team and an opportunity to skate beside Nilsson and Hedberg again, this time on the biggest stage in the sport, bigger than Chicago, far bigger than Winnipeg or Hartford. There were no hard and fast promises but a chance to go out on his own terms was worth a gamble on his part. He was never much on self-doubt.

Dave Maloney: "The guys were pretty excited about the idea of Bobby coming in. I know I was. He was my idol growing up. We had played an exhibition game against Bobby, Ulf and Anders when they were in Winnipeg. Ulf was so good with the puck, a real magician and Anders was like lightning, going straight forward and creating room for Bobby. They had the skill and speed to be really intimidating by themselves, but then Bobby would come in late [in the rush] and they'd find him."

New York was just like the other stops, exceptional only in being the briefest and least painful of last chapters.

It was a time of transition on the ice and in the executive suite for the Rangers. Phil Esposito had retired and Freddie (The Fog) Shero had been fired. Craig Patrick and coach Herb Brooks had been brought in to Madison Square Garden as the brains and heart of the U.S. team that famously upset the Soviets en route to Olympic gold in Lake Placid the previous year. Rangers ownership hoped the magic would translate into the pro game. Patrick had one foot in the past, being just the latest generation of Patricks in charge of the Blueshirts. Brooks, ostensibly, had one foot in the future, believing he had a vision of how the game would be played in future generations. He had a large group of young players that he could school.

Just as they had with the Whalers, the initial reports out of the Rangers' training camp seemed promising. Hull was a physical marvel. He skated hard in the off-season and arrived as perhaps the fittest player in camp. "It looked like he was going to be able to play and help us," Rangers center Peter Wallin said. It was probably a case of seeing what you wanted to see, pulling for a story.

Think of how it all comes to an end for other generation-defining players. Dignity: Beliveau with the Cup. Ceremony: Gretzky skating a wide circle before the cheering crowd. Character: Orr staggering about the ice on one leg. For others whose decisions came in the off-season, they came away with a sense of integrity, having gone out the same way they came in, playing one last game, like a thousand others. Their last games provided a last statistic, a game played, maybe a goal or an assist or a shutout tagged on their career records.

Hull's exit was contentious. His last game wasn't even an official game. No GP. It occurred farther away from the mainstream than Winnipeg. Hull is so far the only great player whose last game in an NHL sweater was played in Sweden, the only one to finish his career with a preseason game. However good the comeback attempt might have been in theory, the underlying reality was another thing entirely. It's a wonder that the parties involved didn't see that it was doomed from the start. Hull was in the wrong place at the wrong time.

Herb Brooks was trying to put his own stamp on the team. "Herb had this vision of a game of weaving forwards and puck possession, playing keep-away," Tom Laidlaw said. "It just wasn't the game that we had ever played before. I don't know if it was ahead of its time—it was something like the European game."

That almost sounds like a thumbnail description of the game that Hull, Nilsson and Hedberg had played in Winnipeg. And when Hull arrived in camp, Brooks took credit for the idea of reuniting the former Jets stars. It sounded like a potential fit. It never came together quite like that, though. Nilsson suffered a bad knee injury that knocked him out of the lineup and limited him the rest of his career. Hedberg went down with an injury in the preseason as well.

Because the Rangers had Nilsson, Hedberg and three other Scandinavian players on their roster, management had scheduled exhibition games in Stockholm and Helsinki in the preseason. Half the Rangers, Hull included, made the trip. It was his last road trip. It was probably one of the happiest ones of his long career. Preseason with the Rangers in Scandinavia was almost like a fantasy camp for him: before the rest of his life began, he was getting one last chance to be in the company of players, in this case a bunch of players who grew up watching him play.

"We'd go out to lunch and we sat around Bobby for three or four hours and he told one story after another," Dave Maloney said. "He was really good with the young players like me." He told true stories and fish tales. He joked about fathering children on every continent. At least they thought he was joking.

Those who were on the trip say that Hull's play was good enough. It was the same message when the Rangers' touring team came back from Europe. Positive reviews. And then, on the eve of the regular season, an opener in Winnipeg, the Rangers announced that it was over. It was a strange sequence of events, not how stars go out. There was a snag—Hartford was putting a claim on Hull and wanted compensation—but that seemed only enough to delay things, not to bring them to an end.

Herb Brooks expressed disappointment. "I was a bit shook up and a bit choked up, as much as a fan as I was as a coach," he said. "My first reaction was this: How can we repay Bobby Hull for the past 30 days, for showing our younger players how a Hall of Famer acts, for his enthusiasm and energy?"

In the *Hockey News* Brooks was even more expansive, saying that he would "have gone to bat for Bobby." The Rangers coach claimed that Hull had gone to him expressing doubts about the hang-up with compensation for Hartford and, in fact, his will to stick it out. Brooks said he was all for letting Hull work out for as long as he wanted, until he considered himself ready and any red tape could be unsnarled. "I feel bad because I was the one who had the idea that he could possibly be reunited with Anders and Ulf," Brooks said. "I told him the first day that he reported that I was not going to push him too soon just because of my respect for him and his great reputation."

It sounds like PR spin rather than truth. "Great reputation" wasn't what people thought of Bobby Hull in the fall of 1981. The likeliest scenario—and those who played on that team will confirm it—was that Brooks wanted Hull gone. Just as he had with the American squad in Lake Placid, he wanted to be the defining figure in the organization. "It would have been hard for Herb to make it his team with Bobby in the room," Tom Laidlaw said. 'Hard' undersells it: given Hull's force of personality and his contempt for coaches, he might have been the biggest obstacle imaginable for Brooks's plans. He wanted players he could mold and Bobby Hull was an old dog, set in his ways, unwilling and unable to learn new tricks. Brooks was not there to be a travel secretary. There would have been no way to get Hull in his corner.

Hull never has claimed that he was treated poorly in New York by Patrick and Brooks specifically. In the wake of his aborted comeback with the Rangers he suggested that there was a vast, league-wide conspiracy. Once, his name was on major trophies and on a Stanley Cup, then it was on a million-dollar check, and by 1981, he hinted that it might be on a one-man blacklist. "Whether there is something more behind [my not playing] as far as one, New York is concerned; two, Hartford; three, Winnipeg; or even four, the NHL is concerned, I really don't know. I wouldn't want to surmise."

Thirty years later, the indignation seems to have faded or, at least, Hull has mellowed. He has said that he wasn't physically up to playing the way he wanted to. Unimaginably for Hull, the spirit was willing, the flesh weak.

It was strange, how it went down, but it wasn't momentous, like Gretzky going to L.A., or poignant, like Orr desperately trying to hang on with body failing. And it didn't change the game in the stroke of a pen, like Hull's signing with the WHA. Bobby Hull's career was over and the hockey world noticed, but mostly shrugged. He was so 1972.

• • •

Hull has never had a job on the hockey side of an NHL franchise in 30 years. He was effectively out of the NHL as soon as the Rangers experiment was aborted. Reporters would ask league executives about Hull and they'd deny that he was blackballed. In Chicago Bob Pulford would just say that it never came up, that Hull had never approached the team. True, as far as it goes. Hull's hard feelings toward his original NHL club in general and Pulford in particular intensified when the Hawks' general manager didn't show any interest in Brett when he was a draft eligible player or when he was an established NHL All-Star on the free-agent market. Hull felt like Pulford was doing it all over again, a replay of the run-around in '79 when Hull was in a Chicago sweater on a hockey card but not on the ice with the team.

Many stars become employees-for-life with the teams they played for, Jean Beliveau for example. Some become employees for a time with organizations that had them late in their career, like Gordie Howe going to work for the Whalers after he finally retired from the game. Others land in unusual places, for example, Ken Dryden working in Toronto or Steve Yzerman in Tampa Bay. None of these scenarios came to pass for Bobby Hull. Asked about it, he'll say that he wasn't interested in coaching—a reasonable position consistent with his low regard for coaches. He wanted to start in an executive position—not as uncommon as it sounds, that's exactly how it came to pass for the aforementioned. But their personalities are at odds with Hull's. He can be entertaining as hell and insightful about the game but work with others or for someone? Hull as a general manager or an assistant GM is not a pretty picture.

Hull's hockey after-life has been the mining of his celebrity. You could buy his autograph at signings. You could pay him to come to your golf tournament, although his shoulders leave him wincing with each drive. Your company could bring him in to make a speech—one agency priced him at $100,000 for a corporate stem-winder to inspire the sales force. And, yes, auctioning off his memorabilia was another way of financing a comfortable retirement—not up there with the high-six or seven figures he'd make in an executive position in the league but not having to depend on his grand-a-month pension that the league paid him. To build his inventory of golden-era *tchotchkes* he went so far as reclaiming memorabilia he had loaned to the Belleville Sports Hall of Fame.

Grudges abound in hockey. The staring contest between Hull and the Hawks was hockey's greatest. Hull had one eyeball each for Bill Wirtz and Bob Pulford and none blinked, until Wirtz's eyes shut forever upon his death in 2007. The culture of the organization changed overnight. For as long as Wirtz lived, the Hawks were locked into a short-sighted television strategy that went out of fashion everywhere 40 years ago: home games were not broadcast in the Chicago market. For as long as Bill Wirtz lived, the franchise, one that should have been a league cornerstone, regarded history as baggage and worked on a shoestring. Hull's No. 9 had hung in the rafters for years but it had a spectral quality. The man who wore it was seen in the arena on only a handful of occasions. Wirtz's son Rocky assumed control of the team and he sought out Hull to repair the relationship. Rocky Wirtz appointed John McDonough, a former executive with the Cubs, to the Blackhawks' presidency and then dispatched him to talk to Hull. "At a certain time, you have to lay down your swords and say no more grievances—we have to get away from the feuding," McDonough told the *Chicago Tribune*. "It was imperative that we got that done. Before this franchise can move forward, we have to step backward and extend ourselves to the Golden Era." Hull aired his grievances—McDonough said he did "a lot of listening." Once McDonough assured Hull that Pulford was out of the mix—assigned to a non-hockey office in the Wirtz Corp.—he accepted a role as an "ambassador." It was going to be a step up from the role of "greeter," the former celebrity who would stand outside a casino to shake hands and pose for pictures with suckers soon to be separated from their money. There was some dignity to Hull's role with the Blackhawks, proximity to a generation of players as young as his grandchildren. But he had long wanted to run a team. "I had a lot of ideas about how you would put a team together," he said. If that window had ever been opened just a crack, it was long ago slammed shut and locked.

As it turns out, Rocky Wirtz ended up getting Bobby Hull back for a price not so very far from what it would have taken to keep him happy in the first place. The Blackhawks are reputed to be the most generous of NHL clubs in their compensation of ambassadors: Hull receives six figures for coming out to selected games and team functions. And he genuinely seems to enjoy interacting with the players on the current-day Blackhawks. "Jon Toews is just a great player and a great young man," Hull says, with no affectation at all.

Still, it's one thing to be able to have conversations with players and another to manage them.

Maybe Hull would have been an effective hockey executive but then again he might have been no better than Brett, a figurehead as a top exec with the Dallas Stars for a brief time. Everyone remarks about the similarities between the father and son in mannerisms and personality. Maybe the father would have shown no more inclination to put in a full day's work than Brett did in Dallas, where he seemed to look at his duties as either a part-time job or a hobby.

Maybe Bobby could have become an agent like many former players, foremost among them Bobby Orr, who, despite being burned by Alan Eagleson, became one of the most powerful men in the business. Orr was able to get a foot in a lot of doors because of history. Maybe Bobby Hull would have become an agent if he had been able to land the one big client he made overtures to, his son Brett, who decided to go another way, perhaps because of history of a different sort.

Because of Bill Wirtz's death and Rocky Wirtz's reaching out, Hull was on hand for parts of the Blackhawks' run to their first Stanley Cup in 49 years in the spring of 2010. So were Stan Mikita and Tony Esposito, among Chicago alumni. And a few months after the publication of the coffee-table book that Hull was flogging at Gretzky's, he and Mikita and other teammates from the '61 Black Hawks received an ovation at the United Center. The team also announced that bronze statues of Hull and Mikita had been commissioned to join the famous metal likeness of Michael Jordan standing outside the arena. It's a point of debate. Some think it's more appropriate to honor Jordan on the United Center grounds because he actually played there and, in fact, the power of his celebrity was the reason the arena was built. Hull and Mikita never played there. Though Mikita was on good terms with the team after his retirement, Hull made a point of staying away. It seems overly harsh to criticize the gesture. Now, if it were a statue of Bill Wirtz, that would be another matter entirely. It would likely be toppled like the statue of Saddam Hussein in Baghdad.

Epilogue
High, Hard and Often

Three days after Hull's appearance at Gretzky's, members of his family back out Point Anne way will gather at a church in Picton for a memorial for his sister Maxine Messer. She was the older sister who, as the one-liner goes, would have been the third-best player in the Hull family behind Bobby and Brett (and ahead of Dennis) if she had been allowed to play. She had died the year before. Though it's only a two-hour drive from Toronto, Hull won't be in attendance. He'll be back in Florida. "We didn't hear from him and we didn't expect we would," Messer's daughter Carrie Saunders would say later. "My mother froze her feet off taking him out on the bay when he was just a tyke. She went down to Woodstock or St. Catharines when he first went away so that he wouldn't be homesick. Later in life she and my father did all the work setting up his cattle sales. But when my mother was dying he said, 'Just phone when you've got the funeral date.' We did, but he had his phone turned off and never returned the call. Not a word since. That's how it is with a lot of the family I guess. I don't have a good word to say about him and I don't think any of the rest of the family does either."

Bobby Hull isn't disconnected with the place where he grew up. He's still in touch with many he played peewee hockey with. He still gets out to Big Island in the summer, still has an interest in cattle, still makes the rounds. He had long been estranged from Maxine, however, and others—he's even quite cool about his brother Dennis. The air temperature in the room drops five degrees when he says that the "luckiest thing for [Dennis] is that he's got my last name." He gets back on his schedule and his schedule only.

A camera crew from an online site comes by the restaurant to shoot an interview. Hull turns on the charm like it's the first inter-mission of the Stanley Cup final on Hockey Night in Canada.

The interviewer, born sometime after Hull's last game, asked him about the importance of hockey in developing character and values. Hull launches into a practiced routine. "I was raised in a little town in eastern Ontario called Point Anne," he begins. "When you say minor hockey is important you've understated it. I did every-thing but crawl to Belleville to play bantam hockey. I lived for the winter to come so I could play hockey . . ."

That rings true. He talks about values, being "a team player." But for a brief time in Winnipeg, when his marriage was rocky, when he had to be disillusioned about the loss of Nilsson and Hedberg to the NHL and his sense that the WHA was crumbling, he was nothing less than a team man. Did some people think him arrogant? Yes, no doubt. "When he walks into a room, it's like 'Well, I'm Bobby Hull'," a former teammate from Hartford said. But that's boundless confidence mistaken for arrogance. Did he *think of himself as The Whole Show? Yes, but it would have been disingenuous to do otherwise. Did he work hard on his game? No one worked harder, in the beginning, at the peak of his skills, and even when he was hanging on by his fingernails with the Rangers. Those who remember him walking or skating seven miles to Belleville never thought of him as arrogant—confident, outgoing, yes, but arrogant, no.*

There is, however, something else in play. I keep thinking about the hairpieces he wore over the years even though fans knew his real hairline was back near his crown. His pieces couldn't have fooled total strangers. His indifference to his wife and family all those years; his emotional wounds from dealings with others, from the wars with the Wirtzes to the slightest of unintended slights; his practiced public persona in opposition to his private self—these aren't hallmarks of arrogance so much as narcissism. He was at once Canadian Adonis and Canadian Narcissus. The root causes of the narcissistic personality date back to childhood: a parent telling a kid that he's special and a parent's abusive behavior are two causes cited by experts. Bobby Hull experienced both. He earned those values of being a team player at the rink but he picked up other values as well, from the man who taught him the game, his father. As those who grew up with him say, his father was a hard man at best and a cruel and abusive man at his worst. He was cruelest to his wife and his loved ones, which sounds too much like his son. Joanne saw it. Others did. And at its roots, narcissism originates not with arrogance but with insecurity—in some way, when you see Bobby Hull, you're looking at a needy man.

The interview rolls along. His advice for kids playing the game could serve as a credo for his game and his life. "Kids, when you shoot, shoot high, shoot hard and shoot often," he says. "'Cause if you do, you can get one of these." At this point he holds up his Stanley Cup replica ring. That's a take. The camera is packed up, handshakes exchanged.

High, hard and often. Bobby Hull was always as subtle as a 100-m.p.h. slapshot whistling by a helmetless head. His voice was always loudest in the room, the happiest or the maddest. Hull never did anything in moderation. He didn't need a big contract but rather the biggest. He didn't need to score goals but rather the most goals. One child? Not when he can have five with Joanne, at least one or two others before Joanne or at other junctures. How many women? As Joanne said he told her: "You'll never know."

The rewards for that credo, though, might be like that replica ring: less than fulfilling. Life sometimes calls for moderation. Could he have worked less hard on the farm and spent more time with his wife and kids? Could he have lived not as fast? Could he have protected his marriage and his financial interests so that he might be holding up his real Stanley Cup ring, which is probably on display in a collector's home? He went about his life as if greatness in the game guaranteed good fortune. Sitting here in Wayne Gretzky's doesn't look like good fortune. As Oscar Wilde said, we are each our own Devil and we make this world our Hell.

Bobby Hull is at a stage of life when there's more call for retrospection than looking ahead. Hull says that he looks back and likes what he sees. He says that he has lived a great life, that he has lived it to the fullest. "I'd do it all again," he says.

The divorce. The scandal it brought on him. The distance from his children for years. The estrangement from his daughter. No regrets.

Leaving Chicago for Winnipeg. Losing a chance to play in the Summit Series and to win another Stanley Cup. Playing great hockey that went mostly unseen. Waiting in vain for the phone to ring with an offer for a job in the game. No regrets.

Regrets are an admission of doubts and weakness and Hull learned all about confidence and strength at the rink. Bad memories are like shots wide and shots saved. He has laid them to rest, can't remember or has successfully forgotten them. No regrets.

Hull is capable of candor. In 1997 he told Michael Clarkson of the Toronto Star: *"I've always felt that things would have turned out differently, if [the Hawks] had kept me or traded me. There mightn't have been a WHA. And you know what? Ego and greed prompted the decision." Such candor is rare. And even if it were ego and greed or any combination of the seven deadly sins or some toxic cocktail of all seven at once, he'd do it all again. No regrets.*

He was always the most social of animals in so many ways He signed autographs until pens ran dry. He turned on the charm like it was controlled with a toggle switch. He homed in on the center of attention like an airborne drone. And yet, like his father, he worked hard and worked best when alone, his father next to the fiery kiln, he tossing a bale of hay like it was a bag of cotton balls.

A stewardess who had served Hull Bloody Marys on the flight in to Toronto the day before arrives at the bar. "She makes a hell of a drink," Hull says. He looks at her lasciviously and when her head is turned, he asks me: "Know what my old Northland looked like?" He looks at her and curls up his tongue.

The stewardess is with him at a book signing at Chapters in downtown Toronto that night. The bookstore's manager has assembled folding chairs in front of a makeshift stage. Hull seems tired and not up to making a speech. "Okay, where do I sign?" he asks and he's pointed to a table. An announcement is made: "Mr. Hull will only be signing copies of his book." When he sits down, he's able to flash the charm with those who have bought books and he poses for pictures with them. If they have something else to sign, he gives it a few strokes with his Sharpie. Good humored when measured to the standards of celebrity athletes, though he's not the lovable extrovert that we remember from his heyday. He's in that most curious of times and circumstances: he has outlived his image.

Index